Being Digital Citizens

Engin Isin and Evelyn Ruppert

ROWMAN & LITTLEFIELD
INTERNATIONAL

London • New York

Published by Rowman & Littlefield International, Ltd.
Unit A, Whitacre Mews, 26-34 Stannary Street, London SE11 4AB
www.rowmaninternational.com

Rowman & Littlefield International, Ltd. is an affiliate of Rowman & Littlefield
4501 Forbes Boulevard, Suite 200, Lanham, Maryland 20706, USA
With additional offices in Boulder, New York, Toronto (Canada), and London (UK)
www.rowman.com

British Library Cataloguing in Publication Information Available
A catalogue record for this book is available from the British Library

ISBN: HB 978-1-7834-8055-5
ISBN: PB 978-1-7834-8056-2

Library of Congress Cataloging-in-Publication Data

Isin, Engin F. (Engin Fahri), 1959–
Being digital citizens / Engin Isin and Evelyn Ruppert.
pages cm
Includes bibliographical references and index.
ISBN 978-1-78348-055-5 (cloth : alk. paper)—ISBN 978-1-78348-056-2 (pbk. : alk. paper)—ISBN
978-1-78348-057-9 (electronic)
1. Internet in public administration. 2. Internet—Political aspects. I. Title.
JF1525.A8I68 2015
323.6'502854678—dc23
                                        2014048134

♾™ The paper used in this publication meets the minimum requirements of American
National Standard for Information Sciences Permanence of Paper for Printed Library
Materials, ANSI/NISO Z39.48-1992.

Printed in the United States of America

Being Digital Citizens

Contents

Acknowledgements

We are grateful to Marianne Franklin, Matthew Fuller, and Adrian Mackenzie, who read an earlier version of the manuscript and provided brilliantly incisive comments that can only be made by those who truly understand the help needed during the last stages of writing a book. We are also thankful for the insightful comments of four anonymous reviewers. Anna Reeve of Rowman & Littlefield International spurred the idea for this book and has been a superb editor. We gratefully acknowledge her attentiveness and responsiveness, which made publishing this book a pleasurable experience. We also acknowledge that the research leading to this book was supported by funding from the European Research Council (ERC) Advanced Research Grant 249379 (Isin) and Consolidator Grant 615588 (Ruppert).

ONE

Doing Things with Words and Saying Words with Things

That things we say and do through the Internet have permeated our lives in unprecedented ways is now a cliché that needs not repeating. That this has happened practically throughout the world despite a digital divide is also accepted. That both corporations and states have become heavily invested in harvesting, assembling, and storing data—for profits or security—about things we say and do through the Internet is practically the strongest evidence of the significance attached to our connected digital lives. That for many people Aaron Swartz, Anonymous, DDoS, Edward Snowden, GCHQ, Julian Assange, LulzSec, NSA, Pirate Bay, PRISM, or WikiLeaks hardly require introduction is yet further evidence. That presidents and footballers tweet, hackers leak nude photos, and murderers and advertisers use Facebook or that people post their sex acts are not so controversial as just recognizable events of our times. That Airbnb disrupts the hospitality industry or Uber the taxi industry is taken for granted. It certainly feels like saying and doing things through the Internet has become an everyday experience with dangerous possibilities.

The worldwide debate over the social, economic, and cultural consequences of digital life connected to the Internet has been in full swing for about twenty years now.[1] Early and notable books such as Sherry Turkle's *Life on the Screen* (1995) and Nicholas Negroponte's *Being Digital* (1995) were by and large celebrations of digital lives being connected to the Internet and enabling people to do things through it.[2] Yet within twenty years the mood has decisively changed. Evgeny Morozov's *The*

1

Net Delusion (2011), Turkle's own *Alone Together* (2011), or Jamie Bartlett's *The Dark Net* (2014) strike much more sombre, if not worried, moods. While Morozov draws attention to the consequences of giving up data in return for so-called free services, Turkle draws attention to how people are getting lost in their devices. Bartlett draws attention to what is happening in certain areas of the Internet when pushed underground (removed from access via search engines) and thus giving rise to new forms of vigilantism and extremism. Perhaps the spying and snooping by corporations and states into what people say and do through the Internet has become a watershed event.[3] Seen from another angle, novels such as William Gibson's *Neuromancer* (1984) and Dave Eggers's *The Circle* (2013) practically bookmark an era. While Gibson projects an experimental and explorative, if not separate and independent, cyberspace, almost like a frontier, Eggers announces the arrival of the guardians at the gates of the frontier. As Ronald Deibert recently suggested, while the Internet used to be characterized as a network of networks it is perhaps more appropriate now to see it as a network of filters and chokepoints.[4] The struggle over the things we say and do through the Internet is now a political struggle of our times, and so is the Internet itself.

If indeed what we are saying *and* doing through the Internet is dramatically changing political life, what then of the subjects of politics? If the Internet—or, more precisely, how we are increasingly acting *through* the Internet—is changing our political subjectivity, what do we think about the way in which we understand ourselves as political subjects, subjects who have rights to speech, access, and privacy, rights that constitute us as political, as beings with responsibilities and obligations? Like those who approach the study of the Internet as remaking social networks, identities, subjectivities, or human-technology interactions, we are interested in how the Internet involves the refashioning of relations not only between people but between people and vast arrangements of technologies and conventions that have become part of everyday language, such as tweeting, messaging, friending, emailing, blogging, sharing, and so on. We are specifically interested in the consequences of these conventions for political life, which we think is being reconfigured in novel ways. Moreover, with the development of the Internet of things—*our* phones, watches, dishwashers, fridges, cars, and many other devices being always already connected to the Internet—we not only do things with words but also do words with things. (We are going to elaborate on this awkward but necessary phrase 'saying and doing things through the Internet' and its two sides, 'doing things with words' and 'saying words with things,' in chapters 2 and 3 when we discuss the figures of the citizen and cyberspace and then speech acts and digital acts.) These connected devices generate enormous volumes of data about our movements, locations, activities, interests, encounters, and private and public relationships through which we become data subjects. When joined up with other data collected by private or public authorities concerning our taxes, health, passport, travel, and finance, the data profiles that can be compiled about people is staggering.[5] Who owns the data generated by the digital traces of people and their devices?[6] The Internet has not only permeated our social, cultural, and economic lives but also resignified political life by creating an interconnected web of relations among people and things. It has influenced almost every aspect of politics, and its presence in politics is ubiquitous. It has created new kinds of politics where there is ostensibly no previous equivalent. It has also given rise to new subjects of politics such as Anonymous, cypherpunks, hacktivists, and whistle-blowers.

Along with these political subjects, a new designation has also emerged: digital citizens. Subjects such as citizen journalists, citizen artists, citizen scientists, citizen philanthropists, and citizen prosecutors have variously accompanied it.[7] Going back to the euphoric years of the 1990s, Jon Katz introduced the term to describe generally the kinds of Americans who were active on the Internet.[8] For Katz, people were inventing new ways of conducting themselves politically on the Internet and were transcending the straitjacket of at least American electoral politics caught, as it were, between conventional Democratic versus Republican party politics. Considering this as the birth of a new political subjectivity entirely owing to the Internet, Katz thought that although digital citizens were libertarian, they were neither alienated nor isolated. Rather, digital citizens were a political movement struggling to come together with a common cause mobilized by values of sharing, prosperity, exchange, knowledge, and openness.[9] Katz's optimism has not been entirely borne out by our subsequent (and international) experience.[10] A recent website, for example, calling on people to become digital citizens seems to be more about personal safety and personal security than Katz's libertarian political subjects dedicated to openness and sharing.[11] It promises, for example, that through becoming digital citizens you will 'learn how to protect yourself and your family. Be a voice for real solutions. Help us take our online neighbourhood back from the criminals and predators.' As this signals, these different imaginaries of being or becoming digital citizens are contested. This contestation is not entirely a product of the Internet, as we shall see later, and perhaps expresses the paradox of the late modern citizen with conflicting and ambiguous callings.[12] The question that we face in relation to this contestation or struggle as both an object of theorizing and of politics is: What kind of political subject, if not a citizen, is coming into being through the Internet? What are the callings that mobilize people with ever more force to become digital citizens, and what are the closings that generate dread and motivate them to withdraw?

In posing these questions our focus is thus on the political subject that arises from acting through the Internet. To state from the outset, we understand the political subject not as a coherent and unified being but as a composite of multiple subjectivities that emerge from different situations and relations. We ask how it is possible for political subjects to make rights claims about how their digital lives are configured, regulated, and organized by dispersed arrangements of numerous people and things such as corporations and states but also software and devices as well as people such as programmers and regulators. This question concerns not only by now well-known activists who are mostly male and Euro-American but also the innumerable and often anonymous subjects whose everyday acts through the Internet make claims to its workings and rules. And as we have already suggested in the questions raised above, how these everyday acts come to produce a political subjectivity that we call digital citizens is our central concern. We have already implied two key ideas of this book; let us now specify them.

First, by bringing the political subject to the centre of concern, we interfere with determinist analyses of the Internet and hyperbolic assertions about its impact that imagine subjects as passive *data subjects*. Instead, we attend to how political subjectivities are always performed in relation to sociotechnical arrangements to then think about how they are brought into being through the Internet.[13] We also interfere with libertarian analyses of the Internet and their hyperbolic assertions of *sovereign subjects*. We contend that if we shift our analysis from how we are being 'controlled' (as both determinist and libertarian views agree) to the complexities of 'acting' —by foregrounding *citizen subjects* not in isolation but in relation to the arrangements of which they are a part—we can identify ways of being not simply obedient and submissive but also subversive. While usually reserved for high-profile hacktivists and whistle-blowers, we ask, how do subjects act in ways that transgress the expectations of and go beyond specific conventions and in doing so make rights claims about how to conduct themselves as digital citizens?[14] Second, by focusing on how digital citizens make rights claims through the Internet, we ask, how are their relations mediated, regulated, and monitored, and how is knowledge generated, ordered, and disseminated through the Internet? We consider both of these concerns as objects of struggle and ones through which we might identify how we *otherwise* conduct ourselves as digital citizens when we engage *with* others and act through the Internet.

When the sociotechnical arrangements and subjects that make up the Internet traverse not only national borders but also legal orders, both borders and orders become permeable *and* reinforced simultaneously. The implications of this are evident in struggles over the Internet; from Anonymous to WikiLeaks, from activists to security professionals alike, acts can and do cut across national borders and multiple legal orders.[15] Some of the Internet's novel aspects, such as the speed and reach of interactions and transactions, have spurred concerns about high-frequency trading, the hacking of financial and banking services, state and corporate spying on citizens, deliberate cross-border virus attacks, covert cyberwars among states, and the rise of often anonymous racism, xenophobia, and homophobia along with cyberbullying and issues of freedom of speech. These are just a few prominent issues of how technical, material, cultural, ethical, and political matters collide and collude across multiple and overlapping orders.[16] The challenge we set for ourselves in this book is to find ways of investigating how people enact themselves as citizens by negotiating their rights such as privacy, access, openness, and innovation and their rights concerning data. We investigate these rights not in terms of their substance but in relation to who the subject is of these rights, or more precisely, who is constituting themselves as political subjects of these rights by saying and doing things—and thus making rights claims—through the Internet.

BETWEEN DIGITAL LIFE AND POLITICAL LIFE

So far there has been a remarkably limited discussion, let alone theorization, of the relationship between citizens and the Internet.[17] It has been
limited in two senses. First, discussions of the relationship have focused
on issues concerning the provision and delivery of public services
through the Internet, variously described as e-government and measured
by indicators such as the United Nations e-government readiness index
or other indices and metrics.[18] This is also the case for studies of government transparency and citizen rights to open data that have lead to initiatives such as the G8 Open Data Charter.[19] Although open data and the
provision and delivery of public services through the Internet are important aspects of contemporary citizenship, to limit citizenship to these
meanings is obviously too narrow for understanding various broader, if
not fundamental, issues we have just mentioned. Second, those who consider such broad issues that we discuss under the rubric of 'digital citizens' seem to overlook how citizenship itself in contemporary societies is
undergoing fundamental changes that are related to a series of other
transformations similar to and different from those concerning the Internet. The issues of transnational mobility and migrations, resurgence of
nationalism, assertions of sovereignty, internationalization of capital, the
decline of the social state, and the rise of neoliberalism are all forcing the
boundaries of citizenship as an issue of concern. Just as the extensity of
the Internet enables digital life to flow across state regulatory jurisdictions, so too do the rights claims of citizens increasingly traverse multiple
legal orders.

To an extent, these issues are now being addressed in the field of
digital studies.[20] Questions concerning who shapes the Internet, who
uses it, and who shapes law and regulation regarding it are now being
debated. It is well recognized that digital studies concerns itself with not
only underlying digital technologies but how these technologies are embedded in sociotechnical arrangements and subjects who shape these arrangements both as users and producers. More significantly, digital studies spans both social sciences and humanities as well as science and technology studies and asks questions concerning the relation of digital technologies to social and cultural change. For Arthur and Marilouise Kroker
especially, critical digital studies revisits the question concerning technology and its embodiment in political, social, and cultural lives.[21] For Krok-

er and Kroker 'What is truly *critical* about critical digital studies is the emphasis on not only understanding the dominant codes of technology, politics, and culture in the digital era but also on digital studies that excel in breaking the codes and in introducing new visions of the digital future by disrupting the codes, disturbing boundaries, and adding uncertainty to established patterns of (code) behaviour.'[22] As we shall see in chapter 6, breaking codes or conventions is an essential aspect of the performativity of digital acts, and hence being critical is inherent in a performative understanding of acts.

If indeed we want to engage with critical digital studies concerning the connectivity of people and things through the Internet, our premise is that even in critical digital studies that explore 'the politics of the Internet', the figure of the citizen makes a faint appearance. As we explain below, we do not mean that either the term 'citizens' or 'citizenship' is absent from digital studies. On the contrary, since the 1990s, the terms 'citizens' and 'citizenship' have been used to describe politics of and on the Internet. The question is, rather, concerned with the faint appearance of the figure of the citizen as a subject making rights claims. A brief survey of exceptions to this absence will help us explain what we mean by this.

An early work by Kevin Hill and John Hughes, *Cyberpolitics: Citizen Activism in the Age of the Internet* (1998), explores the role and impact of the Internet on democratic politics in America.[23] Hill and Hughes conclude that 'politics on the Internet is dominated by a relatively savvy, conservative minority', and perhaps for this reason, 'the Internet is not going to radically change politics'.[24] More recently, R. J. Maratea's *The Politics of the Internet: Political Claims-Making in Cyberspace and Its Effect on Modern Political Activism* (2013) also explores the politics of making claims in cyberspace. Maratea argues that 'the ability to publicize claims and have them disperse through cyberspace does not guarantee that they will connect with prospective supporters, because the Internet has increased audience fragmentation'.[25] Yet for Maratea it is clear that the increased state surveillance of the Internet has shown that those with power will use Internet technologies 'to expand social control and disseminate propaganda'.[26] What is important to recognize is that although the Internet may not have changed politics radically in the fifteen years that separate these two studies, it has radically changed the meaning and function of being citizens with the rise of both corporate and state surveillance.[27]

It is also in those fifteen years that several studies have demonstrated that gradually, if not quite significantly, what it means to be a citizen on the Internet has changed. This includes studies that continue to monitor and assess the impact of the Internet on citizen politics, especially in the United States and United Kingdom, as illustrated in studies of online conduct, participation, and engagement.[28] Karen Mossberger, Caroline Tolbert, and Ramona McNeal, for example, demonstrate in *Digital Citizenship: The Internet, Society, and Participation* (2008) how online participation in society has become a necessary element of democratic citizenship.[29] By defining 'digital citizens' as 'those who use the internet regularly and effectively—that is on a daily basis', they have shown how inclusion in prevailing forms of communication have affected the ability to participate as democratic citizens. Stephen Coleman and Jay Blumler in *The Internet and Democratic Citizenship: Theory, Practice and Policy* (2009) have shown that the Internet has a huge potential to deepen democratic citizenship when invested by imaginative governments.[30] Phillip Howard, by contrast, has shown in *New Media Campaigns and the Managed Citizen* (2006) how information technologies are used in producing a managed digital citizen.[31]

These studies have also started to expand in scope beyond the United States and United Kingdom to include international developments.[32] In part, this reflects the increased involvement in the politics of the Internet of social groups such as youth, women, and minorities whose actions increasingly cross national borders and legal orders and have opened up various meanings and functions of being citizens.[33] Mark Poster, for example, argues that these involvements are giving rise to new political movements in cyberspace whose political subjects are not citizens, understood as members of nation-states, but instead netizens.[34] By using the term 'digital citizenship' as a heuristic concept, Nick Couldry and his colleagues also illustrate how digital infrastructures understood as social relations and practices are contributing to the emergence of a civic culture as a condition of citizenship.[35] Yet, they argue, it is not quite clear what kinds of subjects are emerging from these digital citizenship practices.

We argue that despite this proliferation of the term 'citizen' the figure of the citizen is lost in digital studies by both its presence and absence. When it is present, the figure of the citizen appears as a recipient of rights, a figure that already exists, and whose conduct already pertains to good civic behaviour such as participation. The citizen, it is observed, engages (or fails to), participates (or fails to), and receives (or fails to) rights and entitlements. The figure, then, is largely an already present figure or a problem figure. To put it differently, the figure of the citizen is a problem of government: how to engage, cajole, coerce, incite, invite, or broadly encourage it to inhabit forms of conduct that are already deemed to be appropriate to being a citizen. What is lost here is the figure of the citizen as an embodied subject of experience who acts through the Internet for making rights claims. We will further elaborate on this subject of making rights claims, but the figure of the citizen that we imagine is not merely a bearer or recipient of rights that already exist but one whose activism involves making claims to rights that may or may not exist.

The figure of the citizen is also lost in description of the experiences of subjects who act through the Internet. This absence is evinced by the fact that the figure of the citizen is rarely, if ever, used to describe the acts of crypto-anarchists, cyberactivists, cypherpunks, hackers, hacktivists, whistle-blowers, and other political figures of cyberspace. It sounds almost outrageous if not perverse to call the political heroes of cyberspace as citizen subjects since the figure of the citizen seems to betray their originality, rebelliousness, and vanguardism, if not their cosmopolitanism. Yet the irony here is that this is exactly the figure of the citizen we inherit as a figure who makes rights claims. It is that figure that has been betrayed and shorn of all its radicality in the contemporary politics of the Internet. Instead, and more recently, the figure of the citizen is being lost to the figure of the human as recent developments in corporate and state data snooping and spying have exacerbated. As Rikke Jørgensen has documented, increasingly, rights to privacy, access, and protection are solely articulated as human rights arguments.[36] There are, of course, exceptions to this, perhaps most famously Edward Snowden's pseudonym *Citizenfour* and scholars such as Timothy Luke and Mark Poster.[37] Nevertheless, the figure of the citizen is dimly visible and instead is either a problem subject of government or a problem subject of human rights.

The situation in citizenship studies is the opposite of digital studies. It is the figure of cyberspace that is practically lost in citizenship studies. We also observe cyberspace in relation to both its presence and absence. When the figure of cyberspace is present, it often refers to a nebulous space, often separate if not independent of physical space and one to which only some people belong. There is a certain mysticism that surrounds the figure. Its absence is often evinced during major political events such as Occupy Wall Street, *los indignados* of 15M, or Arab uprisings by the difficulty of accounting for the role of digital media in them.[38] But the figure of cyberspace is also absent in citizenship studies as scholars have yet to find a way to conceive of the figure of the citizen beyond its modern configuration as a member of the nation-state. Consequently, when the acts of subjects traverse so many borders and involve a multiplicity of legal orders, identifying this political subject as a citizen becomes a fundamental challenge. So far, describing this traversing political subject as a global citizen or cosmopolitan citizen has proved difficult if not contentious.[39]

To summarize, when we say that the figure of the citizen is lost in digital studies and that the figure of cyberspace is lost in citizenship studies, our aim is to bring attention to the question concerning political subjectivity in cyberspace. So rather than defining digital citizens narrowly as 'those who have the ability to read, write, comprehend, and navigate textual information online and who have access to affordable broadband' or 'active citizens online' or even 'Internet activists', we understand digital citizens as those who make digital rights claims, which we will elaborate in chapter 2.[40]

So to understand what it means to be digital citizens requires theorizing between digital life (and its digital subjects) and political life (and its political subjects). Both are simultaneously undergoing transformation, and understanding the dynamics of these changes is a challenge. It is a challenge that critical citizenship studies amply illustrates by focusing on citizenship as a site of contestation or social struggle rather than bundles of given rights and duties.[41] It is an approach that understands rights as not static or universal but historical and situated and arising from social struggles. The space of this struggle involves the politics of how we both shape and are shaped by sociotechnical arrangements of which we are a part. From this follows that subjects embody both the material and immaterial aspects of these arrangements where distinctions between the two become untenable.[42] Who we become as political subjects—or subjects of any kind, for that matter—is neither given or determined but enacted by what we do in relation to others and things. If so, being digital and being citizens are simultaneously the objects and subjects of political struggle, and understanding the relations between these struggles is the aim of this book.

Towards developing an understanding of being digital citizens, we draw on a number of scholars who typically study the technical workings of digital devices and platforms and their social, cultural, and political effects. We have learned a lot from the burgeoning literature on the Internet.[43] Our goal is not to focus on the specificities of how technologies like Google or Twitter algorithms work. Although we do give many examples, our aim is to develop an empirically grounded but theoretical conception of the digital citizen as a political subject. We also recognize that our examples are predominantly from Anglo-American sources, which in part says a lot about the concentration of technologies, ownership, and the scandals of our digital lives. We mention these issues to especially foreground that our focus is on *theorizing* what we call digital acts and being digital citizens and that such theorizing is necessary to clear the ground for more detailed and penetrating investigations. It is an approach we share with others and especially with J. L. Austin's *How to Do Things with Words,* work that we take up in chapter 3 to develop our conception of digital acts drawing on his theory of speech acts.[44] Austin understands language as a means of social action. We take this up to interpret digital acts as a kind of speech act and means of social struggle. At present, studies of the Internet and empirical analyses of specific digital platforms are proliferating, yet we lack concepts for framing and interpreting what these mean for being digital citizens. Many of the conventional concepts with which we are familiar, such as online, offline, virtual, and real, for example, do not hold up to critical scrutiny but instead serve as placeholders in search of concepts. Yet having concepts is critical because they shape our perceptions and imaginaries, and it is through concepts that we make sense of our experiences. Our aim, then, is to provide a conceptual apparatus that might help us to think across the numerous studies and accounts so that when we consider Twitter, for instance, we can ask: How do conventions such as microblogging platforms configure actions and create possibilities for digital citizens to act?

BECOMING DIGITAL CITIZENS

We use the term 'critical' to indicate a tradition that is marked by critical reflexivity but also by an open, engaging, and political style of thought. More specifically, however, 'critical' designates a style of thought where we investigate the acts of those who rupture contemporary conventions of being political and enact creative, autonomous, and inventive ways of becoming political. Through this approach, we have marked out what we consider to be several moves in how we theorize being digital citizens. We outline them here, recognizing that one can grasp their fuller meaning and function only by reading the chapters that follow.

In chapter 2, we develop an understanding of the space of digital life as the figure of *cyberspace* and an understanding of the figure of the *citizen* that we inherit. Rather than a separate or independent space constituted by the digital interactions and transactions of people, we define it as a space of relations between and among bodies acting through the Internet. We develop our approach to being digital citizens by drawing on Michel Foucault to argue that subjects become citizens through various processes of subjectivation that involve relations between bodies and things that constitute them as subjects *of* power. We focus on how people enact themselves as subjects of power through the Internet and at the same time bring cyberspace into being. We position this understanding of subjectivation against that of *interpellation*, which assumes that subjects are always and already formed and inhabited by external forces. Rather, we argue that citizen subjects are summoned and called upon to act through the Internet and, as subjects of power, respond by enacting themselves not only with obedience and submission but also subversion. If indeed we understand cyberspace as a space of relations *between and among bodies* acting through the Internet, ways of being digital citizens is a site of struggle between virtuous, malicious, righteous, and indifferent acts. Our performativity always involves relations between ourselves and others. In this way, conducting ourselves means to act *with* others as we place ourselves and take up and carve out social positions—something that Foucault captured by defining power as 'action upon action' or 'conduct of conduct'.

Chapter 3 develops a conception of how we say and do things through the Internet by defining digital acts as a kind of speech act. We do this by taking up Austin's definition of five classes of speech acts that have performative force: judgments, decisions, commitments, acknowledgements, and clarifications. To this we introduce a *sixth class of speech act*, which we think these classes do not account for: *claims*. We arrive at this through our consideration of the citizen subject who articulates 'I, we, they have a right to'. While subjects perform all classes of speech acts and not only through the Internet, making rights claims are specific to our definition of citizens as not sovereign rights-bearing but performative rights-claiming subjects. We argue that making rights claims involves not only performative but also legal and imaginary forces. We then argue that *digital acts* involve conventions that include not only words but also images and sounds and various actions such as liking, coding, clicking, downloading, sorting, blocking, and querying. If Austin showed *how we do things with words*, we also try to show *how we do words with things*.[45] We argue that these digital acts resignify four political questions about the Internet: anonymity, extensity, traceability, and velocity.

In chapters 4, 5, and 6 we then specify how these contestations are enacted through three groupings of digital acts—callings, openings, and closings—and outline the various conventions and actions that compose them. Chapter 7, rather than considering the substance of digital rights, attends to the processes involved in *enacting digital rights claims*. We do so by bringing together those political subjects who make digital rights claims by their acts through the Internet (performativity) and those who make digital rights claims in or by what they say about those rights in declarations, bills, charters, and manifestos (imaginary) and call upon authorities for the inscription of those rights (legality).

Collectively, these moves refine our approach to enacting digital citizens. We work through a complex terrain of openings and closings that cyberspace occasions but also raise a fundamental—and increasingly universal—question: How do we conduct ourselves through the Internet? Given the rights cyberspace occasions and we demand, should we embrace it without question? Given the perils it elicits, should we avoid it? Given the dangers it creates, should we abandon it? Given its potentialities, should we tout the dawn of a new era? All these questions are being asked today, yet they may not be the questions that really matter. Given its pervasiveness and omnipresence, avoiding or shunning cyberspace is as dystopian as quitting social space; it is also certain that conducting ourselves in cyberspace requires, as many activists and scholars have warned, intense critical vigilance. Since there cannot be generic or universal answers to how we conduct ourselves, more or less every incipient or existing political subject needs to ask in what ways it is being called upon and subjectified through cyberspace. In other words, to return again to the conceptual apparatus of this book, the kinds of citizen subjects cyberspace cultivates are not homogenous and universal but fragmented, multiple, and agonistic. At the same time, the figure of a citizen yet to come is not inevitable; while cyberspace is a fragile and precarious space, it also affords openings, moments when thinking, speaking, and acting differently become possible by challenging and resignifying its conventions. These are the moments that we highlight to argue that digital rights are not only a project of inscriptions but also enactment.

NOTES

1. We recognize that digital life has preceded the Internet. The connectedness of digital lives is a more recent phenomenon associated with the Internet, especially the World Wide Web protocol. Our focus in this book is the political consequences and implications of digital lives being connected through the Internet rather than digital lives in general. See J. E. Cohen, *Configuring the Networked Self: Law, Code, and the Play of Everyday Practice* (Yale University Press, 2012); N. Negroponte, *Being Digital* (Hodder and Stoughton, 1995); Z. Papacharissi, ed., *A Networked Self: Identity, Community and Culture on Social Network Sites* (Routledge, 2011).

2. Negroponte, *Being Digital*; S. Turkle, *Life on the Screen: Identity in the Age of the Internet* (Simon & Schuster, 1995).

3. E. Morozov, *The Net Delusion: How Not to Liberate the World* (PublicAffairs, 2011); S. Turkle, *Alone Together: Why We Expect More from Technology and Less from Each Other* (Basic, 2011).

4. R. Deibert, "The Geopolitics of Internet Control: Censorship, Sovereignty, and Cyberspace," in *Routledge Handbook of Internet Politics*, ed. A. Chadwick and P. N. Howard (Routledge, 2009), 324.

5. M. Venkataramanan, "The Data Industry Is Selling Your Life," *Wired*, Nov. 2014; L. Harding, *The Snowden Files: The Inside Story of the World's Most Wanted Man* (Vintage, 2014). As we shall see below, what is also staggering is the emergence of a commercial and noncommercial security industry that advises data subjects that they are individually responsible for protecting their privacy and safety, thereby individualizing what is essentially a political and hence a collective problem.

6. A. Hern, "Sir Tim Berners-Lee Speaks out on Data Ownership." *Guardian* 2014 [accessed 8 October 2014], bit.ly/1t2DEPR.

7. O. Bowcott, "Bullied Man Uses Video from Sunglasses to Mount Private Court Case," *Guardian*, 7 October 2014 [accessed 12 October 2014], bit.ly/ZVoTBF.

8. J. Katz, "The Digital Citizen," *Wired* 5, 12, Dec. 1997, 5.

9. Ibid., 7–8.

10. W. J. Miller, "Digital Citizen," in *Encyclopedia of Social Media and Politics*, ed. K. Harvey (Sage, 2014), 2.

11. Digital Citizens Alliance, "Become a Digital Citizen: Get Involved in Making the Internet Safe 2014" [accessed 26 September 2014], bit.ly/1utQ7vz.

12. S. White, *The Ethos of a Late-Modern Citizen* (Harvard University Press, 2009).

13. D. Bigo, "The Transnational Field of Computerised Exchange of Information in Police Matters and Its European Guilds," in *Transnational Power Elites: The Social and Global Structuration of the EU*, ed. N. Kauppi and M. R. Madsen (Routledge, 2013); D. Bigo, "Security, Surveillance and Democracy," in *Routledge Handbook of Surveillance Studies*, ed. K. Ball et al. (Routledge, 2012). For Bigo, the rights of data subjects depend

on their behaviour within digital networks. If their behaviour conflicts with targets identified by algorithms, their rights will come under question.

14. This is a question posed with respect to surveillance by Z. Bauman et al., "After Snowden: Rethinking the Impact of Surveillance," *International Political Sociology* 8, 2 (2014). The authors raise the question about how multiple actors would need to resist surveillance strategies but also the question of how Internet users will adjust their everyday conduct. It is an open question whether Internet users 'will continue to participate in their own surveillance through self-exposure or develop new forms of subjectivity that is more reflexive about the consequences of their own actions' (124).

15. Ibid., 128. Using the Möbius strip as a metaphor to capture the transversal nature of the Internet, especially concerning surveillance, Bauman et al. argue that 'while big data collection blurs categorizations of what is "domestic" and what is "foreign," the consequent reconfiguration of the boundaries of the sovereign state into a Möbius strip has in turn become a site, in and of itself, of political struggles, resistance and dissent. Along the Möbius strip, states, social movements, and individuals can play a variety of games, reenacting the meanings of sovereignty and citizenship, security, and liberty.'

16. We must heed Didier Bigo's work, which documents how an international field of security professionals emerged and how its professionals are heavily invested in the hyperinflation of dangers and threats of cyberspace. Often, Bigo argues, interventions to quell such dangers serve to expand the security apparatus itself rather than enhancing security. See Bigo, "Security, Surveillance and Democracy," 278.

17. Some examples include T. W. Luke, "Digital Citizenship," in *Emerging Digital Spaces in Contemporary Society: Properties of Technology*, ed. P. Kalantzis-Cope and K. Gherab Martín (Palgrave Macmillan, 2011); M. Poster, "Digital Networks and Citizenship," *Proceedings of Modern Language Association of America (PMLA)* 117, 1 (2002).

18. K. Mossberger et al., *Digital Citizenship: The Internet, Society, and Participation* (MIT Press, 2008); K. Mossberger et al., "Measuring Digital Citizenship: Mobile Access and Broadband," *International Journal of Communication* 6 (2012).

19. E. Mayo and T. Steinberg, "The Power of Information: An Independent Review," June 2007 [accessed 12 October 2014], bit.ly/ZVoZct.

20. The field of digital studies not only comprises the impact of digital technologies but also their increasing connectedness. As such, digital studies includes but is broader than another incipient field, that of Internet studies. The broad scope of Internet studies includes not only the technologies that make the Internet possible but also uses of these technologies and the development of national and international policies to govern and regulate their functioning. C. Ess and M. Consalvo, "Introduction: What Is 'Internet Studies'?," in *The Handbook of Internet Studies*, ed. M. Consalvo and C. Ess (Wiley-Blackwell, 2013); W. H. Dutton, "Internet Studies: The Foundations of a Transformative Field," in *The Oxford Handbook of Internet Studies*, ed. W. H. Dutton (Oxford University Press, 2013).

21. A. Kroker and M. Kroker, *Critical Digital Studies: A Reader*, 2nd ed. (University of Toronto Press, 2013).

22. Ibid., 14.

23. K. A. Hill and J. E. Hughes, *Cyberpolitics: Citizen Activism in the Age of the Internet* (Rowman & Littlefield, 1998).

24. Ibid., 180, 182.

25. R. J. Maratea, *The Politics of the Internet: Political Claims-Making in Cyberspace and Its Effect on Modern Political Activism* (Lexington, 2014), 117.

26. Ibid., 126.

27. This is quite evident in a large collection of already established essays on the politics of the Internet. W. H. Dutton and E. Dubois, eds., *Politics and the Internet*, 4 vols. (Routledge, 2014).

28. S. Coleman, "The Lonely Citizen: Indirect Representation in an Age of Networks," *Political Communication* 22, 2 (2005); Mossberger et al., *Digital Citizenship*; P. N. Howard, *New Media Campaigns and the Managed Citizen* (Cambridge University Press, 2006); S. Coleman and J. G. Blumler, *The Internet and Democratic Citizenship: Theory, Practice and Policy* (Cambridge University Press, 2009).

29. Mossberger et al., *Digital Citizenship*.

30. Coleman and Blumler, *The Internet and Democratic Citizenship*.

31. Howard, *New Media Campaigns and the Managed Citizen*.

32. J. C. Santora, "Crossing the Digital Divide: Do All Global Citizens Have Their Passports?," *Academy of Management Perspectives* 20, 4 (2006); J. James, "The Digital Divide across All Citizens of the World: A New Concept," *Social Indicators Research* 89, 2 (2008); G. Yang, *The Power of the Internet in China: Citizen Activism Online* (Columbia University Press, 2009); K. L. Schlozman et al., "Who Speaks? Citizen Political Voice on the Internet Commons," *Daedalus* 140, 4 (2011); K. Tartoussieh, "Virtual Citizenship: Islam, Culture, and Politics in the Digital Age," *International Journal of Cultural Policy* 17, 2 (2011); M. Gillespie, "BBC Arabic, Social Media and Citizen Production: An Experiment in Digital Democracy before the Arab Spring," *Theory, Culture & Society* 30, 4 (2013).

33. T. Kern and S.-h. Nam, "The Making of a Social Movement: Citizen Journalism in South Korea," *Current Sociology* 57, 5 (2009); W. Y. Lin et al., "Becoming Citizens: Youths' Civic Uses of New Media in Five Digital Cities in East Asia," *Journal of Adolescent Research* 25, 6 (2010); Tartoussieh, "Virtual Citizenship: Islam, Culture, and Politics in the Digital Age"; L. Herrera, "Youth and Citizenship in the Digital Age: A View from Egypt," *Harvard Educational Review* 82, 3 (2012); Y. M. Kim, "The Shifting Sands of Citizenship: Toward a Model of the Citizenry in Life Politics," *Annals of the American Academy of Political and Social Science* 644 (2012).

34. Poster, "Digital Networks and Citizenship," 101–3.

35. N. Couldry et al., "Digital Citizenship? Narrative Exchange and the Changing Terms of Civic Culture," *Citizenship Studies* 18, 6–7 (2014).

36. R. F. Jørgensen, *Framing the Net: The Internet and Human Rights* (Edward Elgar, 2013).

37. Poster, "Digital Networks and Citizenship"; M. Poster, "Cyberdemocracy: Internet and the Public Sphere," in *Politics and the Internet*, ed. W. H. Dutton and E. Dubois (Routledge, 2014); Luke, "Digital Citizenship."

38. Neither of the two major handbooks on citizenship studies surveying the entire field globally, for example, features a chapter on digital citizens or discusses broadly the impact of the Internet for citizenship studies. H.-A. Van der Heijden, ed., *Handbook of Political Citizenship and Social Movements* (Edward Elgar, 2014); E. F. Isin and P. Nyers, eds., *The Routledge Handbook of Global Citizenship Studies* (Routledge, 2014).

39. The debate over global or cosmopolitan citizenship is now extensive, but it has proved to be a contested concept. H. Schattle, *The Practices of Global Citizenship* (Rowman & Littlefield, 2007); D. Archibugi, *The Global Commonwealth of Citizens: Toward Cosmopolitan Democracy* (Princeton University Press, 2008).

40. Mossberger et al., *Digital Citizenship*, 140.

41. J. Clarke et al., *Disputing Citizenship* (Policy Press, 2014).

42. K. Hayles, "The Materiality of Informatics," *Configurations* 1, 1 (1993).

43. Cohen, *Configuring the Networked Self*; E. G. Coleman, *Coding Freedom: The Ethics and Aesthetics of Hacking* (Princeton University Press, 2013); R. Deibert, *Black Code: Inside the Battle for Cyberspace* (McClelland & Stewart, 2013); C. Fuchs, *Social Media: A Critical Introduction* (Sage, 2014); P. Gerbaudo, *Tweets and the Streets: Social Media and Contemporary Activism* (Pluto, 2012); T. Jordan, *Cyberpower: The Culture and Politics of Cyberspace and the Internet* (Routledge, 1999); L. Lessig, *Code: Version 2.0* (Basic, 2006); Morozov, *Net Delusion*; Papacharissi, ed., *A Networked Self*; H. Postigo, *The Digital Rights Movement: The Role of Technology in Subverting Digital Copyright* (MIT Press, 2012); J. van Dijck, *The Culture of Connectivity: A Critical History of Social Media* (Oxford University Press, 2013).

44. J. L. Austin, *How to Do Things with Words* (Oxford University Press, 1962).

45. This is inspired by Bruno Latour's reversal of Austin's statement—doing things with words—to 'doing words with things'. Though he does not refer to Austin when he uses this phrase in this chapter, we think his approach very much follows Austin's conceptualization of speech acts. B. Latour, "The Berlin Key or How to Do Words with Things," in *Matter, Materiality and Modern Culture*, ed. P. Graves-Brown (Routledge, 2000). However, in another writing, Latour references Austin's *How to do Things with Words* in his analysis of how legal texts are made up of not declarative but performative statements. There he argues that a weakness of Austin's concept of speech acts is his reliance on grammar and short interactions rather than 'the whole regime of enunciation.' B. Latour, *An Ethnography of the Conseil d'Etat* (Polity, 2010), 225.

TWO

Citizens and Cyberspace

If indeed the premise of this book is that there is an emerging political subject called 'the digital citizen', we cannot assume that this subject is without history and geography. We cannot simply assume that being a citizen online already means something (whether it is the ability to participate or the ability to stay safe) and then look for those whose conduct conforms to this meaning.[1] The understanding of citizenship and political subjectivity associated with it has a complex history and geography that should not be simplified as participation, safety, security, or access, although obviously these are arguably important aspects of being a citizen. To say that 'digital citizenship is the ability to participate in society online' leaves out too much to properly understand the impact of the Internet on a central figure of political life—the citizen.[2] So any attempt at theorizing 'digital citizens' ought to begin with the historical figure of the citizen before even shifting focus to the digital. Moreover, confining the digital to the Internet or the online overlooks how digital citizens come into being through the meshing of their online and offline lives.[3] For us, this means developing a robust conception of cyberspace that moves beyond this binary trope and ostensibly virtual versus physical or 'real' spaces. This chapter aims to accomplish these two objectives. We first summon a figure of the citizen as a historical and geographical figure by drawing on critical citizenship studies. Then we summon a figure of cyberspace as a space of acts—digital acts—by drawing on critical digital studies. We then develop a first set of propositions on citizens and cyberspace that guide the following chapters.

THE FIGURE OF THE CITIZEN WE INHERIT

Over the past three decades, just when the Internet has become prominent, there has also been a growth of studies on citizenship in the social
sciences and humanities. This has led to the development of a field called
'citizenship studies' that is large and diverse enough that it is impossible
to outline, let alone discuss its basic tenets.[4] The field begins with citizenship defined as rights, obligations, and belonging to the nation-state.
Three rights (civil, political, and social) and three obligations (conscription, taxation, and franchise) govern relationships between citizens and
states. Civil rights include the right to free speech, to conscience, and to
dignity; political rights include voting and standing for office; and social
rights include unemployment insurance, universal health care, and welfare. Although conscription is rapidly disappearing as a citizenship obligation, taxation is still fundamental; voting, although declining, remains
vital. The field of critical citizenship studies makes two basic interventions on this understanding. First, it recognizes new rights, such as sexual
rights, cultural rights, and environmental rights, and documents struggles over their institutionalization (e.g., the struggles over same-sex mar-
riage in the United States and Europe).[5] Second, it also recognizes that
increasingly, whether traditional (i.e., civil, political, social) or expanded
(cultural, economic, environmental, sexual, transnational, and urban),
rights and obligations are negotiated through supranational institutions
such as the United Nations (e.g., Universal Declaration of Human
Rights), the Council of Europe (e.g., European Court of Human Rights),
and the European Union (e.g., European Court of Justice) as well as de-
volved institutions such as regional parliaments (e.g., Quebec or Scottish
parliaments) and traditions of minority communities (e.g., applications of
Sharia law) that question the assumption that citizenship is membership
in only a nation-state.[6] Moreover, critical citizenship studies is distinguished from conventional citizenship studies by its performative understanding of rights and that the polities that give rise to and protect those
rights are various. If we begin thinking about citizenship as 'a membership in the nation-state', we are already approaching it in conventional
ways. Rather, critical citizenship studies often begins with the citizen as a
historical and geographic figure—a figure that emerged in particular historical and geographical configurations and a dynamic, changing, and
above all contested figure of politics that comes into being by performing

politics.[7] How does the figure of the citizen function in critical citizenship studies?

The figure of the citizen as it is inherited from the European Enlightenment is paradoxical. This is born out of two contradictions that it embodies: a contradiction between freedom and obedience and a contradiction between universalism and particularism. Étienne Balibar has drawn attention to both of these contradictions in his response to Jean-Luc Nancy's question 'Who comes after the subject?'[8] Nancy asked a question about the status of the speaking and acting subject of Enlightenment *after* the critique of the sovereign subject—or the Cartesian subject—that was the linchpin of political theory since the Enlightenment.[9] To put it schematically, modern political theory created a divide between modernity and tradition where a subject to power (tradition) was *replaced* by a subject of power (modernity). To put it differently, if on the one side of the divide stood a subject of the sovereign (subject to power), on the other side stood the sovereign subject (subject of power). Modern political theory hailed the arrival of the latter *as* the displacement of the former.[10] Critical political theory questions both the divide and displacement. Instead, it asserts that a subject is a composite of multiple forces, identifications, affiliations, and associations. The subject is divided by these elements rather than by tradition and modernity. It also asserts that a subject is a site of multiple forms of power (sovereign, disciplinary, control) that embodies composite dispositions (obedience, submission, subversion). The question, then, was if we reject the sovereign subject behind every act or deed, then how can we understand the acting subject today composed of, as it were, these multiple identifications, powers, and dispositions?

Balibar's response to this question was surprisingly straightforward: what comes after the subject has already a name, and it is the citizen.[11] Balibar highlighted the paradoxical aspects of the figure of the citizen. To begin, Balibar thought that the very idea of the rights of the citizen institutes a historical figure that is not merely *subject to power* or the *subject of power* but embodies both.[12] This move is quite significant: if being a subject *to* power requires obedience, being a subject *of* power requires disobedience. But these are not pure forms; rather, the citizen subject embodies these as potentialities. Being a subject *to* power is marked by the citizen's domination by the sovereign, and her rights derive from that which is given to her by the (patriarchal) sovereign. Being a subject *of* power means being an agent of power, even if this requires submission. There is an important difference between obedience and submission. If being *subject to power* means obedience to the sovereign, then it requires domination as a mode of power. Whether this is total obedience or resistant obedience depends on the circumstances. By contrast, being a *subject of power* means *submission* to authority in whose formation the citizen participates and its potential *subversion*. What distinguishes the citizen from the subject is that the citizen is this composite subject of obedience, submission, and subversion. The birth of the citizen as a *subject of power* does not mean the disappearance of the subject as a *subject to power*. The citizen subject embodies these forms of power in which she is implicated, where obedience, submission, and subversion are not separate dispositions but are always-present potentialities.

This is, at any rate, our reading of Balibar, and we obviously read him through Michel Foucault's rethinking of the transformation from ancient to modern forms of power with his emphasis on the simultaneous presence of obedience, submission, and subversion. Expressing the basic question that motivated his studies on power, knowledge, and ethics, Foucault said, 'How is it that in Western Christian culture the government of men demands, on the part of those who are led, not only acts of obedience and submission but also "acts of truth," which have the peculiar requirement not just that the subject tell the truth but that he tell the truth about himself, his faults, his desires, the state of his soul, and so on?'[13] For Foucault, it was 'acts of truth' that afforded possibilities for the subject to constitute herself as a subject of power. For us, this also means that acts of truth afford possibilities of subversion. Being a subject of power means responding to the call 'how should one "govern oneself" by performing actions in which one is oneself the objective of those actions, the domain in which they are brought to bear, the instrument they employ, and the subject that acts?'[14] In describing this as his approach, Foucault was clear that the 'development of a domain of acts, practices, and thoughts' poses a problem for politics.[15] It is in this respect that we consider the Internet in relation to myriad acts, practices, and thoughts that pose a problem for the politics of the subject in contemporary societies.

To our knowledge, Balibar is the only scholar who describes Foucault's contribution as describing 'the birth of the citizen subject.'[16] This is intriguing. It shifts our attention on how subjects become citizens through various processes of subjectivation that involve relations between bodies and things that constitute them as subjects *of* power.[17] If we focus on how people enact themselves as subjects of power through the Internet, it involves investigating how people use language to describe themselves and their relations to others and how language summons them as speaking beings. To put it differently, it involves investigating how people do things with words and words with things to enact themselves. It also means addressing how people understand themselves as subjects of power when acting through the Internet. This requires exploring how people come into being through the Internet not only as speaking subjects who use language but also other modes of engaging and acting. For Balibar 'the citizen's becoming-a-subject takes the form of a dialectic, this is because there are necessary contradictions between founding a definition of the citizen and the contestations over it.'[18] As we shall see, becoming digital citizens in acting through the Internet is not free of these contradictions.

The citizen then bequeaths us a figure of politics that not only is capable of being obedient but can also be simultaneously a submissive (*to* authority) and a subversive (*of* authority) figure. It also always carries within it the possibility and danger of the obedient subject of sovereign power. The citizen is a subject who submits to government in which she is implicated. This submission makes this figure a subject of subversion capable of questioning the terms of her own submission. To put it differently, the agency of the citizen appears in the gap between the capacity to submit to authority and yet the ability to act in dissent. This is not a sovereign subject in the mastery of her destiny but an embodied subject formed through games of multiple affiliations and of submission and subversion. The rights that the citizen holds are not the rights of an already-existing sovereign subject but the rights of a figure who submits to authority in the name of those rights and acts to call into question its terms. This is the inescapable and inherited contradiction between submission and subversion of the figure of the citizen that can be expressed in a paradoxical phrase: submission *as* freedom.

The second contradiction concerns its universalism against particularism. For the subject to become a citizen, the conditions must be equal for everyone. To become a citizen is predicated on this equality. This equality is universal. Who is then the citizen? Balibar says that the citizen is a person who enjoys rights in completely realizing being human and is free because being human is a universal condition for everyone.[19] We would say the citizen is a subject who performs rights in realizing being political because becoming political is a universal condition for everyone. There is, however, a contradiction here. It is that, historically speaking, while some subjects are considered capable of conducting themselves as citizens, such as white, male, propertied, able-bodied, Christian, and heterosexual beings, the opposites of each of those subject positions will remain subjects. As Mark Poster writes, 'Western concepts and political principles such as the rights of [hu]man[s] and the citizen, however progressive a role they played in history, may not provide an adequate basis of critique in our current, increasingly global condition.'[20] Poster says this is so, among other things, because Western concepts arise out of imperial and colonial histories and because situated differences are as important as universal principles.[21] This contradiction of the figure of the citizen can be expressed in another paradoxical phrase: universalism *as* particularism.

From a critical perspective on citizenship, these contradictions are the sources of the vitality of the figure of the citizen. These contradictions constitute the figure of the citizen as a subject of claims *for* rights. Each claim that a citizen articulates *against* an authority puts her *under* demands of that authority. If rights of citizenship come into being in law, the citizen comes into being through the performance of that law or performance of the right to claim rights. If the citizen comes into being performatively through rights, the imaginary of citizenship mobilizes this figure of the citizen as a subversive subject. She is a subject of power whose acts of citizenship are simultaneously of submission and subversion. Acts of citizenship embody these two contradictions. On the one hand, acts produce universalism because its subjects claim that everyone can act; on the other hand, and simultaneously, acts produce particularisms against those who are rendered unable or incapable to act or whose acts cannot be recognized.

If indeed we understand this dynamic of taking up positions as subjectivation, we then identify three forces through which citizen subjects come into being: legality, performativity, and imaginary. These are neither sequential nor parallel but simultaneous and intertwined *forces of subjectivation*. We will explain why we call these 'forces' in more detail later, in chapter 3. For now, let us briefly describe each in turn. The legality of citizenship inscribes the figure of the citizen as that person with the right to claim rights. Since the late eighteenth century in Europe and postcolonial societies, this figure of the citizen has acquired certain rights that define it: civil, political, and social rights. Civil rights, such as the right to free speech, the right to privacy, the right to due process, freedom from arbitrary power, freedom to associate, the right to dignity, and the freedom of conscience, are outcomes of social struggles over these liberties and required simultaneously submission to authority and its subversion (e.g., dissent, resistance, protest). Similarly, political rights, such as the right to vote representatives to the parliament, to run for office, to organize political parties and movements, to protest, to assembly, and to civil disobedience are political rights that overall define the figure of the democratic citizen. The social rights of citizenship have their history of struggles, too. The right to universal benefits, welfare, allowances, and health and other social services are not only won through social struggles but also establish a principle: the figure of the citizen, to be an effective political figure, has to acquire not only a modicum of civil life but also social existence. The charters, bills, and declarations claiming rights—with all the symbolic dates associated with them of 1689, 1776, 1789, 1835, 1945—are largely about inscribing again and again rights as claims through social and political struggles both the origins and effects of which are the figure of the citizen.[22]

If making rights claims is performative, it follows that these rights are neither fixed nor guaranteed: they need to be repeatedly performed. Their coming into being and remaining effective requires performativity. The performative force of citizenship reminds us that the figure of the citizen has to be brought into being repeatedly through acts (repertoires, declarations, and proclamations) and conventions (rituals, customs, practices, traditions, laws, institutions, technologies, and protocols). Without the performance of rights, the figure of the citizen would merely exist in theory and would have no meaning in democratic politics. As Karen Zivi writes, if we consider citizenship as making rights claims, it is because it is a performative practice.[23] For Zivi, 'we make rights claims to criticize practices we find objectionable, to shed light on injustice, to limit the power of government, and to demand state accountability and intervention.'[24] We often focus on the content of these rights rather than rights claiming as the performativity of citizenship. As Zivi writes, '[T]o approach rights and rights claiming from the perspective of performativity means, then, asking questions not simply about what a right is but also about what it is we do when we make rights claims.'[25] So what is it that people do when making rights claims? We will address this question in chapter 3. For now, let us note that making rights claims in or by saying *and* doing 'I, we, they have a right to' involves performing both contradictions inherent in citizenship. We need to make two points here. First, performing citizenship both invokes and breaks conventions. We shall characterize conventions broadly as sociotechnical arrangements that embody norms, values, affects, laws, ideologies, and technologies. As sociotechnical arrangements, conventions involve agreement or even consent—either deliberate or often implicit—that constitutes the logic of any custom, institution, opinion, ritual, and indeed law or embodies any accepted conduct. Since both the logic and embodiment of conventions are objects of agreement, performing these conventions also produces disagreement. Another way of saying this is that the performativity of conduct such as making rights claims often exceeds conventions. As Zivi writes, '[A]nalyzing [citizenship] from a performative perspective means, then, appreciating the extent to which our claims both reference and reiterate social conventions, and yet have forces and effects that exceed them.'[26] We have identified this as the contradiction between submission and subversion or consent and dissent. Jacques Rancière captures this as dissensus.[27] We will return to dissensus in chapter 7. Second, while articulating a particular demand (for inclusion, recognition), performing citizenship enacts a universal right to claim rights. This is the contradiction between the universalism and particularism of citizenship.

Yet for the figure of the citizen to come into being through making rights claims that are expressed in and through law, there has to be an imaginary of citizenship produced through thought, symbols, images, ideas, and ideals of the democratic citizen. This imaginary force of citizenship is indispensable for its performative and legal forces, which cannot be thought without them. The imaginary of citizenship includes a whole series of statements and utterances about what citizenship is, ought to be, has been, will have to be, and so on. The imaginary of citizenship is obviously mobilized by and participates in the formation of the legality of citizenship and its performativity and yet cannot be reduced to them. In a way, how we orient ourselves towards 1689, 1776, 1789, 1835, and 1945 and the contested meanings we attach to them are part of this imaginary work of citizenship.

Let us make it clear that our sketch of a critical perspective on citizenship that involves legality, performativity, and imaginary as three overlapping and yet distinct forces of subjectivation, at least for interpreting *modern* democratic citizenship, is open to disagreements, qualifications, and clarifications. We find it difficult to express it systematically since we have more or less assembled it from various dispersed sources, not least our own writings on the subject. But we hope we make a sufficient case that the figure of the citizen cannot enter into debates about the Internet as a subject without history and without geography—and without contradictions. Rather, a critical approach to the figure of the citizen at a minimum recognizes that it is both a subject *to* power and subject *of* power and that this figure embodies obedience, submission, and subversion as its dispositions. If indeed the citizen subject comes into being legally, performatively, and imaginatively through making rights claims, it inherits these sedimented histories and geographies.

THE FIGURE OF CYBERSPACE

We cannot think, let alone write, without concepts. But concepts are not merely organizing principles of our experience; they emplace us in that experience. We experience the world through and with concepts. The concepts that become dominant parts of discourse shape our perceptions through which we make sense of our own experience. We, in other words, live our lives through concepts we have inherited. Cyberspace became such a concept with which we experience being 'online' and participate in online activities. We mentioned earlier that we are critical of a supposed difference between online and offline lives and politics. This is in part because connected devices such as phones, tablets, and wearable technologies render that difference problematic, as people don't need to use a computer to become connected. It is not only our bodies that are connected through the Internet but also our devices in which our lives are embodied. To put it differently, while being online may be a discontinuous activity, being connected is almost always continuous. For these reasons, the concept of cyberspace is a challenge for theorizing being digital citizens not because we make that choice but because it is a concept that already functions in contemporary discourse.

Yet despite its dominance, the concept of cyberspace is usually used in a way that makes it difficult to theorize being digital citizens. Just consider how ubiquitous three of its derivatives have become: cyberwar, cyber-security, and cybercrime. Confronted with a dominant concept, we could choose to ignore its 'flaws' and use it for convenience; we could entirely 'reject' it; or we could note its flaws but use it cautiously. All approaches have been taken with mixed results. If indeed the figure of cyberspace is not something we can merely 'avoid' or 'critique' as the dominant concept through which we conceptualize our experiences of online life, how do we approach it? To explain why we'd rather analytically focus on 'being digital citizens', we will have to come to terms with the figure of cyberspace and its allure and continue to use it with reservations.

We begin with a banal observation. The Internet and cyberspace are not equivalent things. The Internet is a layered and complex phenomenon. It is certainly an interconnected network of computers (and devices) using standard and negotiated protocols to transmit information converted into binary numeric form known as digital objects. These can be sounds, images (moving or still), words, and numbers. The Internet includes governments, corporations, and organizations that own and operate terrestrial and extraterrestrial infrastructures that transmit digital objects. It also includes Internet service providers (ISPs) who own and operate additional infrastructure that connects users to the Internet. It includes software such as operating systems, code, and cryptography to encrypt and decrypt data, and hardware such as routers, switches, cables, transmitters, receivers, servers, and server clusters. And it also contains all of the people who maintain, operate, and configure these infrastructural elements.[28] Let us now describe cyberspace as a space of transactions and interactions between and among bodies acting through the Internet. But this is hardly uncontroversial. If indeed cyberspace is first a relational space, these relations are between and among bodies through the Internet. These bodies can be collective (institutions, organizations, corporations, collectives, groups), cybernetic, or social.[29] Finally, these acting bodies are neither subservient nor sovereign subjects. To restate our conception in short, *cyberspace is a space of relations between and among bodies acting through the Internet.*[30] Cyberspace is a space of social struggles and no less or more 'real' than, say, social space or cultural space—concepts that also describe relations between bodies and things. Yet this separation between 'real' space and cyberspace is so pervasive and carries a baggage that needs questioning.

The term 'cyberspace' is often attributed to William Gibson's telling of the story of a computer hacker whose adventures in cyberspace drive Gibson's award-winning novel *Neuromancer* (1984). This attribution is both a fact and fiction. There Gibson imagines cyberspace as: 'a consensual hallucination experienced daily by billions of legitimate operators, in every nation, by children being taught mathematical concepts. . . . A graphic representation of data abstracted from the banks of every computer in the human system.' Such is the life of words. Following Gibson, cyberspace became a dominant concept to express a separate and independent sphere of life possibly for 'digital citizens' if not cyborgs. As Gibson himself recognized, it has travelled far from his usage and vision. In the documentary film *No Maps for These Territories* he recounts, '[A]ll I knew about the word "cyberspace" when I coined it, was that it seemed like an effective buzzword. It seemed evocative and essentially meaningless.'[31] This is reminiscent of Nietzsche's genealogical principle that just because something comes into being for one purpose does not mean that it will serve that purpose forever.[32] Cyberspace has now become widely used not only in popular culture but also in social sciences and humanities scholarship. In fact, there is a strong resonance between popular culture and scholarship regarding cyberspace that many social sciences and humanities concepts do not enjoy.

We can't provide a genealogy of cyberspace here, but let it suffice to note two of its pervasive contemporary connotations. First, a different and distinct, if not unique, space exists elsewhere, and it is separate from a space that is said to be physical. Second, this space is (or wants to be) independent. These two connotations function in myriad ways, such as virtual versus actual space, cloud versus real space, online world versus offline world, and nonphysical versus physical world.[33] In the early 1990s, when the concept began taking broader shape, cyberspace was saturated by its libertarian qualities as an independent space. 'A Declaration of the Independence of Cyberspace', written by the cofounder of the Electronic Frontier Foundation, John Parry Barlow, became its poignant and oft-quoted representative. The declaration argued that '[c]yberspace consists of transactions, relationships, and thought itself, arrayed like a standing wave in the web of our communications. Ours is a world that is both everywhere and nowhere, but it is not where bodies live.'[34] The declaration imagines that a new world is being created where everyone is entitled to enter and where no distinctions or backgrounds exist. Being adversely addressed to governments, the declaration states that 'your legal concepts of property, expression, identity, movement, and context do not apply to us. They are all based on matter, and there is no matter here.' Leaving aside the paradox of using an American experience and language for creating a universal 'civilization of the mind', the declaration reveals that cyberspace is to be conceived not only as metaphysical (no bodies and no matter) but also as an autonomous space ('On behalf of the future, I ask you of the past to leave us alone. You are not welcome among us. You have no sovereignty where we gather.')

These two functions—that cyberspace is separate and independent—mobilize not only analytical but also political and, as we shall see, legal arguments about the distinctiveness of cyberspace. Currently, these functions operate so strongly that even the most careful scholars, such as Lawrence Lessig, who routinely question the uses of cyberspace still maintain this distinction.

It is helpful to follow Lessig on this distinction. In 1996 he considers the Internet and cyberspace to be more or less the same thing.[35] For Lessig, cyberspace is a metaphor to understand the Internet and the ways in which it is different from what he called 'real' or nonvirtual space. Arguing that cyberspace is (or used to be) a space of freedom, Lessig writes that 'the technologies of control are relatively crude. Not that there is no control. Cyberspace is not anarchy. But that control is exercised through the ordinary tools of human regulation—through social norms, and social stigma; through peer pressure, and reward.'[36] The main difference between cyberspace and 'real' space for Lessig used to be the way in which conduct upon conduct was regulated—in other words, how power is exercised. The anathema for Lessig is the loss of this freedom in cyberspace. In real space, governing people requires inducing them to act in certain ways, but in the last instance, people had the choice to act this way or that way. By contrast, in cyberspace conduct is governed by code, which takes away that choice. In cyberspace, 'if the regulator wants to induce a certain behavior, she need not threaten, or cajole, to inspire the change. She need only change the code—the software that defines the terms upon which the individual gains access to the system, or uses assets on the system.'[37] This is because 'code is an efficient means of regulation. But its perfection makes it something different. One obeys these laws as code not because one should; one obeys these laws as code because one can do nothing else. There is no choice about whether to yield to the demand for a password; one complies if one wants to enter the system. In the well implemented system, there is no civil disobedience.'[38] What Lessig suggests is that cyberspace is not only separate and independent but constitutes a new mode of power. You constitute yourself as a subject of power by submitting to code. Lessig thinks that cyberspace used to be an open and uncontrolled space and its 'regulation [used to be] achieved through social forces much like the social forms that regulate real space.'[39] At one time it was not zoned, but now it has become so. For Lessig, then, 'the essence of cyberspace [used to be] the search engine—tools with which one crosses an infinite space, to locate, and go to, the stuff one wants. The space today is open, but only because it is made that way.'[40] But Lessig argues that engineers were acquiring too much power in creating zones by code and that people were increasingly filtering themselves out from various zones.[41] Here Lessig attributes almost sovereign power to code and accounts for the loss of freedom of cyberspace with the control of code. This is almost equivalent to the (ancient-modern) divide we described above, between on the one side a subject of a sovereign and on the other side the sovereign subject.

Lessig later develops a slightly more nuanced idea of the difference between cyberspace and the Internet, yet he still insists on a basic difference between cyberspace and real space.[42] Lessig thinks cyberspace, like geographic space, has architecture, and this architecture is the code: algorithms that govern hardware and software switches and regulate access to its specific zones. Lessig writes, '[C]ode is a regulator in cyberspace because it defines the terms upon which cyberspace is offered. And those who set those terms increasingly recognize the code as a means to achieving the behaviors that benefit them best.'[43] For Lessig, the difference between what he calls 'real' space and cyberspace is that real space is structured around public spaces that have access to everyone. By contrast, cyberspace includes many zones that are off limits to many and is constituted by code, which means 'You can resist this code—you can resist how you find it, just as you can resist cold weather by putting on a sweater. But you are not going to change how it is.'[44] We disagree with this view of code. Although we gather from Lessig and other scholars such as Ron Deibert and Julie Cohen the importance of code, we cannot agree that code can or does have such a determining influence.[45] We will, however, explain this later in chapter 3, where we discuss in more detail the importance of language and the irreducible differences between

speech, writing, and code. For now, we want to emphasize that if we are
bound to use the concept 'cyberspace' and compare it to something called
'real' space, we'd better understand the complex registers in which cyberspace exists rather than being opposed to an ostensible 'real' space.

Other scholars such as Julie Cohen and Richard Ford have made this
point. Yet while critical of the uses of the term 'cyberspace', we find them
also implicitly if not inadvertently accepting a distinction between cyberspace and an ostensibly 'real' space. Cohen, for example, rightly notes
that '[c]yberspace is in and of the real-space world, and is so not (only)
because real-space sovereigns decree it, or (only) because real-space sovereigns can exert physical power over real-space users, but also and more
fundamentally because cyberspace users are situated in real space.'[46]
Most scholars of cyberspace, says Cohen, 'ignore both the embodied,
situated experience of cyberspace users and the complex interplay between real and digital geographies.'[47] She concludes that 'theories of cyberspace as space fail not because they lack the proper understanding of
whether "cyberspace" is different from "real space," and indeed that
debate simply muddies the issue. Rather, they fail because they lack appreciation of the many and varied ways in which cyberspace is connected
to real space and alters the experience of people and communities whose
lives and concerns are inextricably rooted in real space.'[48] Although we
find her view agreeable, the question here is why continue to use cyberspace and real space as though they still are different categories while at
the same time arguing that people are embodied beings that connect the
two. It is almost as if having recognized the problem, Cohen is searching
for a way to avoid it but, in our view, without success. It seems it is
difficult to maintain that cyberspace 'is most usefully understood as connected to and subsumed within an emerging, networked space that is
inhabited by real, embodied users and that is apprehended through experience' while avoiding the assumption of some 'real' space or users.[49]

We think Richard Ford experiences the same difficulty. He, too, rightly points out that 'the decision to think of the Internet in spatial terms—
and increasingly only in spatial terms—will not help us to understand
the Internet so much as it will affect the way we understand the Internet.'[50] He also points out that 'cyberspace also encourages us to import
our biases, mythologies, misperceptions, and unreflective habitual practices concerning land and territory into a new domain.'[51] Yet Ford continues to fight against the existence of a separate, if not independent, space

called cyberspace but unintentionally gives it an existence by being against it as a project.[52]

We cannot claim that we will do better, but at least we will attempt to avoid thinking of cyberspace as either a separate or independent space from geographic or physical space. We have already characterized cyberspace as a space of relations between and among bodies acting through the Internet. We noted earlier that 1984 was the birth of the concept of cyberspace. Yet during the very same year, a much less known work, or rather, a work known much more for its title, Jean-François Lyotard's *The Postmodern Condition* (1984), appeared. Being asked to report on knowledge in the most highly developed societies and presented to the now defunct Conseil des Universités of the government of Québec in 1984, Lyotard took as his main premise that the production, dissemination, and exchange of knowledge could not survive what he called 'the computerization of society'.[53] Without assuming that computerization ushered advanced societies into a machine age, as it was commonly understood then and still is today, Lyotard instead argues that computerization was ushering knowledge into a new mode of production. We want to revisit both Lyotard's substantive argument and his method because, writing before the concept of cyberspace, his starting point is not an ostensibly existing space but changing social relations through computerization. That, we think, ought to be the starting point.

Lyotard saw the production, dissemination, and legitimation of knowledge taking on a new principle. He interpreted this principle as commodification of knowledge, where it became a form of capital. Since the means of production, dissemination, and legitimation of knowledge principally involves language, Lyotard saw language as the main site of social struggle. It is not surprising, then, that Lyotard was attracted to Ludwig Wittgenstein and J. L. Austin to develop a method of understanding language as a means of social struggle. Lyotard dubbed this as 'language games' involving different classes of utterances.[54] Again, we will wait until chapter 3 to elaborate these as speech acts. But what is important here is to note Lyotard's conception of language games as being made up of competitive (agonistic) social struggles where performative utterances—or what we will more generally call digital acts—are strategic moves that bring into being rather than point to presumably already existing referents. What we find in Lyotard—albeit in incipient form—is that rather than conceiving a separate and independent space, the point is to recognize that power relations in contemporary societies are being increasingly mediated and constituted through computer networks that eventually came to be known as the Internet.

Lyotard's significant contribution was to recognize that computerization was both mediating and constituting these language games and resulting in new forms of capital, which Pierre Bourdieu would designate as cultural capital.[55] Lyotard anticipates it by imagining 'that a firm such as IBM is authorized to occupy a belt in the earth's orbital field and launch communications satellites or satellites housing data banks. Who will have access to them? Who will determine which channels or data are forbidden? The State? Or will the State simply be one user among others? New legal issues will be raised, and with them the question: "who will know?"'[56] If the computerization of society raises such questions, the analysis of the production, dissemination, and legitimation of knowledge, on which it has a profound effect, cannot be restricted to understanding computerization as communication or computer-mediated communication. Rather, the object of investigation ought to be language games that became possible through what Lyotard saw as networked computers.

The point here is not to claim that Lyotard provides a better description of 'cyberspace' or the Internet. Lyotard himself warned against using his hypotheses as predictive claims. Nonetheless, when we examine the shape that the Internet has taken since 1984 with its social media platforms, access struggles, storage battles, copyright fights, protocol competitions, and so on, it is obvious that what is at stake is the production, dissemination, and legitimation of knowledge and the control of its storage, access, and transmission as objects of intense competitive struggles. Who owns the growing volumes of data generated by saying and doing things on the Internet, who accesses it, who has right to its use, and who has right to profit from it are political problems of our age. So when we conceive cyberspace as a space of relations between and among bodies acting through the Internet, we mean that it is through those relations and struggles that it comes into being as a contested space. This is this approach we develop to contribute to our understanding of the figure at the centre of these competitive struggles: the digital citizen, her claims, and the callings made upon her. Understanding cyberspace as an agonistic space of relations and struggles is our general starting point. Rather than understanding cyberspace as a separate and independent space, we interpret it as a space of relations. Put differently, Donna Haraway's *Cyborg Manifesto* (1984), which is not about the then incipient Internet but about the interconnectedness of humans and machines, is just as relevant to our age of the Internet through which we both say and do things.[57]

We approach cyberspace, then, as a relational space in which digital citizens come into being through digital acts. The Internet—whether it is a network of networks or a network of filters and chokepoints—is a sociotechnical arrangement that makes up only one part of the relations of cyberspace that are not separate from bodies.[58] Deibert rightly argues that 'although cyberspace may seem like virtual reality, it's not. Every device we use to connect to the Internet, every cable, machine, application, and point along the fibre-optic and wireless spectrum through which data passes is a possible filter or "chokepoint," a grey area that can be monitored and that can constrain what we can communicate, that can surveil and choke off the free flow of communication and information.'[59] Not only does this mean that the Internet has material effects such as data centres, server clusters, and code, though this is certainly true and there are studies about these material forms. It also means that cyberspace is a space of relations that comes into being through interactions and transactions between and among bodies acting through the Internet. For this reason, to declare cyberspace as either being actual or virtual, separate and independent from another space, ostensibly physical, is an inadequate starting point. If we make that point emphatically enough, then where do *we* start?

We mentioned earlier how Balibar defines Foucault's contribution as a genealogy of the birth of the citizen subject. It is worth exploring this through Gilles Deleuze's argument that Foucault's theorization about the birth of the subject was spatial.[60] As Foucault provides a genealogy of various forms of power, he assigns certain properties to each in terms of strategies and technologies by which and through which it is exercised. A form of power that works through exclusions, for example, is more appropriate for sovereign power demanding of its subjects obedience. Being *subject to power*, in other words, brings about forms of sociospatial exclusion such as banishment, deportation, expulsion, and so on.[61] The spaces that *sovereign power* produces correspond to such strategies and technologies of exclusion: expulsion, prohibition, banishment, eviction, exile, and deportation are such examples. By contrast, being a *subject of power* mobilizes strategies and technologies of discipline, which require submission but open up possibilities of subversion. The spaces that *disciplinary power* produces are appropriate to such strategies and technologies of discipline: asylums, camps, and barracks but also hospitals, prisons, schools, and museums as spaces of confinement. Each of these spaces is a space of contestation, competitive and social struggles in and through which certain forms of knowledge are produced in enunciations that perform subjects. Neither spaces of exclusion nor spaces of discipline are static or container spaces. They are dynamic and relational spaces. There are no 'physical' spaces separate from power relations and no power relations that are not embedded in spatializing strategies and technologies of power.

The most notable contribution Foucault made to our understanding of the modern subject of power is that this subject was also simultaneously a subject of knowledge. [62] So Foucault often preferred to reflect on relations of power and knowledge and spaces appropriate to them. If we are thinking about spaces of confinement, it requires not only the power relations necessary to constitute such spaces but also what relations of knowledge are produced, disseminated, and exchanged about them. That a subject of power is also a subject of knowledge is a significant aspect for both societies of exclusion and societies of discipline.

These two forms of power—sovereign and disciplinary—were conjoined by another—control—defined by Gilles Deleuze, who, after Foucault's death, thought about power in relation to spaces that were becoming prevalent and in which cybernetic control depended on the movements and conduct of subjects. [63] Deleuze recognized that 'Foucault's often taken as the theorist of disciplinary societies and of their principal technology, confinement (not just in hospitals and prisons, but in schools, factories, and barracks). But he was actually one of the first to say that we're moving away from disciplinary societies, we've already left them behind.' [64] Deleuze was now convinced that '[w]e're moving toward control societies that no longer operate by confining people but through continuous control and instant communication.' [65] The space of control societies was diffuse and dispersed and decisively cybernetic in its modes of government.

For Deleuze, the logic of confinement is analogical: walls, perimeters, streets, checkpoints, height, volume, and depth were prominent features of spaces of confinement for exclusion or discipline. By contrast, the logic of spaces of control is digital: movement, opening and closing of circuits, transmission, and dispersion were its modulating operations. For Deleuze, 'factories formed individuals into a body of men for the joint convenience of a management that could monitor each component in this mass, and trade unions that could mobilize mass resistance; but businesses are constantly introducing an inexorable rivalry presented as healthy competition, a wonderful motivation that sets individuals against one another and sets itself up in each of them, dividing each within himself.'[66] Deleuze thinks that, by contrast, in control societies 'the key thing is no longer a signature or number but a code: codes are *passwords*, whereas disciplinary societies are ruled . . . by *precepts*.'[67] He observes that 'the digital language of control is made up of codes indicating whether access to some information should be allowed or denied.'[68] For Deleuze, control societies function with a new generation of machines and with information technology and computers. For control societies, 'the passive danger is noise and the active [dangers are] piracy and viral contamination. This technological development is more deeply rooted in a mutation of capitalism.'[69] Deleuze cites Guattari imagining a city 'where anyone can leave their flat, their street, their neighbourhood, using their . . . electronic card that opens this or that barrier; but the card may also be rejected on a particular day, or between certain times of day; it doesn't depend on the barrier but on the computer that is making sure everyone is in a permissible place, and effecting a universal modulation.'[70] Deleuze concludes, '[I]t may be that older means of control, borrowed from the old sovereign societies, will come back into play, adapted as necessary. The key thing is that we're at the beginning of something new.'[71] For Deleuze, '[i]t's true that, even before control societies are fully in place, forms of delinquency or resistance (two different things) are also appearing. Computer piracy and viruses, for example, will replace strikes and what the nineteenth century called "sabotage" ("clogging" the machinery).'[72] What Deleuze envisions at the end of the 1980s is the appearance of control societies merging analog and digital forms of controls to create a space—perhaps cyberspace—that is embodied rather than a separate and independent space. As prescient as Deleuze's thoughts on control societies, he did not develop them further. He also made assumptions we cannot agree with, such as the succession of sovereign, disciplinary, and control societies. We see sovereign, disciplinary, and control societies and their power/knowledge spaces as coexisting forms, although they may have come into being in different historical and geographical circumstances.[73]

To start where Deleuze left off and work with cyberspace as a space of acts, we briefly turn to scholars concerned with geographic space who have long developed a critique of physical space as separate and independent.[74] Central to this critique has been to reject the existence of an objective, natural, or physical space separate and independent from represented or lived spaces—a flat ontology, if you like.[75] Following Henri Lefebvre, at least three registers of spaces have been elaborated: conceived space, perceived space, and lived space.[76] The essential point is that inhabiting spaces in three registers, we experience our being-in-the-world through simultaneous but asynchronous registers. Subjects inhabit *conceived spaces* such as objectifying practices that code, recode, present, and represent space to render it as a legible and intelligible space of habitation. People inhabit *perceived spaces* such as symbolic representations of space that guide our imaginative relationship to it. Subjects also inhabit *lived spaces* through things they do in or by living. Lived spaces are the spaces through which subjects act. These three registers of space are distinct yet overlapping but also interacting: by inhabiting them, we make them.[77] Understanding how people come to understand their own experiences and how these experiences come together or stay apart in conceived, perceived, and lived spaces requires doing research: How do bodies position themselves in relation to each other and other things? Having recognized that space exists in various registers, scholars also study such spaces as cultural, social, legal, economic, or political spaces. Their assumption is not that such spaces exist as separate and independent from spaces people inhabit, but these are analytical means to concentrate on a subset of relations that constitute such spaces for deeper understanding of how people inhabit, say, a cultural space, which is simultaneously yet asynchronously a conceived, perceived, and lived space. We have provided here merely a glimpse of how critical scholars have complicated our views of space.[78] The point that we need to make before we proceed is that just as critical geographers understand geographic space as not only physical, so, too, do we understand cyberspace as not only virtual.

CYBERSPACE AS DIGITAL ACTS

We want now to illustrate how we approach cyberspace as a relational space of digital acts. But before we proceed, let us note that we will not continue to use the language of conceived, perceived, and lived space. Instead, we will use the same categories we have introduced to discuss three forces of subjectivation that bring citizen subjects into being: legality, performativity, and imaginary. This is partly because we do not want to introduce yet another vocabulary so as to complicate our discussion further but also because the three forces parallel these three in broad terms. So when we consider the legality of spaces, we will discuss conceived spaces comprising rules, regulations, and other codes that govern (or attempt to govern) that space. When we discuss the performativity of spaces, we will discuss the lived spaces that are brought into being by acts. And when we discuss imaginary spaces, we will discuss the images, ideals, and ideologies of perceived spaces.[79] The parallel is not perfect, but it will serve our purposes of maintaining a grip on the complexities of cyberspace as distinct from other spaces while approaching it from the perspective of acts that constitute it.

Consider what happens when a group of people organize to be at the same place and time through an Internet platform, say, messaging or tweeting, and stage an act of protest. Since 2009 many acts of protest or demonstration have taken place around the world, each receiving different degrees of public attention. The most prominent began in Iran with protests against the president in 2009. In 2011 these gathered pace with acts of protest in Tunisia, Egypt, Libya, and Yemen, uprisings in Bahrain and Syria, and demonstrations in Algeria, Jordan, Kuwait, and Morocco. In 2010 and 2011 acts of protest and riots were staged in English cities. In 2011 acts of protests called 'Occupy' were also staged in New York, London, Madrid, and other cities. In 2013 demonstrators in Istanbul staged acts of protest against the government.[80] In 2014, first Kiev and later in the year Hong Kong were the sites of such protests. Although all of these protests were staged within relatively the same period, there were significant differences, as one would expect, for the reasons, methods, reactions, and effects of these acts. Yet it is fair to say that they all shared two qualities: all these acts were staged in squares and streets and were varyingly enacted through the Internet.[81] This has resulted in numerous interpretations of the relation between the two: squares and social media. It is quite unfortunate at the outset that the interpretive debates about the importance of the Internet in the staging of these acts have been framed in terms of 'social media'. To reduce the wide repertoires of communication and collaboration that activists use to 'social media' such as Facebook or Twitter has had the effect of focusing attention on these (what we shall later call) 'closed' repertoires under the control of a few commercial organizations rather than on open platforms.[82] At any rate, the question has been framed as to the role of social media in these worldwide protests. Christian Fuchs has grouped these interpretations of the relationship between social media and squares and streets into four: first are those who adopt broadly a technological determinism perspective and argue that social media has made these protests possible and that their staging in squares would have been impossible without social media. A second takes an opposite perspective, arguing that social media has had nothing to do with the success or failure of the staging of these acts in squares. A third group accepts that squares were crucial but recognizes that investing in social media paid significant dividends in staging these acts. A fourth group, in which Fuchs sees himself, argues that the objective conditions that led people to protest found mechanisms for expressing subjective positions, thereby helping organize these protests.[83] By emphasizing a difference between the Internet in general and social media, Fuchs identifies three dimensions of Internet usage, especially by the Occupy movement: building a shared imaginary of the movement, communicating its ideas to the world outside, and engaging in intense collaboration.[84] Fuchs also helpfully develops a much wider list of platforms used by the movement rather than dumping them all into an all-encompassing category of 'social media'. Paolo Gerbaudo also examines the squares versus social media debate and attempts to move beyond optimists and pessimists about the role of social media.[85] His argument is that these acts always involved groups of leaders who undertook the essential tasks of organizing and gathering people rather than flat hierarchies or distributed networks that are often attributed to such enactments through the Internet.

Both Fuchs and Gerbaudo remind us of the importance of understanding how these subjects of protest had already been formed into social groups, recognizing each other and summoning each other for action. Without that understanding, could a message or tweet even have the capacity of being understood, let alone the power to summon subjects, as simply recipients of messages? Both Fuchs and Gerbaudo are critical of assuming that there exists another space—cyberspace—separately and independently from squares, but neither then offers a way of conceptualizing cyberspace.[86] Lessig's question, '[S]o where are they when they are in cyberspace?' remains unanswered. Lessig's own response that 'we have this desire to pick: We want to say that they are either in cyberspace or in real space. We have this desire because we want to know which space is responsible. Which space has jurisdiction over them? Which space rules? The answer is both. Whenever anyone is in cyberspace, she is also here, in real space.'[87] Our answer is different from Lessig's. We think that the answer is not both because there are no two different spaces in the first place. Instead, we have characterized cyberspace as a space of relations between and among bodies acting through the Internet. Cyberspace is a space like social space, cultural space, economic space, or psychological space. Each of these kinds of spaces is a space through which we enact ourselves in relation to other bodies in whichever ways our acts derive their legal, performative, and imaginary force. Acting through the Internet, making connections with others, is a new condition of our lives that adds to but does not displace or supplant other ways of acting in social or cultural spaces in which we are embedded.

Moreover, neither Fuchs, nor Gerbaudo, nor for that matter many digital studies scholars ask the question of whether the subjects of cyberspace are citizen subjects. The ubiquitous concept used is 'activist' but it runs the risk of being a homogenous and unified concept that ostensibly works the same way in Cairo, Istanbul, New York, Madrid, Kiev, Tehran, Athens, Hong Kong, or Tunisia. This is partly because the Internet encourages this homogeneous and undifferentiated usage, but in each of these political, economic, and social if not cultural spaces, citizen subjects have different histories and embody different legal, performative, and imaginary forces for their enactment. To begin with, in each of these spaces, rights that constitute citizenship are quite fundamentally different. It is trite to say, but being an American citizen in New York is different from being an Iranian citizen in Tehran and not equivalent regardless of human rights conventions. Second, the boundaries of what is sayable and doable and thus the performativity of being citizens are radically different in, say, Tunis and Madrid. Finally, the imaginary force of acting as a citizen in Athens has a radically different history than it has, say, in

Istanbul. These complexities and differentiations come to make a huge difference in how citizen subjects uptake certain possibilities and act and organize themselves through the Internet.

This is all the more significant since one of the most important developments is the increasing shaping of cyberspace to coincide with the borders of states. Originally, cyberspace came into being as centred on the United States, as governmental and nongovernmental organizations and corporations that made up the Internet networks were located 'there'. It then expanded throughout the world as a network of networks traversing many nation-state borders. More recently, however, through imperatives of capital accumulation led by corporations such as Google, Apple, Amazon, Facebook, Twitter, Instagram, and Tumblr and imperatives of surveillance and security led by states such as the United States, United Kingdom, Iran, China, and India, cyberspace is increasingly overlapping the borders of states. In other words, cyberspace as a space of relations between and among bodies acting through the Internet is anything but a smooth space. Rather, it is striated in the sense that it is differentiated, fractured, segmented, and crisscrossing and in the sense that it embodies a multiplicity of authorizations, controls, filters, choke points, and boundaries.[88] The figure of the citizen traversing the borders of states in cyberspace is rapidly being effaced like a face in the sand at the edge of the sea as waves of filters and choke points wash over it.

Cyberspace, then, is a complex space of becoming citizens. What kinds of digital acts constitute cyberspace? How do these acts produce digital citizens? We address these questions in chapter 3, but here we propose how acting through the Internet has resignified four political questions. These are neither qualities nor properties of the Internet but objects of political contestation more generally. Taken singly, each highlights contentious or contested issues of conflict arising from bodies acting through the Internet. Yet we want to argue that taken together, they point to how acts that constitute cyberspace are distinctive to other political struggles. We will briefly state them here without further elaboration, but we will return to them in chapter 3. The first concerns anonymity. Being anonymous in cyberspace has several complex meanings that are different from being anonymous or even making rights claims to being anonymous. It is not surprising that one of the most recognizable if troubling acts on the Internet is by citizen subjects called Anonymous. If we distinguish privacy from anonymity, we realize that anonymity on the

Internet has spawned a new political development. If privacy is the right to determine what one decides to keep to herself and what to share publicly, anonymity concerns the right to act without being identified. The second concerns the velocity of acting through the Internet. For better or for worse, it is almost possible to perform an act on the Internet faster than one can think. The third concerns the extensity of acting through the Internet. The number of addressees and destinations that are possible for acting through the Internet is staggering. So, too, are the boundaries, borders, and jurisdictions that an act can traverse. The fourth concerns traceability. If it is performed on the Internet, an act can be traced in ways that are practically impossible outside the Internet. Taken together, anonymity, velocity, extensity, and traceability are questions that are resignified by bodies acting through the Internet.

CITIZENS, DIGITAL CITIZENS, CYBERSPACE

If we are going to use the figure of the citizen to describe the subject of power in cyberspace, it requires more than being online or being on the Internet to become digital citizens. Being online and being connected are insufficient metaphors for describing citizens in cyberspace. The kind of historical subject the citizen designates and how this subject is summoned and enacts cyberspace is the object of our analysis. Understanding how digital citizens and cyberspace come into being through digital acts requires exploring both the ways in which this subject—digital citizen— is produced and the ways in which cyberspace emerges as his or her domain of existence. We suggested that enacting ourselves through the Internet has resignified political questions of anonymity, extensity, traceability, and velocity of acts. If we constitute ourselves as digital citizens, we have become subjects of power in cyberspace. This involves the inscription of rights in law (legality), claiming rights through performance (performativity), and responding to callings (imaginary) that, taken together, resignify the digital citizen or its enactment.

To recapitulate the basic premises of this book, let us recall that we consider the subject called the citizen as a *subject of power*. While *subject to power* is produced by *sovereign* societies, the *subject of power* is produced by *disciplinary* and *control* societies. It is absolutely important to make it clear that the contemporary subject embodies *all* these three forms of power. This is the sense in which we consider the citizen subject as a subject of power and as a subject we inherit.

If being *subject to power* involves obedience, being *subject of power* involves obedience, submission, and subversion. The subject called 'citizen' is a paradoxical subject as it already embodies conduct of obedience, submission, and subversion. Conduct always acts upon conduct as embodied conventions. If we understand conventions as sociotechnical arrangements, we recognize that they comprise norms, rules, values, affects, laws, ideologies, and technologies.

Yet what makes a subject a citizen is the capacity for making rights claims. To put it differently, the citizen as *subject of power* comes into being through acts of making rights claims. Conventions are about instituting rights to govern relations between subjects and between subjects and conventions. By making rights claims, citizen subjects govern their relations with themselves, with others, and with conventions. This is the process of the subjectivation of citizen subjects, and it always involves the forces of legality, performativity, and imaginary.

If we understand cyberspace as neither a separate nor an independent space but one constituted by bodies acting through the Internet, then we need to know how, as subjects of power, bodies are called upon to conduct themselves in that space. What actions become possible? What actions are encouraged? What actions are cultivated? What actions are discouraged? What actions are legal or illegal? What actions become performable? What actions can be imagined? By asking these questions, we are compelled to consider both cyberspace as a space of relations between and among bodies acting through the Internet and how it is brought into being through digital acts.

We are not yet ready to define digital acts, but we have already suggested that bodies acting through the Internet resignify political questions of anonymity, extensity, traceability, and velocity of the conduct of citizen subjects. We have so far expressed our basic premises as a series of propositions that we have put forward rather than argued. This is by way of approaching both the figures of the citizen and cyberspace with ideas that we think are important to bear in mind. In chapter 3 we will elaborate both speech acts and digital acts to develop the concept of making rights claims. Then, in chapters 4, 5, and 6, we will specify digital acts—callings (demands, pressures, provocations), closings (tensions, conflicts, disputes), and openings (opportunities, possibilities, beginnings)—as ways of conducting ourselves through the Internet and discuss how these bring cyberspace into being. We return to the citizen subject making rights claims and make a case for its resignification in chapter 7.

NOTES

1. This is a generally used meaning of 'digital citizenship' used most consistently by K. Mossberger et al., "Measuring Digital Citizenship: Mobile Access and Broadband," *International Journal of Communication* 6 (2012); K. Mossberger et al., *Digital Citizenship: The Internet, Society, and Participation* (MIT Press, 2008), expresses it most clearly.

2. Mossberger et al., *Digital Citizenship*.

3. Nathan Jurgenson, for example, writes of the 'false separation' between the 'digital and physical' and argues that they are enmeshed, there is no 'elsewhere,' and that 'what we do while connected is inseparable from what we do when disconnected.' Thus, 'disconnection from the smartphone and social media isn't really disconnection at all: The logic of social media follows us long after we log out. There was and is no offline; it is a lusted-after fetish object that some claim special ability to attain, and it has always been a phantom.' N. Jurgenson, "The IRL Fetish," *New Inquiry*, 28 June 2012 [accessed 8 August 2014], bit.ly/N57s34.

4. The field of citizenship studies is quite extensive. Although T. H. Marshall's work has been considered a key contribution, its Anglo-American bias and historical outlook has been criticized. T. H. Marshall, *Citizenship and Social Class* (1949), ed. T. B. Bottomore (Pluto Press, 1992). See S. White, *The Ethos of a Late-Modern Citizen* (Harvard University Press, 2009); J. Clarke et al., *Disputing Citizenship* (Policy Press, 2014); M. Bulmer and A. M. Rees, eds., *Citizenship Today: The Contemporary Relevance of T. H. Marshall* (UCL Press, 1996). Also see B. S. Turner, *Citizenship and Capitalism: The Debate over Reformism* (Unwin, 1986); B. S. Turner, "Outline of a Theory of Citizenship," *Sociology* 24 (1990).

5. U. Erel, *Migrant Women Transforming Citizenship* (Ashgate, 2009); S. Phelan, *Sexual Strangers: Gays, Lesbians, and Dilemmas of Citizenship* (Temple University Press, 2001); A. Latta, "Environmental Citizenship," *Alternatives Journal* 33, 1 (2007); T. Miller, *Cultural Citizenship: Cosmopolitanism, Consumerism, and Television in a Neoliberal Age* (Temple University Press, 2007).

6. A. McNevin, *Contesting Citizenship: Irregular Migrants and New Frontiers of the Political* (Columbia University Press, 2011); K. Rygiel, *Globalizing Citizenship* (UBC Press, 2010); P. Nyers, "The Accidental Citizen: Acts of Sovereignty and (Un)Making Citizenship," *Economy and Society* 35 (2006); P. Nyers, "Abject Cosmopolitanism: The Politics of Protection in the Anti-deportation Movement," *Third World Quarterly* 24 (2003); A. Ní Mhurchú, *Ambiguous Citizenship in an Age of Global Migration* (Edinburgh University Press, 2014); V. Squire, *The Exclusionary Politics of Asylum* (Palgrave Macmillan, 2009).

7. Clarke et al., *Disputing Citizenship*, 9–11.

8. E. Balibar, "Citizen Subject," in *Who Comes after the Subject?*, ed. E. Cadava et al. (Routledge, 1991).

9. The literature on the subject is quite extensive, but see S. Žižek, *The Ticklish Subject: The Absent Centre of Political Ontology* (Verso, 2000); J. Butler, *Subjects of Desire:*

Hegelian Reflections in Twentieth-Century France (Columbia University Press, 1999); R. Braidotti, *Nomadic Subjects: Embodiment and Sexual Difference in Contemporary Feminist Theory*, 2nd ed. (Columbia University Press, 2011).

10. We recognize here that both 'modern political theory' and 'critical political theory' are rather broad categories. We don't mean to neatly slot political theorists into these categories but rather consider the categories as capturing particular dispositions: those theorists who see such a radical divide between subject to power and subject of power and temporally assume that the latter displaces the former (and hence a belief in modernity) convey that disposition. By contrast, critical political theorists are disposed to question both the divide and displacement. These dispositions can be found in many political theorists and, in fact, sometimes both in the same theorist.

11. Balibar, "Citizen Subject," 38.

12. Ibid., 46. Balibar puts it the following way: 'The idea of the rights of the citizen, at the very moment of his emergence, thus institutes an historical figure that is no longer the *subjectus*, and not yet the *subjectum*.' We designate his 'subjectus' as subject to power and 'subjectum' as subject of power.

13. M. Foucault, *Ethics: Subjectivity and Truth*, ed. P. Rabinow, vol. 3, *Essential Works of Foucault, 1954–1984* (New Press, 1997), 81.

14. Ibid., 87.

15. Ibid., 114.

16. Balibar, "Citizen Subject," 55.

17. This understanding comes first from Foucault's conceptualization of the arrangements (discourses, laws, regulations, physical spaces, etc.) that organize and configure processes of subjectivation. This conceptualization has been advanced in different and not necessarily consistent ways in Deleuze's conception of assemblages. G. Deleuze, *Difference and Repetition* (Columbia University Press, 1995); G. Deleuze, *The Logic of Sense* (Columbia University Press, 1993). It is also captured in understandings of actor-network. B. Latour, *Reassembling the Social: An Introduction to Actor-Network-Theory* (Oxford University Press, 2005); J. Law, *After Method: Mess in Social Science Research* (Routledge, 2004). It is akin to what other scholars in science and technology studies more generally refer to as sociotechnical arrangements. We understand the human body as not a given but a socially produced yet material body adjusted to the sociotechnical arrangements in which it lives. This we consider to be consistent with J. Butler, *Bodies That Matter: On the Discursive Limits of "Sex"* (Routledge, 1993).

18. Balibar, "Citizen Subject," 53.

19. Ibid., 45.

20. M. Poster, "Digital Networks and Citizenship," *Proceedings of Modern Language Association of America (PMLA)* 117, 1 (2002), 99.

21. Ibid., 99–100.

22. These symbolic dates refer to the following inscriptions: 1689, the passage of the Bill of Rights in England; 1776, the Declaration of Independence in the United States; 1789, the Declaration of the Rights of Citizens and Men in France; 1835, the Act of Parliament in Britain; and 1945, the Universal Declaration of Human Rights.

23. K. Zivi, *Making Rights Claims: A Practice of Democratic Citizenship* (Oxford University Press, 2012).

24. Ibid., 4.

25. Ibid., 8.

26. Ibid., 19.

27. J. Rancière, "The Thinking of Dissensus: Politics and Aesthetics," in *Reading Rancière*, ed. P. Bowman and R. Stamp (Continuum, 2011).

28. L. DeNardis, "Hidden Levers of Internet Control," *Information, Communication & Society* 15 (2012). DeNardis provides a useful description of its complexity and layers as objects of control. For a description of cyberspace as a 'medium' that includes all of these elements that we have described as constituting the Internet, see M. Dodge and R. Kitchin, *Mapping Cyberspace* (Routledge, 2001).

29. Butler, *Bodies That Matter*; D. J. Haraway, *Simians, Cyborgs and Women: The Reinvention of Nature* (Free Association, 1991). We follow Butler and Haraway in considering bodies as inherently social and not prior to their socialization. For us, collective, technological, and biological bodies are all social bodies.

30. Adrian Mackenzie describes cyberspace as a condition of wirelessness. He says, 'Wirelessness designates an experience trending toward entanglements with things, objects, gadgets, infrastructures, and services, and imbued with indistinct sensations and practices of network-associated change. Wirelessness affects how people arrive, depart, and inhabit places, how they relate to others, and indeed, how they embody change.' A. Mackenzie, *Wirelessness: Radical Empiricism in Network Cultures* (MIT Press, 2010), 5.

31. M. Neale, *William Gibson: No Maps for These Territories* (Canada: Docurama), documentary.

32. F. Nietzsche, *On the Genealogy of Morality*, ed. K. Ansell-Pearson, trans. C. Diethe (Cambridge University Press, 1994), ii, §12.

33. For an excellent account, see J. E. Cohen, "Cyberspace as/and Space," *Columbia Law Review* 107, 1 (2007).

34. J. P. Barlow, "A Declaration of the Independence of Cyberspace," Electronic Frontier Foundation, 8 February 1996 [accessed 11 July 2014], bit.ly/1r41WqG.

35. L. Lessig, "The Zones of Cyberspace," *Stanford Law Review* 48, 5 (1996): 1403.

36. Ibid., 1407.

37. Ibid., 1408.

38. Ibid.

39. Ibid.

40. Ibid.

41. Ibid., 1410.

42. L. Lessig, *Code: Version 2.0* (Basic, 2006).

43. Ibid., 84.

44. Ibid., 93.

45. J. E. Cohen, *Configuring the Networked Self: Law, Code, and the Play of Everyday Practice* (Yale University Press, 2012); R. Deibert, *Black Code: Inside the Battle for Cyberspace* (McClelland & Stewart, 2013).

46. Cohen, "Cyberspace as/and Space," 217–18.

47. Ibid., 213. However, there are many examples of scholars who undertake empirical studies of Internet users and argue that the online and offline, or the real and virtual, are related rather than isolated; see, for example, D. Miller, *Tales from Facebook* (Polity, 2011).

48. Cohen, "Cyberspace as/and Space," 225.

49. Ibid., 255.

50. R. Ford, "Against Cyberspace," in *The Place of Law*, ed. A. Sarat et al. (University of Michigan Press, 2003), 154.

51. Ibid., 158.

52. Ibid., 177.

53. J.-F. Lyotard, *The Postmodern Condition: A Report on Knowledge* (University of Minnesota Press, 1984), 7.

54. Lyotard was drawing from L. Wittgenstein, *Philosophical Investigations*, 2nd ed., trans. G. E. M. Anscombe (Blackwell, 1958), and J. L. Austin, *How to Do Things with Words* (Oxford University Press, 1962).

55. The debate over Bourdieu's contribution is vast, and his influence on our collective work is deep, but clearly his book *Distinction* has been most influential. P. Bourdieu, *Distinction: A Social Critique of the Judgement of Taste* (Harvard University Press, 1987).

56. Lyotard, *The Postmodern Condition*, 6.

57. Haraway, *Simians, Cyborgs and Women*. The inspiration for Haraway was Norbert Wiener's understanding of cybernetics as the domain of human-machine fusion. N. Wiener, *The Human Use of Human Beings: Cybernetics and Society*, 2nd ed. (Sphere, 1968); N. Wiener, *Cybernetics: Or, Control and Communication in the Animal and the Machine* (Wiley, 1948).

58. This is an understanding advanced by scholars in the social studies of science who argue against distinctions between humans and technologies and nature and society. For example, it echoes what some scholars refer to as postsocial relations mediated by objects, technologies, and data, as defined by K. Knorr Cetina and U. Bruegger, "Traders' Engagement with Markets: A Postsocial Relationship," *Theory, Culture & Society* 19, 5/6 (2002).

59. Deibert, *Black Code*.

60. G. Deleuze, *Foucault* (University of Minnesota Press, 1986).

61. M. Foucault, *Discipline and Punish: The Birth of the Prison* (Vintage, 1979).

62. M. Foucault, *Power/Knowledge*, ed. C. Gordon (Harvester Wheatsheaf, 1980).

63. G. Deleuze, "Postscript on Control Societies," in *Negotiations* (Columbia University Press, 1990).

64. G. Deleuze, "Control and Becoming," in *Negotiations* (Columbia University Press, 1990), 174.

65. Ibid.

66. Deleuze, "Postscript on Control Societies," 179.

67. Ibid., 180.

68. Ibid.

69. Ibid.

70. Ibid., 181–82.

71. Ibid., 182.

72. Deleuze, "Control and Becoming," 175.

73. Similarly, Galloway has also drawn from this short text of Deleuze to explore protocols of the Internet as modes of control. He argues that 'with the advent of digital computing, the term ['protocol'] has taken on a slightly different meaning. Now, protocols refer specifically to standards governing the implementation of specific technologies. Like their diplomatic predecessors, computer protocols establish the essential points necessary to enact an agreed-upon standard of action.' A. R. Galloway, *Protocol: How Control Exists after Decentralization* (MIT Press, 2006), 7.

74. Almost half a century ago Lefebvre was precisely concerned about the dualistic separation of physical space from nonphysical space. His analysis of the three ways of making space has been widely discussed, and we will not rehearse it here. H. Lefebvre, *The Production of Space* (Wiley-Blackwell, 1991).

75. E. W. Soja, *Thirdspace* (Blackwell, 1996); C. Collinge, "The *Différance* between Society and Space: Nested Scales and the Returns of Spatial Fetishism," *Environment and Planning D: Society and Space* 23 (2005); C. Collinge, "Flat Ontology and the Deconstruction of Scale: A Response to Marston, Jones and Woodward," *Transactions of the Institute of British Geographers* 31 (2006). Also see J. Allen, "Three Spaces of Power: Territory, Networks, Plus a Topological Twist in the Tale of Domination and Authority," *Journal of Power* 2 (2009).

76. We are drawing from E. C. Relph, *Place and Placelessness* (Pion, 1976); Y.-F. Tuan, *Space and Place: The Perspective of Experience*, 2nd ed. (University of Minnesota Press, 2001); D. B. Massey, *For Space* (Sage, 2005).

77. This reminds us also what F. Braudel, *On History*, trans. S. Matthews (University of Chicago Press, 1980) called three modes of experiencing time, of which *longue durée* was one.

78. Among those who write about cyberspace are Cohen and Rodgers, who have taken up this conception of space inspired by Lefebvre, *The Production of Space*. Cohen, *Configuring the Networked Self*, chap. 2, and J. Rodgers, *Spatializing International Politics: Analysing Activism on the Internet* (Routledge, 2003), chap. 1.

79. In his study of geek culture, Chris Kelty argues that their formation as a public is guided by a moral imaginary of the Internet as well as the heterogeneous infrastructure of the Internet, which constitutes and constrains their ability to 'become public'. In this regard, he describes geek culture as 'recursive' to capture the interrelation between imaginaries and technologies. C. M. Kelty, *Two Bits: The Cultural Significance of Free Software* (Duke University Press, 2008).

80. We have limited our description of these acts to 'demonstration' and 'protest' to indicate the contested terrain of naming that followed these acts, which ranged from revolution to rebellion to uprisings and riots. Here we are not concerned with the effects of these acts; we want to discuss their relation to the Internet and how to think about cyberspace.

81. By using the term 'choreographed' we are following Paulo Gerbaudo, *Tweets and the Streets: Social Media and Contemporary Activism* (Pluto, 2012).

82. Most scholars have also followed this unfortunate trend of not differentiating open Internet platforms, such as independently run websites, and closed platforms. An exception is C. Fuchs, *Digital Labour and Karl Marx* (Routledge, 2014).

83. Ibid., 325–33.

84. Ibid., 337–38.

85. Gerbaudo, *Tweets and the Streets*.

86. Ibid., 12.

87. Lessig, *Code*, 298.

88. We are using smooth and striated space in the same way as G. Deleuze and F. Guattari, *A Thousand Plateaus* (University of Minnesota Press, 1980), 372–82. See also M. Nunes, "Virtual Topographies: Smooth and Striated Cyberspace," in *Cyberspace Textuality: Computer Technology and Literary Theory*, ed. M.-L. Ryan (Indiana University Press, 1999).

THREE

Speech Acts and Digital Acts

Making rights claims, we have proposed, involves enacting ourselves as citizen subjects through legal, performative, and imaginary forces. To put it differently, we have suggested that making rights claims involves bringing citizens into being legally, performatively, and imaginatively. We discuss in this chapter how rights claims made through the Internet are digital acts that bring digital citizens into being as subjects *to* power and subjects *of* power. If indeed we have defined cyberspace as a space of relations between and among bodies acting through the Internet, how do digital acts bring cyberspace into being? We are not convinced by the dominant view that cyberspace exists separately and independently from so-called real space or the acts of citizen subjects. Cyberspace introduces at least two complexities. First, digital acts traverse borders, boundaries, and jurisdictions much more speedily and imperceptibly through the Internet.[1] The resulting cyberspace is a mesh of national borders and involves a multiplicity of legal orders. When a citizen of a state makes an observation about, say, an athlete who is competing in a competition in another state, whether this act is classified 'racist' or 'misogynist' will involve multiple borders and legal orders that this speech act has traversed. This traversing of acts produces considerable complexities in becoming digital citizens. Second, we need to specify to what extent certain rights claimed by digital acts are classical rights (e.g., freedom of speech), to what extent they are analogous to classical rights (e.g., anonymity), and to what extent they are new (e.g., the right to be forgotten). If indeed digital acts in control societies produce these complexities and bring into

51

being both the subject and cyberspace, then how do we understand digital acts? To address that question we step back in this chapter to develop a critical discussion of speech acts as a way of conceiving digital acts. This discussion then frames the core chapters of this book, which are organized around digital acts that make rights claims possible.

SPEECH ACTS

There is a crucial if not fundamental relationship between the speaking subject and the citizen subject. Yet theorizing the speaking subject is anything but straightforward, and this is further complicated by speech through the Internet: blogs, comments, messages, and tweets are new conventions of speech acts that have not only become more numerous but also brought about fundamental changes in how we do things with words. The speaking subject has moved to the centre of debates over the Internet, and how acting through the Internet creates cyberspace is now a question concerning technology, international law, and politics.[2] The permissibility, legality, legitimacy, privacy, security, and anonymity of things said and done and whether they are sayable or doable are among the major debates of our times. Already, considerable scholarly work has been produced, especially on freedom of speech through the Internet, and it is beyond the task of this book to even try to attempt an outline.[3] Moreover, our concern with the Internet is not the speaking subject as such but how making rights claims brings citizen subjects into being. How do digital acts bring citizen subjects into being? Does the Internet introduce a radical difference for understanding citizen subjects? Does the language of the Internet—code—work like natural language? To address these questions and to characterize digital acts, speech acts theory, developed in the twentieth century, provides our starting point. To anticipate our argument, many of the complexities that arise about acting and speaking through the Internet are in fact complexities of speech acts as such. To address the complexities of enacting ourselves through the Internet, we will need to develop an appreciation of the complexities of enacting ourselves as citizen subjects, legally, performatively, and imaginatively. Then we will need to consider what, if any, difference the Internet makes and the properties of the space that acting through the Internet creates—cyberspace.

We mentioned earlier that François Lyotard had already argued that the emerging Internet was a space of language games.[4] He had observed that computer networks were altering the way knowledge was produced, disseminated, and exchanged. He proposed understanding these language games constituted by performative utterances as strategic moves. Lyotard drew on Ludwig Wittgenstein, who in his later work famously insisted that we must understand language as a human activity rather than as code, which came to be known as ordinary language philosophy.[5] What that meant was to investigate what people are doing with language, with an emphasis on doing, and that this ought to be the central focus of philosophy. To understand language as activity rather than code meant to investigate how people do things with words in everyday language and life. This was the object of J. L. Austin's *How to Do Things with Words*.[6] We have already expressed some scepticism in chapter 2 about arguments treating code as speech.[7] Clearly, on the debate between ordinary language philosophy's focus on language as an activity and analytic philosophy's focus on language as code, we favour the view of language as a social activity. That choice rests on the idea that how people do things with words (or code) is much more creative and inventive than a conception of speaking subjects following rules. If we work with the idea of speaking subjects following rules, we fail to recognize the practical creativity and inventiveness of people in action *with* language.

Although a speech act for Austin often involves doing things with words, he is critical of the dominant view that treats a speech act as a description. Austin designates this descriptive element of speech acts as constatives. When we use statements such as 'I am typing', I am describing what I am doing. It is a constative speech act. It describes a state of affairs; it makes a truth claim; and it can be verified or falsified. As a constative speech act, it is a statement that signifies a meaning. By contrast, when a statement either warns about something or urges someone to do something, it moves from being a statement to being an utterance. It accomplishes an act by its *force*. Austin says that there are many verbs in the English language that can be classified according to these effects of meaning and force. Austin uses three connectives to classify speech acts: 'of', 'in', and 'by'. For 'of', Austin says: the act *of* saying something is a locutionary act. This is a speech act whose *meaning* calls forth a truth versus false distinction and provokes verification or falsification. The effect or consequence of a locutionary act—a constative—is to produce or fail to produce a meaningful description of a state of affairs. For 'in', as *in* saying something we may be doing something, Austin says it produces an illocutionary act. This is a speech act whose *force* creates a *potential* effect in a state of affairs that it seeks to describe. What it invokes is not verification or falsification but whether there is an uptake. To put it another way, whether an utterance is successful (felicitous) or unsuccessful (infelicitous) is its force.[8] For example, in saying, 'I am writing my will', I am indicating that I am bequeathing. Although my speech act places me under an obligation, I haven't done anything yet. In saying something, I have brought forth—performative—conditions for something to happen. Finally, doing something *by* saying something is a perlocutionary act. This is a speech act that must have an effect to be actualized. Like an illocutionary act, a perlocutionary act invokes an evaluation along felicitous or infelicitous lines rather than true or false. By saying that 'I am typing gibberish' (when you are anticipating otherwise), I may have annoyed you. (Perhaps I am under coercion to give a false statement.) By saying something, I have accomplished something. Thus, 'of' saying something has *meaning* (locutionary acts), whereas 'in' or 'by' saying something has *force* (illocutionary and perlocutionary acts).

The crucial insight here is that these distinctions between meaning and force, between statement and utterance, and between constative and performative are key to understanding how speech that acts is different from speech that describes. Austin gives examples of illocutionary acts, such as betting, bequeathing, warning, promising, and so on, and examples of the perlocutionary acts, such as persuading, annoying, thrilling, bullying, frightening, wounding, and so on.[9] By advancing the idea that speech is not only a description (constative) but also an act (performative), Austin ushers in a radically different way of thinking about not only speaking and writing but also doing things in or by speaking and writing.

The brief sketch we have provided does not even skim the complexities that Austin has given rise to, and it is not our aim to go further into speech acts. We need to highlight a few points here to show how Austin helps us articulate an adequate conception of digital acts. First, as far as we're concerned, Austin is more interested in deeds than words; or, more precisely, he is interested in deeds that words perform. He observes that words will never be enough to accomplish an act, despite recognizing that without words at some stage it is difficult to see how any act can be accomplished.[10] So although his examples are from speech, his interest is how words perform acts: 'to say something is to do something; or in which by saying or in saying something we are doing something.'[11] It is perhaps unfortunate that his work is considered to be about 'speech acts', but quite emphatically we consider Austin to be theorizing speech that acts. Second, Austin recognizes that nonverbal forms of speech such as bodily gestures and movements as well as visual and aural forms are almost always involved in the accomplishment of an act, especially in a perlocutionary act. So Austin may not mention bodies much if at all, but bodies and their movements are implicit in speech that acts. To put it differently, speech or writing cannot act without bodies. Third, although almost all of Austin's examples are in the first person, he is not enamoured by the speaking sovereign subject who is the master of her speech situation. On the contrary, as the illocutionary and perlocutionary acts indicate, in acting there are always infelicitous situations. As Cavell writes, Austin recognizes that acts will *also* occur 'unintentionally, unwillingly, involuntarily, insincerely, unthinkingly, inadvertently, heedlessly, carelessly, under duress, under the influence, out of contempt, out of pity, by mistake, by accident [and so on].'[12] To put it differently, Austin's concern with infelicitous is not a regret on his part but a recognition that speech does not only act, it also can fail to act or fail to act in ways anticipated.

We read Austin as trying to understand what he calls total speech situations, where bodies, words, images, sounds, and smells combine to accomplish an act.[13] For Austin, investigating an act would require 'prolonged fieldwork', though he admits that's not what he is doing.[14] But focusing on conventions of, in, and by which we act clears the ground for such investigations. For Austin, both the meaning of statements and force of utterances become possible by their appropriateness to the situation, which means an understanding of conventions governing a speech act situation. In chapter 2 we characterized conventions broadly as sociotechnical arrangements that embody norms, values, affects, laws, ideologies, and technologies. To judge the situation, the speaking subject must understand and perform in relation to the conventions governing what is sayable and doable in that place and time. The acting subject who speaks will have an understanding of not only the situation but also the appropriateness of what can and must be said and not said in that situation.[15] For this reason Bourdieu, also discussing Austin, insists that words themselves do not have inherent *meaning* or *force* but acquire them in appropriate situations. For Bourdieu, speech acts are social acts and draw their force, illocutionary force if you like, not from linguistic forms that govern them but from social conventions that make them possible. The things which render a subject capable of accomplishing an act are precisely the social conventions that guarantee its institution.[16] This is not to deny the power of words. But such power is nothing other than the delegated power of the speaker as a social subject.[17] This is, of course, another way of saying that a speech act is always a social act and the speaking subject a social subject. But do speaking subjects *merely* follow conventions (as Bourdieu seems to think)? The key issue in speech acts becomes whether, and if so to what extent, what is sayable and doable follows or exceeds social conventions that govern a situation.

Austin is quite subtle on this point, but Judith Butler picks it up in a creative way. For Austin, a general consideration is that although a speaking subject will rely on conventions to ascertain the meaning and force of her speech act, neither the meaning nor its force will ever be controllable by her. So while a convention is a necessary condition of an act, almost equally it is also a necessary condition of its misfire—one of the 'ills that all action is heir to'.[18] That it requires conventions to accomplish an act and that it also provokes their transgression turns out to be a significant discovery of Austin. Butler makes use of this in her theorizing of gender by drawing our attention to citation, repetition, and resignification of a convention and how these produce subjects of both submission *and* subversion. If a convention is to be cited to accomplish an act, a repetition of certain norms will be necessary. Yet each repetition will bring new circumstances to bear on the act, so much so that it is a resignification—a new deployment of a convention.[19] But Austin reserves the transgression, or subversion if you like, of a convention only for perlocutionary acts.[20] While illocutionary acts will cite and iterate conventions to enact their performative force, perlocutionary acts will derive their force from the unconventional, undecidable, and unpredictable effects (in Butler's sense of resignification). Contra Bourdieu, this is exactly where Butler locates the agency of the subject not as a sovereign subject but a speaking subject who *becomes* responsible for what she cites, repeats, and resignifies.[21] Thus, as opposed to locutionary and illocutionary acts, perlocutionary acts will rupture conventions, and their performative force will derive from this rupture. Following Derrida on this, Butler says: 'The force of the performative is thus not inherited from prior usage, but issues forth precisely from its break with any and all prior usage. That break, that force of rupture, is the force of the performative, beyond all question of truth or meaning.'[22] For political subjectivity, 'performativity can work in precisely such counter-hegemonic ways. That moment in which a speech act without prior authorization nevertheless assumes authorization in the course of its performance may anticipate and instate altered contexts for its future reception.'[23] To conceive rupture as a systemic or total upheaval would be futile. Rather, rupture is a moment where the future breaks through into the present.[24] It is that moment where it becomes possible to *do* something different in or by *saying* something different.

We have described cyberspace as a space of relations between and among bodies acting through the Internet. We have discussed that for Austin, speech acts mean that 'in' and 'by' saying something, we are doing something. By advancing the idea that speech is not only a description (constative) but also an act (performative), Austin ushered in a radically different way of thinking about not only speaking but also doing things in or by speaking. As Felman writes, Austin '[demystified] . . . the illusion upheld by the history of philosophy according to which the only thing at stake in language is its "truth" or "falsity."'[25] For Felman thought that Austin eradicated the difference between saying and doing.[26] For Austin, even constative speech acts that are statements describing a state of affairs cannot remain without effects. It is in this sense that Austin makes us think about ourselves as those beings who always know how to do things with words, even though our chances of accomplishing things we set out to do remain precarious since our words will occasionally (perhaps more so than we would like) misfire and accomplish things we did not intend.

But what about saying something in or by doing something? Or, to put it differently, what about saying something in or by doing things? This question may appear redundant since Austin is said to have erased the difference between saying and doing. But Austin never considers speech situations where things perform words. It was Bruno Latour who raised the question of how we may accomplish words in or by doing things—hence reversing Austin's phrasing.[27] For Latour, without mentioning Austin, it was important to recognize that actions can accomplish words.[28]

This reversal enables us to address a question we have not yet articulated. It is the question of acting bodies. Now Austin does not explain what is an action that accomplishes an act. He implicitly recognizes that action is a bodily movement that accomplishes something, but he does not explicitly recognize that to perform an act involves bodily movements. We may raise our hand, for example, in a particular way to indicate we are taking an oath—an act of promising. Here, raising a hand is an action, but the conventions governing the situation indicate that this action is performing an act of promise. An action is a bodily movement that accomplishes something. Strangely, Austin says to perform illocutionary acts does not require action. This is because the illocutionary force of an act consists in its potential. When I say 'I promise', I indicate that in saying so I commit myself to doing something. But this act of commitment is as yet unfulfilled, and its completion is not guaranteed because I haven't fulfilled it *yet*. What I've done is place myself under an obligation. By contrast, the accomplishment of a perlocutionary act requires action. Doing something means performing an action. This is strange because, as Butler says, 'when one declares that one is a homosexual, the declaration is the performative act—not the homosexuality, unless we want to claim that homosexuality is itself nothing but a kind of declaration, which would be an odd move to make.'[29] So the question of the body should make us think about the difference between speech and bodies, acts and action.

It is just unconvincing that illocutionary acts will not require actions and that perlocutionary acts will. If we return to the example of an act of promising above, where we raised our hand by taking an oath, the situation there may have not required words at all but simply raising hands. Similarly, in certain situations we may perform an act of promising simply by an action of nodding heads, which will indicate a promise. Austin, in other words, despite his cautions, is unable to consider the possibility of saying something in or by doing something, or how to do words with things.

A reason Austin is perhaps compelled to make this distinction between illocutionary and perlocutionary acts (former requiring no action and latter requiring it) is a result of his examples, which (a) are exclusively linguistic *and* (b) involve the first person. Austin is aware of both limitations.

We said that the idea of a performative utterance was that it was to be (or to be included as a part of) the performance of an action. Actions can only be performed by persons, and obviously in our cases the utterer must be the performer: hence our justifiable feeling—which we wrongly cast into purely grammatical mould—in favour of the 'first person', who must come in, being mentioned or referred to; moreover, if the utterer is acting, he must be doing something—hence our perhaps ill-expressed favouring of the grammatical present and grammatical active of the verb. There is something which is *at the moment of uttering being done by the person uttering.*'[30]

Although Austin concedes that 'there is something which is *at the moment of uttering being done by the person uttering*', he does not consider a moment where something being *done* may constitute *uttering* something.[31] Nor does he consider what happens when we move from the first person to the second and third—from individual to collective bodies. There is then really no reason to assume that an act can be accomplished without bodies in action, whether illocutionary or perlocutionary.

It was Shoshana Felman who brilliantly teased out the implications of Austin's understanding of action, body, and acts.[32] Felman says the act calls into question the difference between language and the body: 'the act, an enigmatic and problematic production of the speaking body, destroys from its inception the metaphysical dichotomy between the domain of the "mental" and the domain of the "physical," breaks down the opposition between body and spirit, between matter and language.'[33] Although we are inspired by this reading of Austin, it is actually a resignification of Austin rather than a description.

The importance of recognizing that we know how to do not only things with words but also words with things will become apparent soon, when we further specify digital acts. When we develop the idea in more detail, that it is the relations between and among bodies acting through the Internet that brings cyberspace into being, it will become apparent that we need to understand numerous digital actions. If for Felman 'the scandal [of the body] consists in the fact that the act cannot know what it is doing', we need to recognize here that when bodies act through the Internet, they are not only doing by speaking but also speaking by doing. This is the principal reason why we need to investigate not only things done in or by speaking through the Internet but also things said in or by doing things through the Internet.[34]

'I, WE, THEY HAVE A RIGHT TO'

We have provided a sketch of basic issues concerning speech acts as characterized by Austin and as repeated, cited, iterated, and resignified by his recent interlocutors. Let us provide a description of what *we* gather from Austin, Bourdieu, Butler, Derrida, Felman, and Latour for resignifying acts for our purposes. Since we act of, in, and by saying something, language calls us into being as speaking subjects of acts. To be addressed by and addressing others in language is a social act (Bourdieu). It involves our bodies not as always already given but as *responsive* agents (Butler). It involves our subjectivity (the way in which we understand our bodies and their embeddedness with others through language) not as always already given but as *responsible* agents (Butler). Being responsive means being called upon by others and to call upon others. We accomplish acts through conventions. Yet we cannot control or master our responsiveness: how we cite, iterate, and resignify conventions. We fail. This is the scandal of the body (Felman). This is the scandal of submission. Yet we make choices on what to cite, how to iterate, and where to repeat. We perform our responsibility in resignifying the conventions by which to act. This creates the space for agency. It is also the time of rupture by which conventions are deconstructed by performative force (Derrida). This creates the space for subversion (Butler). We succeed. There are distinctions between speech acts and actions (Butler). We not only in or by saying something do things but also in or by doing things say something (Latour).

So far, so good. But Austin and his interlocutors do not speak about citizen subjects making rights claims. Butler comes closest since she is interested in articulating a 'politics of the performative', but her primary concern is not the citizen subject who claims 'I, we, they have a right to'. We noted in chapter 2 that we will return to the argument that making rights claims involves in or by saying and doing 'I, we, they have a right to'. We can now add that citizen subjects who make such claims should not be conflated with the rights-bearing subject who already exists and whose claim is to already existing rights. On the contrary, citizen subjects performatively come into being in or by the act of saying *and* doing something—whether through words, images, or other things—and through performing the contradictions inherent in becoming citizens.

To understand citizen subjects who make rights claims by saying and doing 'I, we, they have a right to', we are moving from the first person to the second and the third, from the individual to the collective. We need to consider two additional forces that make acts possible. The two forces are the force of the law and the force of the imaginary. Arguably, various examples that Austin provides address the force of law. Austin calls two classes of speech acts as judgements and decisions, and regarding judgements, most of his examples are court verdicts. Yet we still think that the performative force of a convention's legality is different enough that the force of law should be considered as a separate force. Breaking a convention will have significantly different effects, depending upon whether that convention is constituted as legal or illegal. This is not to say that Austin does not provide room for legality, but it is to say that it requires analytical separation.

Similarly, the force of the imaginary is undeniably a significant force in making an act possible, which Austin does not consider.[35] We use the term 'imaginary' as originally used by Cornelius Castoriadis, who asks a seemingly simple and yet quite a challenging question: What holds together any given thing called a society? To put it differently, what gives a society its apparent cohesion, unity, and organization?[36] To address that question, Castoriadis says that we ought to understand the institution of society. The institution does not mean organizations but conventions by which individuals conduct themselves. The institution of society requires norms, values, language, tools, procedures, and methods of dealing with relations and differentiations—in short, conventions. This institution requires coercion and sanctions as well as support, adherence, legitimacy, belief, and consensus. It cultivates individuals who know how to negotiate these sanctions and adherences. The institution of society through which individuals conduct themselves through conventions would be impossible without what Castoriadis calls social imaginaries. These include spirits, gods, God, polis, citizen, nation, state, party, commodity, money, capital, interest, taboo, virtue, sin, and so forth. These are imaginaries not because they fail to correspond to concrete and specific experiences or things but because they require acts of imagination. They are social because they are instituted and maintained by impersonal and anonymous collectives. Being both social and imaginary, these institute society as coherent and unified yet always incoherent and fragmented. How each society deals with this tension constitutes its politics. Castoriadis thinks that this tension is especially acute in democracy as it cultivates an individual who remains at home with this tension. This individual is autonomous not because it is separate or independent from society but as its product retains the capability to question its own institution. Castoriadis says that this new type of being is capable of calling into question the very laws of its existence and has created the possibility of both deliberation and political action. The imaginary institution of society for Castoriadis is much more complex than we depict it here, but what we want to recognize is that not only does the imaginary institution of society require making and breaking conventions, but these conventions can be sustained only through the force of the imaginary: myths, stories, and values that inhabit people and their sense of the world.[37] In fact, what we describe as the 'call' to act would be impossible without the force of the imaginary. There is understandably an overlap between legal, performative, and imaginary forces of acts, but separating them analytically allows us to emphasize their distinct qualities.

Our understanding of how the citizen subject comes into being through enacting herself legally, performatively, and imaginatively should indicate that the citizen subject is both a result and an effect of making claims about rights that may or may not yet exist. By making rights claims in or by saying and doing 'I, we, they have a right to', people enact themselves as citizen subjects. To put it our way, it is by making rights claims by the forces of legality, performativity, and imaginary that we enact and bring ourselves into being as citizen subjects.

Yet we still have to demonstrate specifically how the citizen subject as a speaking subject is called into making rights claims. To do this, we need to return to Austin briefly and then show how his classification of speech acts requires expansion to understand citizen subjects making rights claims in or by saying and doing something. Austin considers five classes of acts with performative force: judgements, decisions, commitments, acknowledgements, and clarifications. (1) There are judgements, such as acquitting, convicting, measuring, characterizing, ranking, calculating, and placing. These are typified by giving a verdict. As we mentioned earlier, we would separate legal judgements from practical judgements and value judgements. (2) There are decisions, such as appointing, excommunicating, sentencing, nominating, resigning, bequeathing, pleading, and pardoning. These are typified by exercising power, influence, and authority. (3) There are commitments, such as guaranteeing, pledging, consenting, espousing, embracing, and proposing. Promising or undertaking to commit to doing something typifies these. These also include declarations or announcements of intention. (4) There are acknowledgements, such as apologizing, congratulating, commending, cursing, and challenging. They are typified by action that involves socially oriented and evaluated expression. (5) There are clarifications, such as conceding, illustrating, assuming, postulating, or replying. They are typified by the declarations 'I argue', 'I postulate'.

This classification of acts is clearly useful for developing our view on acts of citizen subjects. But it should also be clear that Austin (and his interlocutors) do not pay enough, if any, attention to the subject who thus speaks 'I, we, or they have a right to'. What kinds of acts are those that make rights claims? They are not judgements, decisions, commitments, acknowledgements, or clarifications. They are claims. When Karen Zivi argues for a performative approach to understanding rights, she suggests that 'it means asking questions about what we are doing together when we say we have rights, about the realities we create and the relationships we engender through the making of rights claims, and about the effects that our utterances may have, intended or otherwise, on both ourselves and others.'[38] This, in turn, for Zivi, requires 'appreciating the extent to which our claims both reference and reiterate social conventions and norms, and yet have forces and effects that exceed them.'[39] Thus, she argues 'that we treat claims such as "I have a right to privacy" or "We have a right to health care" as performative utterances, asking not just whether the particular claim corresponds to law or morality as if it were simply a constative utterance but also what it is a speaker does in or by making a particular claim. We need to analyze rights claiming, in other words, as an illocutionary and a perlocutionary activity.'[40] Yet, ironically, claiming as a class of speech acts is not on Austin's list.

We have already suggested as a first move to expand the forces that make speech acts possible to include not only performativity but also legality and imaginary. Having proposed that, we now name the class of acts that involves 'making rights claims' as 'claims'. In other words, we are proposing to add a new class of acts to Austin's: claims. People making rights claims in or by saying and doing 'I, we, they have a right to' enact themselves as citizen subjects. It is imperative to reflect further on how in or by saying and doing 'I, we, or they have a right to' produces a citizen subject.

The citizen subject, we have argued, is both a submissive and subversive speaking and doing subject. How does 'I, we, or they have a right to' *function* as a claim? First, it places the citizen subject under conventions that constitute callings on her. Making rights claims in or by saying 'I, we, or they have a right to', the citizen subject recognizes—explicitly or tacitly, consciously or unconsciously—that she acts under certain conventions. Saying 'I have a right to' is possible only within a convention from which it derives its legal, performative, or imaginary force. This is essentially an act of submission.[41]

Yet, and second, the utterance 'I, we, or they have a right to' also provokes closings or openings. What we mean by this is that as a claim, the utterance 'have a right to' places demands on the other to act in a particular way. This can activate the force of the law, for example, when citizen subjects claim that a right is being violated. Or it can mobilize a performative force in or by breaking a convention. Or it can invoke an imaginary force by appealing to a convention that is out of place or time. This is the sense in which the rights of a subject are obligations on others and the rights of others function as obligations on us. By virtue of the legal, performative, or imaginary forces, 'I, we, or they have a right to' can provoke openings and closings as possibilities. For this reason, we think of the relation between callings, openings, and closings as not sequential or separate but simultaneous and intertwined aspects of making rights claims. The conversion between submission and subversion can be instantaneous. In or by saying and doing something and making a rights claim as a speaking citizen subject may have aimed at subversion of a convention, yet it may well have functioned, as a misfire would, as an act of submission to that convention. Or an act of obedience, for that matter. How an act functions in making rights claims through callings, closings, and openings and how a citizen subject is produced through these are ultimately matters of empirical research and cannot be elaborated *only* theoretically.

If callings summon citizen subjects, they also provoke openings and closings for making rights claims. We consider openings as those possibilities that create new ways of saying and doing rights. Openings are those possibilities that enable the performance of previously unimagined or unarticulated experiences of ways of being citizen subjects, a resignification of being speaking and acting beings. Openings are possibilities through which citizen subjects come into being. Closings, by contrast, contract and reduce possibilities of becoming citizen subjects. We discussed earlier the imaginary institution of society by Castoriadis. We highlighted a basic tension to which he draws our attention between conventions and their resignification. He also sees this tension playing out as openings and closings. The principle of closure always directs itself to maintaining the institution of society, while the principle of opening constantly threatens its institution. The principle of closure intensifies coercion and sanctions, while the principle of opening calls into question their institution with imaginary significations.[42] Our sense of openings and closings draws on Castoriadis's articulation of this tension as constitutive for the imaginary institution of society and subjects that it spawns.

To sum, by adding claims as a class of acts to Austin's judgements, decisions, commitments, acknowledgements, and clarifications, we have identified making rights claims with 'I, we, they have a right to' as acts of citizen subjects. We now have to discuss how digital acts are a special case of speech acts that we resignify in this chapter.

DIGITAL ACTS

Making rights claims, whether this is through the Internet or not, will occasion callings, openings, and closings and will involve conventions and negotiations among and between obedience, submission, and subversion. The same issues are practically present in all speech acts. All speech acts uttered through the Internet—which we will refer to as digital acts—such as blogging, messaging, emailing, tweeting, posting, liking, and commenting can have the same qualities of being locutionary, illocutionary, and perlocutionary acts. Similarly, the felicity or infelicity of such acts, whether speaking subjects have understood adequately the appropriateness of the situation in which they have spoken, and whether there were misfires (an appropriate description for emails or tweets gone awry) or effects in their performativity are not peculiar to digital acts. Moreover, one prevalent issue is whether subjects can control the effects of their acts and, if so, to what extent, and another is how their acts exceed their intentions. Acting through the Internet illustrates particularly well the inoperability of the sovereign subject yet also her emergent agency. Finally, the perlocutionary force of digital acts through the Internet and to what extent they rupture conventions are legal and political issues. Thus making rights claims to privacy, anonymity, accessibility, or the right to be forgotten all have the qualities of making rights claims through digital acts.

Yet making rights claims is possible through a class of acts—claims— that, although related, is irreducible to one of the classes of speech acts that Austin enumerates. The premise of this book is that the citizen subject acting through the Internet is the digital citizen and that this is a new subject of politics who also acts through new conventions that not only involve doing things with words but doing words with things.

A complicating aspect of digital acts is that they involve computer programming languages—code—which is similar to but distinct from human languages. We have mentioned in chapter 2 that we find the idea of code as architecture proposed by Lessig as misleading. It conflates what code is with what code does. Or, now using Austin, we suggest that in or by saying and doing something with speech and code people produce illocutionary or perlocutionary effects. If Lessig persists in using 'architecture' to describe the effects of code, then clearly, code is not architecture. Rather, in or by using code, the architecture or the conventions of the Internet are created. Nevertheless, we think the metaphor of architecture is also misplaced, a point that is captured in Alexander Galloway's description of code as the creator of protocol.[43] He argues that 'a computer protocol is a set of recommendations and rules that outline specific technical standards. The protocols that govern much of the Internet are contained in what are called RFC (Request For Comments) documents. Called "the primary documentation of the Internet," these technical memoranda detail the vast majority of standards and protocols in use on the Internet today.'[44] But Galloway recovers a broader conception of protocol to include 'any type of correct or proper behavior within a specific system of conventions.'[45] It is the use of code to create conventions that gives code its potent force in the age of computer networks.[46] For Galloway, 'now, protocols refer specifically to standards governing the implementation of specific technologies. Like their diplomatic predecessors, computer protocols establish the essential points necessary to enact an agreed-upon standard of action.'[47] What is code, then? Arguing that computer languages and natural languages are very similar, Galloway writes that 'like the natural languages, computer languages have a sophisticated syntax and grammar. Like the natural languages, computer languages have specific communities and cultures in which the language is spoken.'[48] For Galloway, then, code is a language. But unlike natural languages, it is a special kind of language. He contends that '*code is the only language that is executable.*'[49] 'So [for Galloway] code is the first language that actually does what it says—it is a machine for converting meaning into action.'[50] With Austin (and Wittgenstein), this conclusion comes as a major surprise to us. As we have argued in this chapter, for Austin (and Wittgenstein) language is an activity, and in or by saying something in language we do something with it—we act. To put it differently, language *is* executable.[51] There is no uniqueness to code in that regard, although while code is like language, it is different. We think that difference is to be sought in its effects and the conventions it creates through the Internet rather than in its ostensible unique nature.[52]

To develop the difference that code makes for speech, let us recall here the four political questions that acting through the Internet resignifies, which we briefly discussed in chapter 2: anonymity, extensity, traceability, and velocity. We can now say that these are effects of in or by saying and doing something through the Internet. To put it differently, digital acts through the Internet and the space that these acts create—cyberspace—are marked by these effects and distinguish them from other speech acts. If we consider briefly the question of anonymity, we may begin to realize its immensity. For speech acts to have illocutionary or perlocutionary effects, speakers do not have to identify themselves. Nor would they need to necessarily locate themselves. Consider a demonstration in a public square. To perform it as a political act, people assemble, sing, shout, clap, thump, and disassemble. Despite all the contemporary surveillance technologies such as cameras, to identify each and every person in this act is quite difficult. To maintain anonymity in squares and streets is still a possibility, and the convention called 'demonstration' requires it. By contrast, acting through the Internet has disrupted this convention. Often, digital acts give rise to a multiplicity of performative utterances that want to and, more importantly, as we shall see, claim the right to remain anonymous. But to remain anonymous on the Internet is a battle.[53] Thus, the political struggle over anonymity when one acts is among the defining struggles of our time. Similarly, digital acts introduce enormous velocity to the performative force of utterances. Digital acts will not eliminate distance (we understand distance here as not merely quantitative but also a qualitative metric), but the speed with which digital acts can reverberate is phenomenal. When we consider this along with extensity, or the reach of digital acts, it becomes even more significant.

Finally, the transmission, recording, and storage of utterances of digital acts also make them durable in unpredictable ways and amenable to tracing. It is well nigh impossible to make digital utterances without a trace; on the contrary, often the force of a digital speech act draws its strength from the traces that it leaves. As we said in chapter 2, each of these questions raised by digital acts can arguably be found in other technologies of speech acts—the telegraph, megaphone, radio, and telephone come to mind immediately. But it is when taken together that we think digital acts resignify these questions and combine to make them distinct from speech acts, in terms of both the conventions by which they become possible and the effects that they produce.

We touched upon a distinction between speech acts and action above. We argued that to accomplish performative acts requires bodies in action. To accomplish the performative force of speech requires performing an action or series of actions. To put it differently, we argued that we not only do things with words but also do words with things. Is it the same for digital acts? Do digital acts require acting bodies as speech acts do? The answer is yes, but differently. Consider a more or less total speech act situation. There will be conventions creating spaces for possible performative utterances. There will be bodies to perform, witness, and enjoin those utterances. There will be constative speech acts about the situation. There will be illocutionary utterances. There will be perlocutionary utterances. Some conventions will be cited, iterated, and repeated. Some conventions will be resignified. Some will be broken. Each of these acts will come into being through legal, performative, and imaginary forces. They will also bring into being subjects who will act this way or that way. There will be various actions to bring about these things if indeed we are imagining a space of movement and performance. We say this is 'more or less' a total speech act situation because depicting a 'total' speech act situation is impossible. Yet this gives a fairly good description of what transpires in a scene of speech acts. The important thing is to separate acts (locutionary, illocutionary, perlocutionary), forces (legal, performative, imaginary), conventions, actions, bodies, and spaces that their relations produce.

If we consider digital acts with this scene in mind rather than imagining a separate and independent cyberspace from an ostensibly real space, we will begin to give a description of what conventions have arisen that enable digital acts, what sorts of digital acts have become possible, what kinds of actions make those acts performative, and what kinds of openings and closings arise. Consider the conventions that have emerged through the Internet that made possible new actions such as emailing, blogging, coding, messaging, tagging, posting, and pirating. These conventions include platforms such as Bitcoin, BitTorrent, Facebook, GitHub, Pirate Bay, Tor, WikiLeaks, and YouTube. These platforms have come into being for various purposes: communicating, evading, collaborating, networking, whistle-blowing, programming, or downloading. Each of these platforms makes possible various actions: aggregating, blogging, coding, downloading, emailing, filtering, firewalling, following, friending, liking, mashing, messaging, mining, pirating, posting, trending, tweeting, and uploading. Note that each of these may involve words but not necessarily so: they can also involve citations involving images and sounds. But they can also involve repetitions such as retweeting, forwarding, and downloading; and they can involve resignifications such as classifying and linking. To accomplish an act would require one or more of these actions. Since to perform these actions is possible only through the Internet, digital acts would require them. What are digital acts, then? When people perform digital acts in or by saying and doing things through the Internet, they become digital subjects. When people perform digital acts in or by saying and doing 'I, we, they have a right to', they enact themselves as citizen subjects; they are making digital rights claims.

We want to recognize digital rights claims as those made through the Internet and through which people claim 'I, we, or they have a right to'. We do not yet want to give content to this claim separate from how making digital rights claims has evolved over the past decade or so. *But for now, we are proposing that becoming digital citizens in cyberspace involves making digital rights claims.* Through digital acts and making rights claims, digital citizen subjects are brought into being. Two points to remember here are the traversing of digital rights across multiple national borders that invoke multiple legal orders and the transferability of rights from classical to digital domains. Both these issues create considerable complexities around which numerous struggles are already occurring.

Combined, these two issues raise one big question: Who is the subject of digital rights? We pose this question not in the sense of subjects that already exist as the bearers or holders of rights but as their claimants. The difference is important. If we ask this question about the bearers of rights, then we would be embroiled in a debate over whether digital rights are human rights or citizenship rights. If not, then the question we must ask is: Who are digital citizens? If their acts traverse national borders, surely they cannot be called citizens since we do not have transnational legal arrangements—save the European Union, whose legal scope and competence on citizenship is limited by its derivative character. Arguably, human rights are distributed across various regional conventions which certainly lack not only scope and competence but also the force of law in protecting those rights. Accordingly, most legislation that governs digital rights is enacted by nation-states, and their scope and competence are applicable only within their borders. To put it simply, while digital acts traverse borders, digital rights do not. This is where we believe thinking about digital acts in terms of their legality, performativity, and imaginary is crucial since there are international and transnational spaces in which digital rights are being claimed that if not yet legally in force are nevertheless emerging performatively and imaginatively. Yet, arguably, some emerging transnational and international laws governing cyberspace in turn are having an effect on national legislations. To put it differently, the classical argument about the relationship between human rights and citizenship rights, that the former are norms and only the latter carry the force of law, is not a helpful starting point. We are going to return to the question 'Who is the subject of digital rights?' in chapter 7 as we conclude the book. Before we reach that point, we need to demonstrate, in chapters 4, 5, and 6, how callings, closings, and openings of cyberspace bring that subject—the digital citizen—into being by examining various digital acts.

THE SEARCH FOR A METHOD

We mentioned earlier that the way we approach the citizen subject is inspired by a method Michel Foucault practiced, Gilles Deleuze elaborated, and Étienne Balibar articulated. We have expanded it through the speech acts theory of J. L. Austin and his interlocutors Jacques Derrida, Pierre Bourdieu, Shoshana Felman, Judith Butler, and Bruno Latour. We have further expanded speech acts to digital acts by recognizing not only their performative force (illocutionary and perlocutionary) but also their legal and imaginary forces. We have then developed a concept—making rights claims—that connects the figure of the citizen subject to acts. We developed this by first identifying a sixth class of acts as claims. This class of acts, just as Austin would argue about his classes of acts, is not mutually exclusive but simultaneous and overlapping with those articulated by Austin. Clearly, investigating making digital rights claims in cyberspace would involve all six classes of acts. What distinguishes the citizen subject is making rights claims in or by saying and doing 'I, we, they have a right to'. We consider this book as a contribution to laying the groundwork for undertaking empirical investigations of digital acts, their principles, concepts, and methods concerning specifically making rights claims in cyberspace as a question of the subject of digital rights.

For us, the most important proposition we have developed here is that through making rights claims in or by saying and doing 'I, we, they have a right to', people enact themselves as citizen subjects. By including all persons in the claim (singular, plural, and third), we want to indicate that making a claim never brings a singular subject into being but that a subject is always already plural. For this reason, the citizen subject who speaks thus, 'I, we, or they have a right to', is neither the rights-bearing subject who already enjoys rights nor the sovereign subject in mastery of the effects of her acts. If indeed conventions and their resignification are necessary conditions of acts, as we argued earlier, then making rights claims produces obedient, submissive, and subversive citizen subjects in the sense that making rights claims enters the subject into a play of power. To understand digital acts we have to understand speech acts or speech that acts. The speech that acts means not only that in or by saying something we are doing something but also that in or by doing something we are saying something. It is in this sense that we have argued digital acts are different from speech acts only insofar as the conventions they repeat and iterate and conventions that they resignify are conventions that are made possible through the Internet. Ultimately, digital acts resignify questions of anonymity, extensity, traceability, and velocity in political ways.

For us, the most important recognition we have developed is that digital acts traverse national borders and legal orders in unprecedented ways. That the resulting cyberspace often (if not always) crosses a multiplicity of borders and involves a multiplicity of legal orders is something that complicates the legality, performativity, and imaginary of becoming digital citizens. To put it differently, making rights claims in cyberspace complicates the subject of rights and of which rights those claims are subject.

We described above a scene enacted by the relations between or the coming together of bodies, acts, actions, and conventions through the Internet. There we identified some of those actions, acts, and conventions that make possible digital acts. We mentioned actions such as emailing, messaging, chatting, and blogging that have now been incorporated into platforms such as Facebook, YouTube, WikiLeaks, GitHub, Tor, Bitcoin, and BitTorrent. We said that people are now acting in relation to these platforms and are performing conventions such as communicating, collaborating, networking, whistle-blowing, and so on. Each of these conventions involves citing, iterating, repeating, and resignifying various actions: aggregating, blogging, coding, downloading, emailing, filtering, firewalling, following, friending, liking, mashing, messaging, mining, pirating, posting, trending, retweeting, and uploading. We next will discuss some of those digital acts and actions and the citizen subjects that they produce.

NOTES

1. As Bauman et al. write, through the Internet, 'states, social movements, and individuals can play a variety of games, reenacting the meanings of sovereignty and citizenship, security, and liberty.' Bauman et al., "After Snowden: Rethinking the Impact of Surveillance," *International Political Sociology* 8, 2 (2014): 128.

2. The concept 'speech acts' has also been used in security studies. Jef Huysmans recently argued that this usage was heavily slanted towards 'speech' as linguistic utterance. Critiquing this approach, he argues that it should instead slant towards 'acts'. He writes, 'The conception of act that is at work in the security speech act thus combines two political elements. First, the speech act of security is a creative move that ruptures a given state of affairs. Second, the political conception of rupture is folded into an exceptionalist scripting of the act—breaking the normal rules of the game on existential grounds.' J. Huysmans, "What's in an Act? On Security Speech Acts and Little Security Nothings," *Security Dialogue* 42, 4–5 (2011): 375. But Huysmans finds fault in Austin's original conception when he says, 'Arguably, this dimension of the conception of act takes it outside of the Austinian framing of speech act, which is heavily embedded in instituted structures of meaning' (374). We think, however, that this 'fault' has more to do with the appropriation of his work in security studies than Austin's 'speech acts' theory. As we argue below, Austin was indeed quite keen on 'speech that acts' rather than 'speech acts'.

3. D. C. Nunziato, *Virtual Freedom: Net Neutrality and Free Speech in the Internet Age* (Stanford University Press, 2009).

4. F. Lyotard, *The Postmodern Condition: A Report on Knowledge* (University of Minnesota Press, 1984).

5. L. Wittgenstein, *Philosophical Investigations*, ed. P. M. S. Hacker and J. Schulte, trans. G. E. M. Anscombe, 4th ed. (Blackwell, 1998), §23.

6. This is a rather short yet influential book by J. L. Austin, who originally delivered it as William James Lectures at Harvard in 1955. Austin, *How to Do Things with Words* (Oxford University Press, 1962). After Lyotard and following Wittgenstein and Austin, a number of scholars have made creative use of the performativity of language. Of special importance to us are J. Derrida, *Limited Inc*, trans. G. Graff (Northwestern University Press, 1988); J. Derrida, *Without Alibi*, ed. P. Kamuf (Stanford University Press, 2002); S. Cavell, *Philosophical Passages: Wittgenstein, Emerson, Austin, Derrida* (Blackwell, 1995); S. Cavell, *Must We Mean What We Say? A Book of Essays*, 2nd ed. (Cambridge University Press, 2002); J. Butler, *Gender Trouble: Feminism and the Subversion of Identity* (Routledge, 1990); J. Butler, *Excitable Speech: A Politics of the Performative* (Routledge, 1997). However, as Vikki Bell has argued, the concept of performativity has now moved well beyond a focus on language. V. Bell, *Culture and Performance: The Challenge of Ethics, Politics, and Feminist Theory* (Berg, 2007), 11–17. Latour wrote a brilliant short essay, which does not mention Austin but nevertheless makes a significant intervention in resignifying Austin's influential phrase 'how to do things with words' as 'how to do words with things'. Latour may never have intended his piece as an intervention in the debate over Austin. Latour, "The Berlin Key or How to Do Words with Things," in *Matter, Materiality and Modern Culture*, ed. Paul Graves-Brown (Routledge, 2000).

7. J. E. Cohen, *Configuring the Networked Self: Law, Code, and the Play of Everyday Practice* (Yale University Press, 2012); R. Deibert, *Black Code: Inside the Battle for Cyberspace* (McClelland & Stewart, 2013); L. Lessig, *Code: Version 2.0* (Basic, 2006).

8. As Shoshana Felman writes, '[S]ince . . . to speak is to act, performative utterances, inasmuch as they produce actions, and constitute operations, cannot be logically true or false, but only successful or unsuccessful, "felicitous" or "infelicitous".' S. Felman, *The Scandal of the Speaking Body: Don Juan with J. L. Austin, or Seduction in Two Languages* (Stanford University Press, 2003), 7. Also see Bell, *Culture and Performance*, 115.

9. S. Cavell, *A Pitch of Philosophy: Autobiographical Exercises* (Harvard University Press, 1994), 81.

10. Austin, *How to Do Things with Words*, 8.

11. Ibid., 12.

12. Cavell, *A Pitch of Philosophy*, 87.

13. Austin, *How to Do Things with Words*, 52, 147.

14. Ibid., 148.

15. Ibid., 8–9, 13, 26, 29, 34, 81–82.

16. P. Bourdieu, *Language and Symbolic Power* (Harvard University Press, 1993), 125–26.

17. Ibid., 107.

18. Austin, *How to Do Things with Words*, 16, 25, 27, 105.

19. Butler, *Gender Trouble*, 173, 177–79; J. Butler, *Undoing Gender* (Routledge, 2004), 218, 224.

20. Austin, *How to Do Things with Words*, 120–21.

21. Butler writes: 'Whereas some critics mistake the critique of sovereignty for the demolition of agency, I propose that agency begins where sovereignty wanes. The one who acts (who is not the same as the sovereign subject) acts precisely to the extent that he or she is constituted as an actor and, hence, operating within a linguistic field of enabling constraints from the outset.' Butler, *Excitable Speech*, 16.

22. Ibid., 152.

23. Ibid., 164.

24. Toni Negri in conversation with Deleuze. G. Deleuze, "Control and Becoming," in *Negotiations* (Columbia University Press, 1990), 170.

25. Felman, *Scandal of the Speaking Body*, 6.

26. Ibid., 65. Felman writes: 'If the problem of the human act thus consists in the relation between language and body, it is because the act is conceived—by performative analysis as well as by psychoanalysis—as that which problematizes at one and the same time the separation and the opposition between the two. The act, an enigmatic and problematic production of the speaking body, destroys from its inception the metaphysical dichotomy between the domain of the "mental" and the domain of the "physical," breaks down the opposition between body and spirit, between matter and language.' Moreover, Felman considers this as 'Austinian materialism is a materialism of the residue, that is, literally, of the trivial: a materialism of the speaking body' (109).

27. Latour, "The Berlin Key or How to Do Words with Things."

28. Latour illustrates this through the example of an individual trying to make a key open a door in Berlin and how such an action is capable of accomplishing words: 'If I take my key with two bits that authorizes me to re-enter my house and obliges me to bolt the door at night and forbids me to bolt it during the day, am I not dealing with social relations, with morality, with laws? Of course, but made of steel' (19).

29. Butler, *Excitable Speech*, 22.

30. Austin, *How to Do Things with Words*, 60 (emphasis in original).

31. Ibid.

32. Felman, *Scandal of the Speaking Body*.

33. Ibid., 65.

34. Ibid.

35. See C. Castoriadis, *World in Fragments: Writings on Politics, Society, Psychoanalysis and the Imagination*, ed. D. A. Curtis (Stanford University Press, 1997), 3–18.

36. Ibid., 3–4.

37. C. Castoriadis, *The Imaginary Institution of Society*, trans. K. Blamey (Polity, 1987).

38. K. Zivi, *Making Rights Claims: A Practice of Democratic Citizenship* (Oxford University Press, 2012), 19.

39. Ibid.

40. Ibid., 15.

41. Let us note that an act of submission is also a creative act despite its negative connotation. That's why it is more nuanced to think of power being exercised through three inseparable modes of obedience, submission, and subversion.

42. Castoriadis, *World in Fragments*, 9–12.

43. A. R. Galloway, *Protocol: How Control Exists after Decentralization* (MIT Press, 2006).

44. Ibid., 6.

45. Ibid., 7.

46. Also see A. Mackenzie and T. Vurdubakis, "The Performativity of Code: Software and Cultures of Circulation," *Theory, Culture & Society* 22, 1 (2005): 4. They argue that code is to be understood not only as software 'but also in terms of cultural, moral, ethical and legal codes of conduct.'

47. Galloway, *Protocol*, 7.

48. Ibid., 164.

49. Ibid., 165.

50. Ibid., 165–66.

51. A. Mackenzie and T. Vurdubakis, "Codes and Codings in Crisis Signification, Performativity and Excess," *Theory, Culture & Society* 28, 6 (2011).

52. Although N. Katherine Hayles develops a nuanced understanding of speech, writing, and code, she also seems to agree with Galloway that code is the only language that is executable. N. Katherine Hayles, *My Mother Was a Computer: Digital Subjects and Literary Texts* (University of Chicago Press, 2005), 50–51.

53. For most hackers, hacktivists, cyberactivists, and Internet activists, this has been a major issue, and there exist complex countertechnologies to maintain anonymity when acting through the Internet. These are advocated as strategies by organizations such as the Electronic Frontier Foundation, the Open Rights Group, Riseup.net, and Tactical Technology Collective. The struggle over Tor, a method of browsing the Internet anonymously, is itself a case study in how anonymity has become a defining struggle of our time. See J. Bartlett, *The Dark Net: Inside the Digital Underworld* (Heinemann, 2014) and Deibert, *Black Code*.

FOUR

Callings

Participating, Connecting, Sharing

If the citizen comes after the subject—as a subject of power—then what are the various digital acts through which citizen subjects perform themselves? How are citizen subjects called upon to conduct themselves in cyberspace? As we have argued, digital citizens do not already exist as subjects who now access, communicate, participate, work, and shop online.[1] We cannot simply assume that being a digital citizen already means something, such as the ability to participate, and then look for whose conduct conforms to this meaning. Rather, digital acts are refashioning, inventing, and making up citizen *subjects* through the play of obedience, submission, and subversion. As we noted in chapter 2, the citizen embodies and is implicated in the formation of all of these forms of power, a composite subject of possibilities of obedience or submission to authority but also of potential subversion.

To repeat, if we are going to designate the emerging political subject of cyberspace as the digital citizen, we ought not to use that concept in its conventional meaning as the ability to participate in cyberspace. Being digital citizens is not simply the ability to participate.[2] We discussed in chapter 1 how Jon Katz described an ethos of sharing, exchange, knowledge, and openness in the 1990s. Today, these have become callings to perform ourselves in cyberspace through actions such as petitioning, posting, and blogging. These actions repeatedly call upon citizen subjects of cyberspace, and here we want to address their legal, performative, and imaginary force.

Consider the force of openness, an imaginary that places numerous demands upon the digital conduct of citizens.[3] The liberating promises of digital technologies include the demands that what we do be shared or exchanged and be open to others. This was exemplified in Katz's optimism, which embraced cyberspace as part of an emerging political libertarian ethos of connectivity, the free exchange of information and spreading of ideas, the creation of new communities and forms of democratic participation, and the reconnection of people to institutions that govern their lives. All of these values are related to openness. Today, being open has become a demand on organizations and individuals to share everything from software and publications to data about themselves. From open data, open government, open society to open access, open source, and open software, both individuals and collectives are compelled to make available through the Internet what they produce, what they do, their processes and traces.[4] These demands come from not just governing authorities or commercial interests but also from social, political, cultural, and work relations with others when we are called upon to share and collaborate digitally. But also the demands come from subjects who through habit, necessity, or desire engage digitally for a variety of purposes, from those of pleasure and politics to mere convenience, and call on others to do so as well.

However, openness also gives rise to uneasy tensions between calls for 'free culture' and access to knowledge and calls for privacy and copyright, albeit for different reasons and with different effects.[5] Julie Cohen, for example, emphasizes that the imaginary of 'protecting intellectual rights', enforced through copyright laws, commodifies and marketizes knowledge. Moreover, privacy laws inhibit the free flow of knowledge and stand in the way of efficient markets, meeting consumer needs, and securing public safety. Cohen argues that copyright often trumps privacy because the latter is interpreted as 'second order' to broader commercial interests. Yet copyright and privacy are debated as though they are unrelated legal domains; however, they share underpinning political and theoretical ideals, or we would say *imaginaries*, of information as freedom versus control.

We agree with Cohen on the seemingly paradoxical relation between imaginaries of openness (copyleft, commons) and closedness (copyright, privacy) and their connection to information freedom and control. She is right to argue that this paradox cannot be resolved in legal theory for two main reasons. First, freedom and control are not separate but require each other, and how this plays out involves calibration within specific situated practices.[6] Second, and relatedly, legal theory depends on a conception of abstract liberal autonomous selves rather than subjects that emerge from the creative, embodied, and material practices of situated and networked individuals.[7] It is in relation to the latter that Cohen understands subjectivity, self-formation, and the networked self and how these are configured by the imperatives and tensions of openness.

While fruitfully opening up legal theory to social theory in challenging ways, Cohen reproduces the legal strategy of instituting an imaginary of the citizen based on broad abstract principles upon which specific laws and policies can then be enacted. In doing so, she elides an understanding of the specific actions through which political subjects come to *act* in cyberspace. It is by making and responding to callings (and the various actions that these mobilize) that subject positions as ways of acting come into being.[8] Without specifically investigating these callings, how they are made, how they are responded to, and the actions that they engender, it would be difficult to understand the kind of citizen subject they bring into being. It is often forgotten that the citizen subject is not merely an intentional agent of conduct but also a product of callings that mobilize that conduct.

If we focus on callings and the actions they mobilize and how they make acts possible, we also shift our focus from a freedom versus control dichotomy to the play of obedience, submission, and subversion. This is a play configured by the forces of legality, performativity, and imaginary which call upon subjects to be open and responsible and through which mostly governmental but also commercial and nongovernmental authorities try to maintain their grip on the conduct of those who are their subjects.[9] How do subjects of power act within such a play of obedience, submission, and subversion? That is the question that this chapter addresses through an examination of callings that mobilize a series of actions that make possible digital acts in cyberspace. We focus on three acts that symbolize particularly well the demands for openness—participating, connecting, and sharing. These acts are not all inclusive; there are certainly other acts, but they cover what we suggest are key digital acts and their enabling digital actions. And while we treat these acts analytically as separate, it is with the understanding that they are interrelated yet have distinctive aspects that need specifying.[10]

PARTICIPATING

Acts of participating in cyberspace are now seen as democratizing. Being active 'in' cyberspace was a defining characteristic of digital citizens advanced in the 1990s. This understanding was confined to democratic politics and the ability to access, communicate, and participate online, which was understood as a virtual space separate and independent from 'real' space. Many writers such as Clay Shirky, Yochai Benkler, and Chris Anderson continue to celebrate the participatory and social-change promises of the Internet, especially in the age of Web 2.0, which Tim O'Reilly has referred to as providing an 'architecture of participation.'[11] But such universal claims have increasingly been challenged, especially in arguments that the Internet is implicated in the production of digital inequality and a 'digital divide' along lines of class, gender, race, and ethnicity, which reflects and reinforces already existing inequalities in contemporary societies.[12] Both the existence of already formed subjects and virtual and real spaces are assumed in these accounts. For this reason it is imperative to begin thinking about participating in relation to how a digital divide is being conceived.[13]

Inequality is expressed as leading to two divisions: between those who do and do not have access and between those who do or do not contribute to content or leave digital traces. In either case, certain groups are left out, and the concern is either their participatory or methodological exclusion, the former referring to the representativeness of who is 'online' and the latter pointing to who leaves digital footprints that can be analysed by different knowledge-making practices. Being left out is also argued to lead to further exclusions: 'A "digital divide" is never only digital; its consequences play out wherever political and economic decisions are made and wherever their results are felt.'[14] Halford and Savage, for example, argue that many scholarly studies see lack of access to the Internet as both arising from and reinforcing existing social inequalities since citizens are denied information about employment or social services or opportunities for involvement in politics, social networking, and consumption. In this way, access to the Internet, they say, is interpreted as a neutral good that can be converted into other goods and so it is through access that life chances can be changed. Solutions put forward to reduce such digital divides and increase social inclusion often include education, training, and the delivery of publicly accessible and subsidized technology.[15]

For Halford and Savage, whether liberating or dividing, cyberspace (or what they refer to as the 'Web') is always considered as an already given space, and its subjects are separate, independent, and preformed rather than performed. Rather than assuming that 'pre-formed social groups "use" (or don't use) technologies', they identify a 'more complex process of mutual interaction and stabilisation' where digital technologies are not separated from social processes but instead involved in constituting subjects in diverse and pervasive ways.[16] In other words, they advance that the Web is not independent from the actions of subjects. Though they refer to a vague conception of the 'Web', Halford and Savage are right about the digital divide and social divide being interrelated. What they identify as complex social processes between digital technologies and the formation of subjects, we specify as the digital acts through which citizen subjects are called upon by legality, performativity, and imaginary.

Becoming a digital citizen involves responding to callings where participating is one of them. Participating demands specific actions of skilling and tooling that citizens need to undertake to equip themselves. Governments and international organizations, such as the United Nations World Summit on the Information Society (WSIS), which promotes the principles of connectivity, access, and capacity, security, governance, equity, and diversity, often issue this calling. For governments, participating involves digital access to not only information but also transactions and services such as registrations, service requests, licences, voting, and so on. For example, in the United Kingdom, 'starting with the citizen' is a policy concerned with a transactional relationship and about digitally doing 'business' with government.[17] The same demand extends to transacting with corporations where online purchasing is promoted as a form of consumer empowerment and where consumer citizens are called upon to access and analyse their transactional data. This is exemplified in the UK government's 'midata' programme, which gives 'people greater access to electronic records of their past buying and spending habits [to] help them to make better buying choices.' Here, rights to personal data are about giving 'power to consumers.'[18] The empowering possibilities of accessing and working with data also underpin 'open government data' programmes. Openness is extended to making government transparent through a public right to data and freedom to information, a version that is also advanced by civic organizations such as mySociety.[19] These call forth an imaginary of citizens as data analysts equipped with the skills necessary to analyse their commercial transactions and thus make better decisions or to analyse the transactions of governments and thus hold them to account.[20]

For governments, corporations, civic organizations, and many scholars, a digital citizen is thus a subject who is called upon to equip herself so that she can participate on the Internet. Mossberger et al., for example, understand digital citizenship as the ability to fully participate in society online, which requires regular access to the Internet, with adequate devices and speeds, technological skills and competence, and information literacy.[21] Equipping thus includes not only hardware, such as installing computers in classrooms and libraries and expanding high-speed broadband services, but also developing skills and capabilities through training courses in computing, coding, and programming.[22] Equipping digital citizens is thus understood as assembling and investing in the material and literary skills necessary for people to participate in cyberspace as a social right. The United Kingdom government's digital inclusion strategy, for example, has been introduced not only to provide access through investments in digital infrastructures but also to 'equip the whole country with the skills, motivation, and trust to go online, be digitally capable and to make the most of the internet. . . . If we succeed, by 2020 everyone who can be digitally capable, will be.'[23] Such digital inclusion is linked to making better financial decisions, finding jobs, accessing services, maintaining social contacts, and addressing equality, social, health, and well-being issues such as isolation. In its response to the strategy, the Labour Party's digital review identified 'digital inclusion' as a necessary condition of access to other social goods, noting, for example, that 'benefits claimants [are being] sanctioned because they can't job search on-line.'[24] For governments, being online is a means of 'digital health literacy' and a 'matter of life and death'; as people who are 'disengaged from the digital world, [they] won't be part of a culture of preventive care' and managing their own health, which are crucial when austerity meets rising demand.[25]

The so-called digitally excluded in the United Kingdom are identified in the government's strategy as 'the most vulnerable and disadvantaged groups in society' and include 'those' residing in social housing, living on lower wages or unemployed, having disabilities, being over fifty-five or between fifteen and twenty-four years of age, or being offenders or ex-offenders. To track national progress on reducing digital exclusion, a nine-point scale measures the performance of digital capability in relation to particular digital services (such as claiming benefits). From people 'who never have and never will' to those who are 'reluctant' or are 'confident' or 'expert', the figure of the citizen is imagined as a progression of digital competencies. Just as corporations are evaluated in relation to their 'digital IQ', so too are citizens.[26] The lack of access to hardware used to separate 'cyber-haves from the cyber-have nots', but now access is conceived as occurring along a 'continuum ranging from, at one end, those who have no Internet access or experience to those, at the other, who have broadband access at home, use the Internet frequently, and are comfortable with a variety of online techniques.'[27]

The examples noted above illustrate different political views and emphases concerning the causes and consequences of a digital divide, a concept that has been variously defined in both government and the academy since its inception in the 1990s. Despite their differences, they do generally share an imaginary of citizen subjects as already formed as subjects of submission, where their participation is a matter of access, skills, and usage. It is an imaginary of a citizen as a subject who is often submissive (if not obedient) and is active only in ways recognized by government policies and programmes. All efforts are aimed at disciplining subjects along digital inclusion scales through actions that involve access, skills, motivation, and trust. It is through repetition that these actions become embodied and through which citizen subjects become governable. Digital inclusion thus places demands on the citizen subject to uptake these actions, to be skilled and tooled, and to learn and become knowledgeable and competent in looking after herself and governing her social needs, from accessing services and jobs to reducing her household bills. But to do so also demands vigilance in maintaining and re-equipping oneself in terms of both skills and infrastructures in the face of constant change: 'System outages, constant software updates, platform redesigns, network upgrades, hardware modifications, and connectivity changes make netizenship in the bitstream a rather challenging way of life.'[28]

Digital inclusion—at least as it is expressed in the United Kingdom—is not imagined as participating in politics digitally through actions such as petitioning, organizing, recruiting, contributing, campaigning, blogging, and so on. But participating can also be understood as including these actions along the lines first celebrated in the 1990s, where the Internet was promoted as a way to improve socioeconomic advantage via the opportunity to get political information and engage in political discussion and exchange.[29] Nevertheless, many studies have found little evidence that socially and economically disadvantaged group participation increases when politics is conducted through the Internet, whether in ways that mimic offline forms, such as petitions, or new ones, such as social media.[30]

What can be said of the political participation of the socially advantaged, then? One common finding of studies is that youth have the highest level of online political participation. This is, however, usually identified to be less than other 'offline' forms.[31] Let us consider a couple of examples. One 2007 study of youth in five cities—Hong Kong, Seoul, Singapore, Taipei, and Tokyo—found youth online participation is lower for forms of digital civic political engagement in much the same way as it is offline (e.g., reading newspapers, voting, signing petitions). Other forms of participating such as fandom, connecting with friends or strangers, peer-to-peer file sharing for music, and so on are more predominant modes. But interestingly, while commercial and entertaining uses dominate, the study found that participating online could increase civic political engagement for youth who are already politically interested. Furthermore, 'social networking can potentially be transformed to mobilizing forces when the time comes'.[32] In another study, American teens were found to sometimes use their online engagement to help them to be political whereby the 'act of hanging out online [was found to have] enormous potential for creating the civic networks that support real-world political engagement.'[33] One more study of youth is worth mentioning here as it points to a problematic differentiation between online and offline worlds that persists in these analyses of participation. A website supported by a local authority but managed and run by youth in Sweden was found to lead to greater civic participation and engagement, but this to a large degree was linked to wider participatory activities such as town hall meetings.[34] It is interesting to note that in all of the examples, the mere fact of participating is key, whether or not it involves simply accessing information or services or participating via interactive or dynamic social media and platforms. Simply put, the production and consumption of political content—political positions, opinions, demands, claims, and so on—are not matters of concern in these studies. When they are discussed, participants are found to do so 'thinly' and without being substantially engaged.[35]

While these are important issues, we have summarized them principally to distinguish our argument, which is that once a superficial distinction is made between online and offline activities, how people conduct themselves through the Internet by meshing their lives is neglected. First, the imaginaries of participating elide how the forces of legality and performativity organize and configure it and are neither neutral nor visible. Participating is treated as a functional demand rather than a political one, where making rights claims is an open object of contestation and struggle. For example, what resources of cyberspace do digitally equipped subjects have the authorization to access as a result of the workings of search algorithms and filters or the protocols that govern and normalize the retention, storage, sharing, and discoverability of information?[36] If legality and imaginary configure the citizen as a subject *of* power and place demands on her to participate digitally (submission), what we find interesting here and in relation to how we have understood being digital citizens is the performativity of participating that provides a glimpse of the citizen as also a potential subject of subversion. How, for example, does participating give rise to subversive actions, such as those of critical citizen science?[37] Or, as Matthew Fuller and Andrew Goffey put it, how do injunctions such as Google's 'Don't be evil' maxim belie the propensities that are activated by relatively unstable sociotechnical arrangements that are generative of 'unintended or secondary effects'?[38] Moreover, the discourse on participation presumes subjects as being already present. Instead, we ask: How can the calling to participate that we have identified produce digital citizens whose acts exceed their intentions? To put it differently, a tension exists between the ways in which the figure of the digital citizen is conceived in hegemonic imaginaries and legal discourses and how she is performatively coming into being through actions that equip her as a citizen in ways that are not acknowledged or always intended.

CONNECTING

If we take the examples of teens noted above, what comes to matter in terms of political participation is in the first instance their 'networking'. Beyond participating as an information or resource-seeking practice is the demand to connect with others and in doing so to be part of digital networks and associations. In relation to teens, danah boyd argues that social media enables them not only to participate but to help create 'networked publics', which are 'constructs' through which teens connect and imagine themselves as part of a community that is not independent from but very much connected to their relations in 'real' space.[39]

Yet understandings of networking or being networked imply that subjects are already constituted and how they network occurs through 'open' systems.[40] Instead, networking is really an effect of a calling that summons subjects to be and remain almost always connected in already given sociotechnical arrangements. The difference is captured in José van Dijck's account of the change that social media has introduced from community-oriented 'connectedness' to platform- and owner-configured 'connectivity.'[41] With the introduction of Web 2.0, she argues that connectivity captures how sociality has become technologically mediated through commercial platforms that organize and manage interaction. So while much is made of the 'networked information society', it is through the calling to connect that subjects engage in actions that come to make up both their subject positions and social networks.[42] But connecting also captures how digital actions are taken not only in relation to others but also with specific sociotechnical conventions of which platforms are just one part.[43] In other words, conventions are what subjects submit to when they connect.[44] It is through actions such as joining social media, emailing, following, gaming, chatting, friending, or messaging that subjects connect and through which they act.

That 2011 was deemed 'the year of the networked revolution' speaks to this, especially in relation to the number of political uprisings that were, to various degrees, mediated by different conventions such as tweeting, blogging, and messaging. Mass political protests and occupations seeking to overthrow dict.........., austerity programs, world banks, media empires, or the rich w........pared to one another not only in terms of a revolutionary ethos bu.......in terms of their mobilization of (especially) social networking platforms as means of expression, dissemination, and organizing.[45] While the conventions of social media have sometimes been attributed as causes of such uprisings, captured in terminology such as 'Twitter revolutions', as we noted in chapters 2 and 3, more nuanced arguments have noted that these were mediated by digital platforms.[46] Or, as we would put it, acting through the Internet and making connections with others does not replace, displace, or supplant other ways of acting in social or cultural spaces in which we are embedded.

In its most mundane and everyday connotation, connecting responds to the demand that subjects become active in relation to various conventions and be available and continuously open to others. That is, in spite of concerns about surveillance, control, privacy, and commercial exploitation (which we discuss in chapter 5), connecting is a social, cultural, economic, and political demand expressing an obligation.[47] These demands of always being connected have fostered numerous critiques. It is in relation to this demand that Sherry Turkle weaves a narrative of everyday practices that moves between connecting as liberating and tethering. She concludes that rather than connecting people, cyberspace is isolating them from more meaningful and 'real' face-to-face human interactions such that 'digitally native' people—especially young people—are now 'alone together.'[48] Numerous other popular critiques such as Nicholas Carr's *The Shallows* and Evgeny Morozov's *Net Delusion* also provide critical analyses of connected lives. Yet others have argued against these critics, especially the arguments that technologies are making people data subjects and rewiring their brains or those that sound a moral panic about teens' obsessive engagement with devices.[49] A key argument of these critiques is that such panics do not attend to what Lovink calls the specific 'user cultures' that are emerging and becoming embedded in social life in relation to actions such as linking, clicking, or liking that extend beyond specific platforms. To put it bluntly, from our perspective, popular critics have become too concerned about cyberspace creating obedient subjects *to* power rather than understanding that cyberspace is creating submissive subjects *of* power who are potentially capable of subversion.

It is through specific actions that subjects connect, and the compulsion is evident when subjects continu to use digital platforms even knowing that their digital traces are tracked and their conception of privacy is being breached. There are different explanations posited for this, such as the 'learned helplessness' of subjects in the face of the unchangeable agreements they enter into with providers to the weighing of the benefits of 'free' apps against costs that are either unknown or not yet evident.[50] Van Dijck concludes that despite these and other constraints on agency and participating, opting out of social media is difficult, especially if being digitally literate and maintaining a critical stance in relation to contemporary culture are of value.[51] Franklin echoes this in her stance that such propositions see 'unplugging' as 'simply a technical matter when evidence shows that there is a little understood psychoemotional component to being and staying in touch via the internet.'[52]

Acts of connecting respond to a calling that persists even in light of the traceability of digital actions and concerns about privacy. Those who are making rights claims to privacy and data ownership are by far out-numbered by those who continue to share data without concern. That a data trace is a material that can be mined, shared, analysed, and acted upon by numerous people makes the imaginary of openness vulnerable to often unknown or unforeseeable acts. But digital traces also introduce another tension. Another calling, that of sharing digital content and traces, is a demand that evokes the imaginary of openness fundamental to the very architecture of shared resources and gift economy that formed the once-dominant logic of cyberspace.[53]

SHARING

Acts of sharing place unique demands on citizen subjects of cyberspace. Most creatively, sharing involves actions of collaborating and co-produc-ing with wikis (e.g., Wikipedia), file sharing (e.g., Dropbox, CiteULike), websites (e.g., mySociety), software (e.g., open source), code (e.g., GitHub), crowdsourcing (e.g., DesignCrowd), recommendations (e.g., TripAdvisor), and social media (e.g., blogs). While all of these conven-tions are concerned with sharing, what is shared, of course, varies, but also the meaning of sharing is organized in platform-specific ways. One-to-many sharing applications, for example, work on different principles: Grindr enables sharing locations with others who are nearby at the same time, whereas LinkedIn organizes sharing via a 'People You May Know' recommender algorithm.[54] To various degrees, the action of sharing can permit and lead to further actions, such as repurposing, adapting, revis-ing, and mashing content. Sharing expertise is also the ethos of hacking events, which are not only forums organized by and for activists but now commonly by governments and corporations. The same can be said of actions that involve collective problem solving as modes of sharing one's labour, skills, and data through initiatives such as the citizen science projects of Zooniverse or, in contrast, Amazon's Mechanical Turk.[55] However, like other one-to-many sharing platforms, these are also organized on different principles. Galaxy Zoo and similar forms of citizen science involve donations of voluntary labour for usually broader public goods and objectives. Be that as it may, they also have their forms of hierarchical organization, such as that of the 'Wikiworkers' of Wikipedia, which is 'predicated on a strict hierarchy, in which higher levels exist to frustrate and undo the activities of participants at lower levels.'[56] In comparison, Mechanical Turk is a commercial marketplace that connects businesses and researchers with workers to complete specific digital microtasks such as transcribing text or responding to surveys. Unregulated and mostly paid at very low rates, 'turkers' constitute a cheap and irregular form of digital labour.[57]

Sharing works in manifold ways. Governments are compelled to be open and transparent to citizens through sharing not only information and reports on websites but also data and metadata as open-government data programmes around the world illustrate. But here the sharing of government data is also directed at commercial bodies towards stimulating a market of applications, platforms, and analytics as well as to innovate services, contribute to a worldwide government data market, and stimulate greater private-sector provision of public services.[58] This understanding of sharing extends to academic research through policies of open-access publishing, where creative commons copyright is increasingly being adopted; the sharing of research outcomes and processes on websites, in university repositories, and in social media; and the sharing of educational resources and courses online via closed virtual learning environments or massively open online courses (MOOCs).

The sharing of data extends to the digital traces generated by the acts of participating and connecting. The ubiquity of various uses of digital traces has made data sharing a norm.[59] Digitally transacting with corporations and governments generates digital traces that citizen subjects are compelled or required to share. For example, the proposal of the United Kingdom government's care.data programme for sharing patient medical records from general practitioners and health-care providers with researchers and other specified groups is justified on the grounds that such sharing of digital traces is in the patient's interest. While data confidentiality and protection concerns have been key matters of concern and have set back its implementation, the underlying assumption is that the well-being of the patient depends on sharing the data of all patients. Technological solutions for protecting and securing health data are thus provided as the solutions, but the ethos of sharing remains intact. [60]

As Luke notes, while government practices of sharing data have been controversial, subjects use many connected digital devices on an everyday basis to 'control their daily schedules, travel routes, personal communications, work lives, and individual identities far more than any intrusive state bureaucracy.' [61] Through the use of these digital devices and apps, subjects continuously generate data about various aspects of their lives, from communicating, sleeping, and exercising patterns to their moods. Popularly known as the 'quantified self', data traces produce a compulsion to not only self-track but share this data so that subjects can monitor themselves in relation to others but also contribute to research on, for example, health conditions. Ironically, while government programmes for sharing health data have been scuppered, the sharing of health information through private organizations such as 23andMe (DNA profiling of more than 700,000 members) and PatientsLikeMe (health conditions of more than 250,000 members) are proliferating and promoting data sharing for the public good of advancing medicine. [62] Governments and corporations alike call upon citizen subjects to share data about themselves as an act of common good. Through disciplinary methods they compel citizen subjects to constitute themselves as data subjects rather than making rights claims about the ownership of data that they produce.

These calls for sharing data extend to the growing development of digital methods by government, corporate, civic, and academic researchers. Many examples can be cited, but one alone can exemplify the valuation and justification of data sharing, especially for research. A controversial Facebook study of users involved the collection of data and manipulation of emotions through targeted posts without informed consent. While raising numerous ethical issues, the study was defended on the grounds that like other scientific pursuits, such uses of data contribute to improvements in social scientific methods and knowledge. [63] Indeed, sharing data—even if it leads to questionable ethical practices—trumps these issues since, it is argued, collective public utility vastly outweighs the risks.[64] While this may become an isolated case, it nevertheless exemplifies the logic of the sharing of data generated by various digital actions.[65]

The example also opens up how sharing data as a public good extends beyond that in commercial and government databases. Myriad conventions are also generative of 'new forms of social data—data generated as a by-product of new forms of popular cultural engagement'.[66] Much attention is paid to how social media and other conventions are active in processes of 'prosumption,' a term that is used to capture how subjects are simultaneously involved in the production and consumption of content through actions such as posting profiles, uploading files, blogging, and tweeting.[67] However, these actions also generate data that circulate, have a 'social life' and liveliness, and through feedback loops come to co-construct and reshape popular culture.[68] Consider how actions such as tagging and posting profiles create social and cultural data. They shape the type of music, books, and friends people will have but without recognizing the workings of the predictive algorithms that underlie such actions.[69] But it also occurs in other automated ways, such as Facebook's 'frictionless sharing', where tastes and preferences—such as online purchases of books—are automatically registered and made available to one's friends.[70]

Sharing digital traces is also key to the operation of location-based platforms, such as Foursquare, which tracks geographic locations of individuals and rankings (restaurants, stores, neighbourhoods, cities) and then makes personalized recommendations based on these and those of 'trusted' friends and experts.[71] These locative recommender applications exemplify how the movement of bodies through physical spaces is constituted by conventions and that a separation between 'real' space and cyberspace is untenable. The 'where' of bodies and their interactions are produced and reproduced by the actions of citizen subjects acting through these conventions, and like the recursive and performative effects of other recommender platforms, their actions feed back to shape locational knowledge and preferences. In these ways, relations between and among bodies acting through the Internet are not separate from but bound up with relations to places. Bodies acting through the Internet thus involve making connections not only with others but with things (products) and places (pubs) and do not displace but are entangled with other ways of acting.

The data configure and shape not only the content and substance of popular culture but also the very functioning and shaping of its conventions made possible through the Internet. Sharing is by default demanded by numerous conventions that require the data generated by the repetitive actions of subjects in order to function. Indeed, end-user licence agreements and contracts often require this sharing of data to ostensibly improve the user experience and without which a platform could be rendered less usable. Users are also repetitively requested via surveys that pop up on platforms or appear as emails to provide feedback about their online experience, to review, or to comment on or like content or products.[72] As noted above, sharing purchasing data or profiles is a built-in requirement of recommender systems that generate suggested products through either collaborative or content-based filtering.[73] But more generally, sharing is the logic on which search engines especially depend, where user queries and clicks on links in search results are signals and data that feed algorithms to autocomplete entries, track trends, build profiles, and index and rank access to content. Echoing the arguments on prosumption, William Gibson recently stated in relation to this point that 'Google is made of us, a sort of coral reef of human minds and their products'.[74] That is, how platforms are configured and navigated is not based on the actions of users but on algorithmic calculations of what all users do and the massive traces they leave.[75] In other words, the sharing of user-generated content is the working and shaping logic of many conventions.

Exploring this logic, Beer and Burrows exemplify what we consider as two kinds of 'speech that acts': sharing through actions such as posting 'user-generated content' as text, images, and sounds in files, blogs, and tweets; and sharing through actions such as clicking, querying, rating, liking, recommending, following, listening, viewing, and retweeting. They exemplify our point that there are two ways of acting through the Internet: in or by saying something but also in or by doing something. In both instances, citizen subjects are acting where the effect is to influence the content and ranking of knowledge.

The imaginary of openness places demands on subjects for sharing through numerous digital actions of which we have covered only a few of a massive number mobilized by this calling. As we have suggested, many digital actions are predisposed to sharing, whether or not this is visible or known. Sharing is a logic fundamental to the operation of many of the conventions that configure and are configured by actions. Openness in relation to sharing thus has multiple meanings and is a matter of political contestation that belies the positive formulations of it as a founding imaginary of cyberspace. On the one hand, it means making governments transparent, democratizing knowledge, collaborating and co-producing, and improving well-being but on the other, exposing, making visible, and opening up subjects to various known and unknown practices and interventions.[76] Along with participating and connecting, sharing generates these tensions, especially in relation to what is often reduced to as questions of privacy. This tension that openness generates increasingly creates additional demands that citizens secure themselves from and be responsible for the potential and even unknowable consequences of their digital conduct.

DEMANDS

If participating, connecting, and sharing place subjects under demands, the tensions that these generate are managed by the formation of new demands and obligations. It is these infinitely demanding calls that concern us. They either cultivate citizen subjects who make rights claims in or by saying and doing 'I, we, and they have a right to', or they cultivate citizen subjects who routinely reproduce conventions governed by commercial or governmental logics. Governments, corporations, civic organizations, and the media persistently issue these demands that favour the latter over the former. Governments call upon citizens to be digital; they also demand that digital citizens know their data rights and apply appropriate security and data-sharing protections. While participating starts with the demand that the subject take up the responsibility of making informed and resourceful decisions, this is accompanied with the demand that she conduct herself responsibly and safely as prescribed by authorities and others such as journalists, authors, and civic organizations.

The inherent tensions in calls for citizen subjects to enact themselves in specified ways are most visible in the discourse on what is euphemistically called netiquette: conventions governing how subjects should digitally conduct themselves. As Lessig argued in the early days of cyberspace, control is exercised through the ordinary tools of human regulation—through social norms and social stigma, through peer pressure and reward.[77] Indeed, some norms that are popularly appealed to are about 'good manners' (such as not texting during meals with others) and sometimes wax nostalgic about predigital forms of communicating and connecting that may never have existed (such as interacting with people in cafés or on public transit).[78] For Sherry Turkle, such netiquette involves establishing social norms about the use of devices in everyday life to reduce social costs such as cybersolitude and being tethered to the demands of devices. For others, such as Douglas Rushkoff, cyberspace is controlling and shaping conduct and the solution lies in freeing citizens from the edicts and control of programming (and programmers). Quite tellingly, his manifesto for freeing citizens consists of 'ten commandments' for promoting 'one set of behaviours over another' for how we conduct ourselves in cyberspace, such as not constantly checking email.[79]

These are popular edicts that both originate from positions about the negative consequences of being digital and at the same time assert that being digital is an inevitable yet controllable part of life. Even critical accounts of privacy recognize that responsibilizing subjects is required; for Julie Cohen, this is captured in her general call for a 'culture of exposure' where subjects have the 'ability to manage boundedness', that is, between what they expose or don't expose about themselves.[80] For boyd, it involves 'helping young people navigate public life safely', and teens 'must develop strategies for handling ongoing surveillance and attempts to undermine their agency when they seek to control social situations'.[81] That subjects can indeed take 'control' is shared in the formation of demands such as cybersecurity and cybersafety, which have become common and regularized aspects of being digital citizens. Participating, connecting, and sharing expose subjects to a number of actions, such as bullying, flaming, abuse, sexism, racism, sexual predation, trolling, shaming, and so on. While not unique to cyberspace, the properties of anonymity and extensity inflect these actions with new performative force. That is, rather than a simple translation of 'offline' conducts, digital actions extend these conducts in pervasive and more insidious ways: in other words, 'viral', as that word is now understood. From vigilance about fraud and reporting spam, phishing, and forms of abuse to ways of securing online privacy and identity, subjects are called upon to protect themselves from the dark web of criminality, terrorism, extremism, and pornography and child abuse. Cyberspace is thus like other spaces that demand securing oneself through materials and technologies but also through habits, norms, and protocols.

Such demands to be a responsible citizen of cyberspace are now pervasive. A United States federal mandate has required that all school districts certify that their staff and students have learned about cybersafety and digital citizenship. One United States school program expresses this as 'the importance of cybersafety to ensure that our students exhibit the characteristics of responsible digital citizens' and provides tips on how to conduct oneself online: be responsible (be careful about what personal information is shared), aware (be vigilant against viruses), cautious (don't respond to emails from unknown sources), and appropriate (use netiquette).[82] These principles echo those promulgated by the technology industry, such as Microsoft's safety and security centre, which defines digital citizenship as digital literacy, ethics, etiquette, online safety, and norms and offers a series of resources especially for youth, educators, and parents.[83]

These calls have in part come out of revelations about what is being done with digital traces beyond the examples we discussed previously. Disclosures about the big data monitoring practices of NSA and GHCQ or even Acxiom's high-tech recycling bins in London, which in one week captured the unique identifier codes of some four million mobile phones of passers-by, have made citizens aware of the extensity of surveillance technologies.[84] In response, citizens are called upon to know their digital data and metadata rights as expressed in end-user licensing agreements or data protection legislation and take responsibility for managing their digital traces. While opting out or changing privacy settings is one set of suggestions, more comprehensively, a range of actions is demanded in order to remain secure against, especially, security agency snooping: implementing services such as Tor to anonymize oneself; encrypting communications; buying a computer that is never connected to the Internet to store confidential documents; and not using commercial encryption software as it will likely have a 'back door'.[85] All of these make further demands on subjects to acquire considerable forms of capital, from technical expertise to financial resources and time. Even though citizen subjects are interpellated to respond to these calls, the solutions are increasingly individualized, personalized, and privatized.

Short of these actions and beyond protecting against the tracing of digital actions, subjects are compelled to manage their privacy and identity against other potential dangers. For social media such as Facebook, Twitter, Google+ and LinkedIn, twenty-nine steps are recommended for 'taking control' of how the platforms operate and the openness and visibility of identity, reputation, and presence by customizing privacy settings or by being stealthy.[86] Identity assurance is another recommendation, such as a program introduced by the United Kingdom Government Digital Service to protect privacy and online identities. It requires that citizens go through a process of registering a profile with contracted and certified private-sector organizations (identity providers), which can be used as part of the process of validating and verifying their identity when transacting with governments or businesses.[87]

These demands, though, raise another and often implicit concern: the problematization of the subject. Like William Gibson, Deibert argues that it is users 'after all, who share and network through social media, and it is we who have entrusted our information to "clouds" and social networking services operated by thousands of companies of all shapes, sizes, and geographic locations.'[88] Similarly, Jonathan Franzen accuses Amazon of turning literary culture into shallow forms of social engagement consisting of 'yakkers and tweeters and braggers' and Twitter as the 'ultimate irresponsible medium.'[89] These misfires produce at least two infelicities. First, inadvertently they end up ascribing more power to such corporations as Amazon or Google than they actually have. While much attention is given to the automated and computational aspects of Google, the workings of the search engine are unstable and rely on the distributed, heterogeneous, and dynamic actions of not only algorithms but also engineers, operators, webmasters, and users.[90] Second, they ascribe less power to people than they actually have. While the rules of Google's algorithm and functions such as autocomplete are a tightly held secret, Google's operation is shaped and mediated by the search-and-find behaviours of citizen subjects.[91] What disappears is the performative force of being digital and the possibilities of citizens being subjects of power who regularly subvert demands in or by saying and doing things on the Internet. We argue that to place further demands on subjects against being ignorant or indifferent completely misses the performativity of being digital: subjects of power in cyberspace have come into being through the accumulation of repetitive actions, through their taking up and embedding of conventions in their everyday lives in homes, workplaces, and public spaces. It is through the acts of participating, connecting, and sharing that these have become demands and learned repertoires that are not separate from but indelibly shaped by and shaping of subjects.

That these demands have emerged in the span of only a few years attests to what we call the 'closings' of cyberspace. These demands and their closings are effects of the way in which acting through the Internet has resignified questions of velocity, extensity, anonymity, and traceability. Velocity calls for regular and ongoing vigilance about rapidly changing technologies, protocols, practices, platforms, and rules about being digital; extensity calls for awareness of where and to whom digital actions reach; anonymity calls for limiting and protecting exposure and being cautious about the presumed identities of others; and traceability calls for managing how actions are tracked, analysed, manipulated, and sorted by unknown others and for unknowable purposes. All of these demands spring not from participating, connecting, and sharing alone but the relations between and among bodies acting through the Internet, which is made up of conventions configured by the actions of dispersed and distributed authorities. It is to these configuring actions, which we call the closings of cyberspace, that we turn to in the next chapter, with a focus on filtering, tracking, and normalizing.

But we first want to clarify that callings are interrelated with closings and openings, which narratively organize the next two chapters. While we address these in turn, this is not to suggest that they happen sequentially or are discrete but rather that they are dynamically interrelated. Callings summon subjects who are not 'always-already interpellated' by the imaginary, legal, or performative forces that mobilize them. Because they are subjects of power, citizen subjects have the potential to subvert such forces through their uptake of actions. However, it is this very possibility of subversion that gives rise to closings, which are attempts by selves and others to control and manage how callings and closings are enacted. So if openness is an imaginary that calls upon citizen subjects to participate, then closings seek to further configure the actions through which participation is done. But this is never settled. The two remain in tension. In turn, as we have argued, new callings arise, new demands, and again new configurations of closings, what Deleuze theorized as modulating controls. These modulations, though, give rise to a third configuration of possibility, what we narratively call openings; because citizen subjects occupy positions in response to callings and closings, they also come to forge new ways of being, or openings that we name digital rights claims. That is, the callings we have outlined in this chapter—of participating, connecting, and sharing—are the very conditions that make possible both closings and openings. It is the analysis of these dynamics that enables us to understand to what extent citizen subjects are able to make digital rights claims in the form of 'I, we, or they have a right to' by resignifying conventions in which they are implicated rather than only obeying or submitting to them.

NOTES

1. For a discussion of participation as the key to democratic principles, see S. Coleman and J. G. Blumler, *The Internet and Democratic Citizenship: Theory, Practice and Policy* (Cambridge University Press, 2009); P. N. Howard, "Deep Democracy, Thin Citizenship: The Impact of Digital Media in Political Campaign Strategy," *Annals of the American Academy of Political and Social Science* 597 (2005).

2. W. J. Miller, "Digital Citizen," in *Encyclopedia of Social Media and Politics*, ed. Kerric Harvey (Sage, 2014), 388–90. See also K. Mossberger et al., *Digital Citizenship: The Internet, Society, and Participation* (MIT Press, 2008).

3. Chris Kelty argues that openness is a 'social imaginary' that carries specific technical and moral meanings of social order. C. Kelty, *Two Bits: The Cultural Significance of Free Software* (Duke University Press, 2008).

4. Evgeny Morozov calls openness a 'sacred cow' and ideology of the Internet. E. Morozov, *To Save Everything, Click Here: The Folly of Technological Solutionism* (PublicAffairs, 2013).

5. J. E. Cohen, *Configuring the Networked Self: Law, Code, and the Play of Everyday Practice* (Yale University Press, 2012), 3. Rushkoff describes this as a tension between sharing and stealing. D. Rushkoff, *Program or Be Programmed: Ten Commandments for a Digital Age* (OR Books, 2010).

6. Cohen draws on Amartya Sen and Martha Nussbaum's capabilities approach, which defines freedom as not simply the absence of restraint, or negative liberty, but also as the access to resources and opportunities necessary for achieving 'substantive equality.' Cohen, *Configuring the Networked Self*, 17.

7. As noted, Cohen's target is largely legal scholarship, but many of her arguments are already well rehearsed in the disciplines of anthropology, sociology, politics and surveillance, and science and technology studies. This is especially evident in her canvasing of literatures to address the question of 'culture' and the taking up of social science methodologies and 'descriptive tools for constructing ethnographies of cultural processes and theoretical tools for modeling them' (19). It is also evident in the structure of her argument, which is a review of numerous social theories that are rather difficult to hold together and are framed mostly in relation to debates and positions within legal theory. Ibid.

8. Cohen's solutions to the tensions between openness and privacy involve the reformulation of legal theories and information law and policy 'to promote human

flourishing in the emerging networked information society', including 'institutional and technical structures that promote access to knowledge, that create operational transparency, and that preserve room for the play of everyday practice' (5). She does not attend to how citizen subjects, through acts, resignify themselves. So while she gives considerable attention to the value of understanding subjectivity as performed, she does not examine how subjects act and do not necessarily accept legal precepts of privacy or openness as givens in their 'always emerging subjectivity' (144). For example, see the discussion of boundary management in chapter 6, 143–46. Ibid.

9. As Mark Poster has argued, platforms from email to electronic discussion lists have their hierarchies of control. M. Poster, "Digital Networks and Citizenship," *Proceedings of Modern Language Association of America (PMLA)* 117, 1 (2002): 102.

10. For example, connecting through the action of joining Academia.edu can also involve sharing articles with others connected to you.

11. As cited in T. Olsson, "'The Architecture of Participation': For Citizens or Consumers?," in *Critique, Social Media and the Information Society*, ed. C. Fuchs and M. Sandoval (Routledge, 2014).

12. See a discussion of these studies and critique of the 'digital divide' in S. Halford and M. Savage, "Reconceptualizing Digital Social Inequality," *Information, Communication and Society* 13, 7 (2010).

13. Fuchs summarizes various conceptions of a digital divide from that of Manuel Castells ('inequality of access to the Internet') to the more 'refined' definition of Jan van Dijk ('the gap between those who do and do not have access to computers and the Internet'). C. Fuchs, *Internet and Society: Social Theory in the Information Age* (Routledge, 2008), 213.

14. J. E. Cohen, "Cyberspace as/and Space," *Columbia Law Review* 107, 1 (2007): 242.

15. Academic studies and reviews largely ascribe the digital divide and solution to issues of access and participation; in addition to references in Halford and Savage, see also J. James, "The Digital Divide across All Citizens of the World: A New Concept," *Social Indicators Research* 89, 2 (2008); N. Helbig et al., "Understanding the Complexity of Electronic Government: Implications from the Digital Divide Literature," *Government Information Quarterly* 26, 1 (2009).

16. Halford and Savage, "Reconceptualizing Digital Social Inequality," 952. See also E. Ruppert, "Doing the Transparent State: Open Government Data as Performance Indicators," in *A World of Indicators: The Making of Governmental Knowledge through Quantification*, ed. R. Rottenburg et al. (Cambridge University Press, 2015).

17. D. Bicknell, "Labour Digital Policy Review Examines Continuous Innovation," *Kable*, 15 April 2014 [accessed 30 July 2014], bit.ly/1kmmKaU. The importance of digital services is underscored by the UK government's appointment (March 2014) of a 'head of digital' who is publicly accountable for ensuring rising levels of satisfaction with the delivery of digital services to the public. Doing business with governments digitally is also related to governments seeing themselves as websites just as people see Amazon as a website.

18. Department of Business Innovation & Skills, "Providing Better Information and Protection for Consumers," *gov.uk* 2014 [accessed 13 November 2014], bit.ly/1trM6qB.

19. mySociety is a not-for-profit organization that creates websites in support of knowledge and data sharing for civic and community purposes: 'We invent and popularize digital tools that enable citizens to exert power over institutions and decision makers.' See mySociety, "We Make Websites and Tools That Empower Citizens," 2014 [accessed 13 November 2014], www.mysociety.org.

20. Ruppert, "Doing the Transparent State"; E. Ruppert and M. Savage, "Transactional Politics," *Sociological Review* 59, s2 (2012).

21. K. Mossberger et al., "Measuring Digital Citizenship: Mobile Access and Broadband," *International Journal of Communication* 6 (2012). These factors also underpin the 'capabilities approach' that many scholars adopt, where resources and opportunities are key to advancing digital equality. See note 6.

22. See, for example, one academic's conception of digital literacy and digital citizenship for high school students: E. Meeks, "Digital Literacy and Digital Citizenship," 2013 [accessed 13 November 2014], stanford.io/1rRME7a. For Rushkoff, participating goes beyond questions of literacy to include knowing code and programming languages. Rushkoff, *Program or Be Programmed*.

23. UK Cabinet Office, *Government Digital Inclusion Strategy* (2014). Working with partners in the voluntary sector, digitalskills.com has been set up 'as a trusted source of information and advice on how to help people and organisations go online.'

24. C. Onwurah, "Labour's Digital Review: The Emerging Themes," *Kable*, 30 June 2014 [accessed 17 July 2014], bit.ly/1tUVWlX. The Labour Party is developing a framework to make digital services work for 'the many' through, for example, access and skills and information rights. Bicknell, "Labour Digital Policy Review."

25. H. Milner, "The Preventative Care Revolution Depends on Closing the Digital Divide," *Guardian Professional*, 1 November 2013 [accessed 17 July 2014], bit.ly/1wzXWfx.

26. The sixth annual survey of corporate digital IQs by PricewaterhouseCoopers identified five behaviours that 'give companies the edge, enabling them to maximize their use of digital technology across the business and position them for better performance.' PricewaterhouseCoopers, "The Five Behaviors That Accelerate Value from Digital Investments: 6th Annual Digital IQ Survey," *PwC*, March 2014 [accessed 4 August 2014], pwc.to/119uVyX.

27. K. L. Schlozman et al., "Weapon of the Strong? Participatory Inequality and the Internet," *Perspectives on Politics* 8, 2 (2010): 489.

28. Luke, "Digital Citizenship," in *Emerging Digital Spaces in Contemporary Society: Properties of Technology*, ed. Phillip Kalantzis-Cope and Karim Gherab Martín (Palgrave Macmillan, 2011), 88.

29. This is the understanding advanced in the definition of 'digital citizen' in the *Encyclopedia of Social Media and Politics*, where being active means engaging in dissemination and deliberation which enhance democratic values, political participation, knowledge, and trust of institutions. Miller, "Digital Citizen."

30. Schlozman et al., "Weapon of the Strong?" Online politics increases participation only for those who have just joined the electorate and especially younger citizens. Indeed, the authors note in another article that every study on Internet access and use shows a sharp decline with age. K. L. Schlozman et al., "Who Speaks? Citizen Political Voice on the Internet Commons," *Daedalus* 140, 4 (2011).

31. Though some studies have also identified that digital citizens are not necessarily youths; in the United States, they are more likely to be in their forties than their twenties. Miller, "Digital Citizen," 2.

32. W. Y. Lin et al., "Becoming Citizens: Youths' Civic Uses of New Media in Five Digital Cities in East Asia," *Journal of Adolescent Research* 25, 6 (2010): 852.

33. d. boyd, *It's Complicated: The Social Lives of Networked Teens* (Yale University Press, 2014), 221. Olsson has made a similar argument, where a study of an online commercial web community can provide a space for interaction and participation that

'sometimes holds civic—or pre-political—dimensions.' Olsson, "The Architecture of Participation," 210.

34. Olsson, "The Architecture of Participation," 210.

35. In his study of American political campaigns, Howard argues that while politically participating through digital technologies, people do so 'thinly' and without being substantially engaged. This is also echoed in Lovink's assessment of the dearth of political discourse and democratic engagement on the Internet. G. Lovink, *Networks without a Cause: A Critique of Social Media* (Polity, 2012).

36. Cohen, *Configuring the Networked Self*, 190. For Cohen, the solution is that legal and information policy should leave 'breathing room' for everyday material practices and more open, playful, creative, and self-directed ways. But in setting this up, she reinforces the binary of freedom and control, that the solution is the creation of 'freer' and less constrained arrangements.

37. Dan McQuillan, for example, calls such practices forms of 'citizen glitching', which can reveal the underpinning assumptions of data and computational processes.

38. This is one aspect of what they refer to as 'evil media', an understanding of mediation as a process of becoming activated in unintended ways that do not conform to what is proscribed and thus open to being condemned as malicious. M. Fuller and A. Goffey, *Evil Media* (MIT Press, 2012), 3.

39. boyd, *It's Complicated*. Rather than evaluating social media against other forms of networking—such as that which occurs in 'real space'—boyd addresses social media on its own terms to think about what teens are actually doing and thinking about it. She also does attempt to link real and cyberspace to argue that they are not autonomous.

40. N. Rossiter, *Organized Networks: Media Theory, Creative Labour, New Institutions* (Institute of Network Cultures, 2006), 14. Rossiter makes a similar argument in relation to his critique of the openness of networks. He differentiates between 'organized networks' that co-emerge with digital technologies and 'networked organizations' that usually precede technologies. The latter involves sociotechnical dynamics that are hierarchical and centralizing modes of organization, whereas the former are horizontal, decentralizing, and distributive.

41. J. van Dijck, *The Culture of Connectivity: A Critical History of Social Media* (Oxford University Press, 2013). William Mitchell defines connectivity as the defining characteristic of the twenty-first-century urban condition. W. J. Mitchell, *Me++: The Cyborg Self and the Networked City* (MIT Press, 2003), 22.

42. Cohen, *Configuring the Networked Self*.

43. While it is important to understand medium-specific formats and the constitutive effects of 'native' features of digital platforms such as hyperlinks and likes, these are just one part of the sociotechnical arrangements that make up the conventions of cyberspace. For a discussion of the natively digital, see, for example, R. Rogers, *The End of the Virtual: Digital Methods* (Amsterdam University Press, 2009).

44. This understanding is in distinction to approaches that study social networks as connections between people, for example, D. Watts, *Six Degrees: The Science of a Connected Age* (Norton, 2003).

45. J. Harris, "The Year of the Networked Revolution," *Guardian*, 13 December 2011 [accessed 18 July 2014], bit.ly/1p2lRTC.

46. Curran, Fenton, and Freedman, for example, argue that social media is not the source but the enabler of political protests that have context-specific grievances and causes. J. Curran et al., eds., *Misunderstanding the Internet* (Routledge, 2012).

47. Author Jonathan Franzen claims that publishers are coercing writers into using Twitter. L. Bury, "Jonathan Franzen Falls Foul of Twitterati after Scorning Social Media," *Guardian*, 3 October 2013 [accessed 1 August 2014], bit.ly/1nSrnsY.

48. S. Turkle, *Alone Together: Why We Expect More from Technology and Less from Each Other* (Basic, 2011).

49. Lovink, *Networks without a Cause*; boyd, *It's Complicated*.

50. One multicountry study of smartphones found that when users were informed of the data-sharing practices of certain apps on their smartphone, most expressed dismay or outrage but continued their usual practices. I. Shklovski et al., "Leakiness and Creepiness in App Space: Perceptions of Privacy and Mobile App Use," in *ACM Conference on Human Factors in Computing Systems (CHI) 2014* (Toronto: ACM CHI, 2014). Cohen has also noted that 'inconsistencies between reported preferences and revealed behavior reflect a combination of resignation and befuddlement; most Internet users do not understand how the technologies work, what privacy policies mean, or how the information generated about them will actually be used.' Cohen, *Configuring the Networked Self*, 107.

51. Van Dijck, *Culture of Connectivity*.

52. M. I. Franklin, *Digital Dilemmas: Power, Resistance, and the Internet* (Oxford University Press, 2013), 185.

53. Rushkoff, *Program or Be Programmed*, 116.

54. Grindr.com was launched in 2009 and is a popular all-male location-based social networking application. LinkedIn.com was launched in 2003 and is a social networking platform oriented to professionals.

55. Zooniverse began with the Galaxy Zoo project in 2007, a crowdsourced astronomy project in which people volunteer to assist in the classification of galaxies.

56. P. Mirowski and D. Plehwe, eds., *The Road from Mont Perlerin: The Making of the Neoliberal Thought Collective* (Harvard University Press, 2009), 422.

57. C. Fuchs, *Social Media: A Critical Introduction* (Sage, 2014).

58. See statements, for example, by United Kingdom cabinet minister Francis Maude on data as 'the new raw material of the 21st century.' J. Dudman, "Francis Maude: Data Is 'the New Raw Material of the 21st Century'," *Guardian Professional*, 2012 [accessed 31 Oct 2014], bit.ly/1yLMtfG.

59. Preston argues that this norm is replacing that of privacy. A. Preston, "The Death of Privacy," *Observer*, 3 August 2014 [accessed 7 August 2014], bit.ly/1pdlWFs.

60. See, for example, discussion of technological solutions in G. Stewart, "The Data Security Threat Is Holding Back Digital Progress in the NHS," *Guardian*, 19 June 2014 [accessed 30 July 2014], bit.ly/1qL0V7F.

61. Luke, "Digital Citizenship," 85.

62. See 23andMe, *Find out What Your DNA Says about You and Your Family*, 2014 [accessed 13 November 2014], www.23andme.com; PatientsLikeMe, *Live Better, Together!*, 2014 [accessed 13 November 2014], www.patientslikeme.com.

63. Duncan Watts, a sociologist at Microsoft Research who models social networks, advanced this argument. D. Watts, "Stop Complaining about the Facebook Study: It's a Golden Age for Research," *Guardian*, 7 July 2014 [accessed 31 July 2014], bit.ly/1nWhefR. He defended the practice of manipulating emotions on the grounds that this is an everyday practice of marketers that we know little about. Thus, studies like this one are necessary in order to know the effects of such practices as the alternative is ignorance.

64. Legal scholar Jane Yakowitz makes this point. She argues that standard practices of anonymization can adequately protect privacy and that legal scholars have overstated the risks of reidentification. J. Yakowitz, "Tragedy of the Data Commons," *bePress*, February 2011 [accessed 11 July 2014], bit.ly/1vvv1ud.

65. One common finding is that the ethos of sharing is more widely held by younger users. A survey of young people aged thirteen to seventeen in the United Kingdom conducted in October 2013 and including 1,004 children nationwide found that not only do they want to engage with government services online (85 percent) but also, subject to assurances on privacy, they support the sharing of their data by public-sector organizations for the purposes of improving service delivery (83 percent). Logicalis, *Realtime Generation: Rise of the Digital First Era*, 2013 [accessed 12 October 2014], bit.ly/1qL2ToH.

66. D. Beer and R. Burrows, "Popular Culture, Digital Archives and the New Social Life of Data," *Theory, Culture & Society* 30, 4 (2013), 49.

67. G. Ritzer and N. Jurgenson, "Production, Consumption, Prosumption: The Nature of Capitalism in the Age of the Digital 'Prosumer'," *Journal of Consumer Culture* 10, 1 (2010). The term is used to capture that subjects are both producers and consumers of content.

68. Beer and Burrows make this point by drawing on the work of Adrian Mackenzie on the 'performativity of circulation.' See A. Mackenzie and T. Vurdubakis, "The Performativity of Code: Software and Cultures of Circulation," *Theory, Culture & Society* 22, 1 (2005); Beer and Burrows, "Popular Culture, Digital Archives and the New Social Life of Data."

69. Beer and Burrows, "Popular Culture, Digital Archives and the New Social Life of Data." Beer and Burrows note how social data also become a source of 'infotainment' and play.

70. V. Campanelli, "Frictionless Sharing: The Rise of Automatic Criticism," in *Society of the Query Reader: Reflections on Web Search*, ed. R. König and M. Rasch (Institute of Network Cultures, 2014).

71. Foursquare has also introduced a related platform called Swarm, which enables subjects to 'check in' and share their real-time location with friends.

72. In this regard, liking and rating can be understood as forms of sharing opinions, experiences, and so on.

73. Collaborative filtering is based on a user's past behaviour (e.g., previous purchases) and the similar decisions of other users to predict items that the user might want. Content-based filtering uses specific characteristics of a purchase to recommend other items with similar properties.

74. W. Gibson, "Google's Earth," *New York Times*, 31 August 2010 [accessed 9 August 2014], nyti.ms/1vm4CP7. Like other critics, Gibson further argues that 'we are its unpaid content-providers, in one way or another. We generate product for Google, our every search a minuscule contribution.' For example, Freedman and Terranova argue that digital subjects are the unpaid labourers of the Internet economy. D. Freedman, "Web 2.0 and the Death of the Blockbuster Economy," in *Misunderstanding the Internet*, ed. J. Curran et al. (Routledge, 2012); T. Terranova, *Network Culture: Politics for the Information Age* (Pluto, 2004).

75. T. Gillespie, "Can an Algorithm Be Wrong?," *Limn*, 2 (2012).

76. Morozov describes some of the chilling effects of, for example, opening up data on election donations or court records that have lead to controversial cases about the exposure of subjects to muckraking and political scrutiny. He also argues that such

open data when decontextualized, repurposed, and linked can be used to generate profiles and be put to purposes that cannot be controlled by subjects or data producers. Morozov, *To Save Everything*.

77. L. Lessig, "The Zones of Cyberspace," *Stanford Law Review* 48, 5 (1996).

78. Turkle, *Alone Together*. In 2014, a charter was drawn up for London theatregoers to keep their mobile phones off during performances as part of a campaign to improve audience etiquette. D. Alberge, "Stephen Fry Backs Charter to Switch Mobiles Off before the Curtain Goes Up," *Guardian*, 2 August 2014 [accessed 5 August 2014], bit.ly/1vm4KOp.

79. Rushkoff, *Program or Be Programmed*, 20. In some ways echoing Lawrence Lessig's focus on the power of code, he argues that the choice to be made is between doing the programming or being programmed, in the first instance by the decisions of technicians, but inevitably then by the technologies themselves.

80. Cohen, *Configuring the Networked Self*, 146.

81. boyd, *It's Complicated*, 38, 217.

82. San Antonio Independent School District, *Creating Responsible Digital Citizens*, 2014 [accessed 13 November 2014], bit.ly/1k6SzUO. Another United States researcher has created a digital citizenship website based on his dissertation that outlines nine elements that make up the 'norms of appropriate, responsible behaviour with regard to technology use', such as digital literacy, etiquette, and rights and responsibilities. The site is especially geared to educators. M. Ribble, *Digital Citizenship: Using Technology Appropriately*, 2014 [accessed 13 November 2014], digitalcitizenship.net.

83. E. Blakemore, "Microsoft Launches Digital Citizenship Resources," *Microsoft*, 8 September 2011 [accessed 26 September 2014], wp.me/p4YHEz-lx.

84. Following newspaper reports of this activity, The City of London ordered Acxiom to cease. H. Mance, "Consumers More Wary of Sharing Data, Finds Poll," *Financial Times*, 1 December 2013 [accessed 15 July 2014], on.ft.com/1oWDB2K.

85. B. Schneier, "NSA Surveillance: A Guide to Staying Secure," *Guardian*, 6 September 2013 [accessed 30 July 2014], bit.ly/1qKAZZY. Additional recommendations put forward in another article include multiple and complex passwords, two-stage security and verification settings for social media, and using small search engines such as DuckDuckGo. J. Kiss, "Online Privacy: How Secure Are You?," *Guardian*, 2 December 2013 [accessed 30 July 2014], bit.ly/1kmo11X.

86. K. Shubber, "29 Ways to Take Control of Your Social Media," *Guardian*, 2014 [accessed 31 July 2014], bit.ly/1s5Z0sq.

87. HM Government, "Identity Assurance: Delivering Trusted Transactions," 14 May 2012 [accessed 26 December 2014], bit.ly/1kmlrc2.

88. R. Deibert, *Black Code: Inside the Battle for Cyberspace* (McClelland & Stewart, 2013), 82.

89. L. Bury, "Amazon Model Favours Yakkers and Braggers, Says Jonathan Franzen," *Guardian*, 13 September 2013 [accessed 1 August 2014], bit.ly/1nSpL2x. Rushkoff also argues that the dark sides of cyberspace include facilitating shallow rather than deep thinking, politics through net petitioning instead of action, exploitative marketing activities, and mob-like behaviours. Rushkoff, *Program or Be Programmed*.

90. See, for example, an ethnographic study of search-engine optimizers and the daily actions of consultants and engineers: M. Ziewitz, "Evaluation as Governance: The Practical Politics of Reviewing, Rating and Ranking on the Web" (PhD dissertation, University of Oxford, 2012).

91. Mahnke and Uprichard make this point in their exploration of forms of intervening and creative playing with the operation of Google's autocomplete function. M. Mahnke and E. Uprichard, "Algorithming the Algorithm," in *Society of the Query Reader: Reflections on Web Search*, ed. R. König and M. Rasch (Institute of Network Cultures, 2014).

FIVE

Closings

Filtering, Tracking, Normalizing

For some, openness is the very essence of the Internet.[1] Yet whether the practical workings of the Internet conform to this imaginary has been called into question. Evgeny Morozov, for example, argues that openness is configured by political choices and in relation to specific 'digital technologies' and that those choices should be both resisted and politically debated. But like the misfires of critics we noted at the end of chapter 4, control is given over to how digital technologies are configured without accounting for how people act through the Internet, the conventions they repeat, iterate, cite, or resignify, and the performative force of their engagements. In this chapter, we consider closings as configured not simply by platform owners in the design of algorithms and databases but also by both authorities and subjects in their decisions about how they act and what they share. These decisions result in struggles over laws or politics of information use, as scholars such as Julie Cohen argue.[2] We consider how closings are dynamically configured by the play between all of these actions, including those of citizen subjects that arise in response to the callings to participate, connect, and share. It is through the interrelated actions of citizen subjects, governments, corporations, and others and their repetitions, iterations, and citations that cyberspace comes into being and knowledge about it is produced and disseminated. Three acts express most strongly the play of obedience, submission, and subversion that citizen subjects engage in the constitution of closings: filtering, where citizen subjects submit to regulate and protect themselves or agree to be protected by authorities, tracking where citizen subjects enter into games of evasion, and normalizing where the ways of being citizen subjects in cyberspace are iteratively modulated towards desired ends by private and public authorities.

FILTERING

Acts of filtering involve numerous actions and conventions (sociotechnical arrangements that embody norms, values, laws, ideologies, technologies, and desires). Although blocking and censoring ('the denial of access to information') have received much attention, we want to attend to subtle yet effective actions through which citizen subjects participate in governing themselves.[3] Acts of filtering, for example, are accomplished through sorting (ranking, ordering, trending, indexing, categorizing) and redacting (deleting, refusing, reporting, burying). It is not that we neglect blocking and censoring. These actions are often performed to ostensibly protect citizens from exposure to pornographic, offensive, or political speech. These are often performed by blocking access to search results, webpages, chat rooms, newsgroups, and so on, not only in authoritarian but also in democratic states.[4] A series of global studies by the OpenNet Initiative (ONI) has documented how states—especially in the Global North—are creating borders in cyberspace by building firewalls at key 'Internet choke points,' an action that is so widespread that '[s]tates no longer fear pariah status by openly declaring their intent to regulate and control cyberspace. The convenient rubric of terrorism, child pornography, and cyber security has contributed to a growing expectation that states should enforce order in cyberspace, including policing unwanted content.'[5] The ONI has documented how these programmes have over the past several years shifted from denying access to normalizing control through a variety of means. Rather than simply 'Chinese-style national filtering schemes, recent techniques are more subtle and flexible, and deploy legal regulations, covert practices, and outsource controls to "third parties" to manage what can be posted, hosted, accessed, or communicated online'.[6] These actions include targeted viruses and distributed denial-of-service (DDoS) attacks, surveillance at key choke points, legal takedown notices, and oppressive terms-of-usage policies. The actions have become so well integrated and widespread that they now have become routinized and taken-for-granted forms of the 'everyday surveillance' of cyberspace.[7] Importantly, the ONI argues that while much attention is given over to state actions, the distributed and increasingly private ownership of the infrastructures that make up the conventions of cyberspace often span multiple legal orders such that the decisions on retaining, filtering, monitoring, and sharing information are dispersed and have political effects for citizens across jurisdictions. Rather than being hierarchically organized, discrete systems, technologies and practices are decentred and dispersed across numerous centres of calculation.[8]

Although blocking and censoring are very important, filtering includes other actions that lead to the submission of citizen subjects occurring almost imperceptibly, and even when the blocking and censoring are visible and protested, the citizen subject is often incorporated into their very workings. While writing this book in the British Library, our search query 'Banksy' for a potential cover image for this book returned the message: 'Access to this site has been blocked by our web filtering software as it is categorized as being inappropriate for use in a public area. If you feel that the site is miscategorized, please email.'[9] The query was categorized as 'criminal activity.' When we protested, the site was unblocked with an apology for any inconvenience caused. The example is telling for illustrating not only how filters operate but also how they invite citizen subject actions such as ours. Through those actions, although we were 'disobedient', we nonetheless submitted to the authority of the filtering programme by engaging with it. Questions remain. Why was there a filter in the first place? Who was being protected? By having unblocked the result of our query, should we have felt relief that our activity was not criminal? How would we have reacted had the British Library continued to block access to Banksy's website?

Citizen subjects also participate in such filtering through everyday actions. Parents are invited to block and censor sites using parental control bars so that their children cannot access content they deem inappropriate, such as adult sites. But so, too, do employers block sites for gambling, social networking, and game playing through software such as the Web Blocker, which also enables monitoring Internet usage histories.[10] And citizen subjects block the content of flagged 'friends' on social networking platforms such as Facebook and Twitter.

Cohen refers to blocking as 'architectures of control' and 'regimes of authorization' that are authoritarian in the generic sense that they favour compliant obedience to authority.[11] Rather than experiencing rules— which need not be explained or disclosed—she argues that users experience their effects, which consist of possibilities for action that networks create. So while concerns about the surveillance and collection of digital traces are most controversial (discussed below), the transparency of network processes and how access to knowledge is being filtered are less visible and controllable. Filtering also occurs through the authorizations attached to content and devices. For example, in many cases, only authorized tablets can access encrypted content, and citizen subjects must submit to elaborate authentication procedures. So while sharing is a calling, it is increasingly only within certain regimes of authorization that sharing operates, and in this regard it can be understood as a form of submission.

Sorting is a filtering action that comes in a variety of forms. It is an action citizen subjects take when they create rules (if-then) in their email software to automatically classify spam and move it to a junk folder. And like the feedback and learning mechanisms of algorithms, through regular checking and updating, email filters can become ever more efficient in sorting 'good' from 'bad' emails.[12] Bookmarking pages and following blogs and tweets or friending on Facebook are also actions through which citizen subjects sort and prioritize content. But more pervasively, sorting includes the ranking and ordering of content by search engines. While blocking is often given more attention, of greater concern is how sorting organizes access to knowledge in more pernicious ways. 'Googling' has become a regularized action for finding knowledge in ways that are often taken for granted or not problematized but so pervasive and dominant that the search engine has given rise to the term 'googlization.' The term is coined to suggest that Google affects everything, including 'us' through its use of personal data, the 'world' through its practices of surveillance and infrastructural imperialism, and 'knowledge' through its organization of access to information.[13]

Rather than simply providing results in response to a query, search engine algorithms are based on complex criteria that serve the interests of users to find not only knowledge but also the aims and understandings of relevance of providers and the demands of their business models.[14] Some scholars have challenged the sorting effects of the Google search engine to highlight that its operation (1) is based on decisions inscribed into algorithms that favour and discriminate content, (2) is subject to personalization, localization, and selection, and (3) threatens privacy.[15]

It is important to recall that initially, search engines sorted results to queries in standardized ways. In 2004, however, the Google algorithm started to filter them into personalized results based on users' digital traces, such as their history of queries and clicks on links. Pariser calls these 'filter bubbles', personalized profiles generated by platforms such as Google and Facebook that operate like 'prediction engines' by 'constantly creating and refining a theory of who you are and what you'll do and want next' based on what you have done and wanted before.[16] In addition to harvesting and exploiting an enormous amount of data about users to do this (discussed below under tracking), filter bubbles sort and narrow the knowledge citizen subjects access and separate them into individualized universes where the rules of their formation are invisible. However, while promoting the benefits of personalization for users, search engines such as Google subtly push users to 'see the world according to criteria predefined by Google' and seem more oriented to serving the interests of advertisers.[17]

Trending is another form of filtering, such as that performed by the Twitter trends filter, which ostensibly processes millions of tweets daily and then indexes the 'most-discussed' terms. However, tweeting during events such as Occupy Wall Street have demonstrated that even when terms spike, they do not necessarily get classified as trending.[18] In this instance, critics protested that Twitter was involved in censoring political content, but others have shown that the complex algorithms of the platform organize and filter content in ways often beyond the intentions of their designers. Rather than a simple measure of popularity, the algorithm is based on a combination of factors, and those that Twitter has revealed include identifying topics that are enjoying a surge in a particular way, such as whether the use of a term is spiking (accelerating rapidly rather than gradually), whether users of a term form a tight single cluster or cut across multiple clusters, whether tweets are unique or mostly retweets of the same post, and whether the term has previously trended.[19]

Tarleton Gillespie argues that tensions between users and the designers of the Twitter algorithm are part of larger stakes in the 'politics of representation.' It is a tension underscored by a conflict between people's will to know and be visible to others and Twitter's imperative to draw new users into new conversations. But significantly, Gillespie notes that such algorithms not only are based on assumptions about the image of a public they seek to represent but also help construct publics in that image. The same could be said of other platforms such as Foursquare, which ranks popular places that users are visiting or talking about, or reddit, a social networking and news platform that enables registered users ('redditors') to post content as well as 'upvote' or 'downvote' content along scales of what is new and popular.[20] While not based on undisclosed algorithms such as those that govern Twitter trends or Google searches, the platform still operates as a filter of thousands of items, making some more visible and accessible than others.

As opposed to sorting, redacting is a form of filtering that involves the deletion of content. For example, to address legal problems that arise from the publication of court records, the redacting of some content is performed to limit identification.[21] But more generally, this can apply to the use of formats such as the digitized images of text, which filter out content because they are not searchable or discoverable. These are forms of deletion that can also extend to automatic expiry dates when content is removed (though still accessible), through the operation of search engine optimizers, or, as highlighted in 'right to be forgotten' and pornography website cases, the burying of content so that it virtually disappears from search engine results. Platform moderators can also refuse content or unacceptable actions, and citizen subjects can similarly report content back to them. Moderating and reporting content include high-profile cases such as the outrage and exposure of 'Internet trolls' who swarmed women with hostile tweets, threatening them with abuse and rape.[22]

For us, these issues epitomize how cyberspace is made up of relations between citizen subjects and conventions that are not independent but part of social struggles in spaces such as those taken by Occupy Wall Street protesters or political confrontations over abuse and misogynist conduct. We are not persuaded by arguments that 'we're not in control of our search practices—search engines are in control of us and we readily agree, though mostly unconsciously, to this domination.'[23] On the contrary, the workings of algorithms depend on citizen subjects and the performative force of their actions—algorithms belong to and are only one part of the conventions of cyberspace. By not only citing, repeating, and iterating but also resignifying, citizen subjects can, and as we shall see in chapter 6 indeed do, break conventions and take responsibility. Critics such as those cited above often slip into determinist and structuralist accounts of the workings of platforms by inferring that users are deceived and unwittingly submit to the results of search queries, newsfeeds, or trends and that these are forces 'shaping' them and societies.[24] This is also evident in their solutions. In chapter 4 we noted that the demand of openness generates tensions about visibility and privacy, giving rise to additional demands that citizens secure themselves from and be responsible for the potential and even unknowable consequences of their digital conduct. Along the same lines, Pariser's suggestions for breaking out of the filter bubble are a set of actions that amount to users changing their behaviours, such as erasing the cookies on browsers to developing 'a basic level of algorithmic literacy'.[25] Yet these are just other forms of submission to the logics and workings of filtering.

TRACKING

As we discussed in chapter 4, sharing raises concerns about privacy and surveillance that are related to one of the political questions about acting through the Internet: traceability. If 'Google knows what you are looking for' and 'Facebook knows what you like' and is manipulating your emotions, then the imaginary of openness includes citizen subjects exposing themselves in ways of which they are often unaware but also which can be tracked.[26] While filtering is a closing because of actions of blocking, sorting, and redacting knowledge, tracking is a closing because of the actions of tracing, mining, linking, and profiling citizen subjects. But filtering and tracking are also related. Consider sorting. It depends on tracking digital actions and feeding this back into the very workings of sorting algorithms. So while social media platforms are spaces of sociality, their data traces have become a key objective and fundamental to their very logic of closure rather than simply an effect of their operation.[27]

But importantly, the distinction between filtering and tracking is necessary to capture that digital traces also get circulated and repurposed and in this regard have social lives beyond the feedback loops of their platforms.[28] Thus, not only is tracking incipient to the functioning of specific conventions, but the data generated has extensity such that it can travel beyond and between conventions. Both the convention-specific and extensive uses of data traces are sources of tension and what we call closings, which begin with the very process of rendering digital actions into data, euphemistically dubbed 'datafying', which we use reluctantly for its recognizability. As we noted in chapter 2, modern subjects of power are also simultaneously subjects of knowledge, and in cyberspace this is constituted through the datafying of actions and the making of data subjects.

Only when tracking involves datafying (the process of rendering an action, attribute, or a thing into a quantified and digital form) can it be digitally analysed.[29] Attached to these data traces are various metadata that can include location, time, date, IP address, and user-supplied information such as name and gender. Importantly, it is through datafying digital actions that citizens are made into subjects of power and knowledge in cyberspace. For some, this is an irony of cyberspace: 'the celebrated freedom of political expression via self-publishing and the ease of connection facilitated in the social networking environments of Web 2.0 also offer a multitude of possibilities for automated gathering, sorting, and targeting.'[30] But such data subjectivation has specific effects or closings. One closing concerns the responsibilizing of citizen subjects we noted in chapter 4, where the imaginary of openness calls upon citizen subjects to anonymize and encrypt their communications and take responsibility for the privacy and anonymity of their digital traces. Responsibilizing thus concerns separating digital actions from identifiable citizen subjects by removing names or other particulars, and this is what privacy laws generally seek to secure.

There is considerable disagreement about whether actions of anonymization can secure privacy. Numerous forms of anonymization also exist, such as those that involve ex post facto removal of metadata, which governments or businesses do when sharing data with third parties. This is distinct from anonymity, which involves actions that avoid identification by using pseudonyms or encryption such as PGP (Pretty Good Privacy). These actions perform the right to act without being identified. With the growing volume of digital traces and the possibility of linking data across multiple anonymized data sets, some critics have argued that it is theoretically possible to 'reverse engineer' data sets to identify individuals.[31] Others such as Jane Yakowitz argue that the risks of such identification are minimal and rarely materialize and that these concerns constitute a 'moral panic, and are out of proportion to the actual threat posed by data dissemination.'[32] Instead, she argues that the public benefits and values of open research data far outweigh the risks, and it is research data that needs protection from the increasing incentives to remove and defensively guard personal data, a trend that she calls a 'modern example of a tragedy of the commons.'[33] Just as in the classic version, subjects who protect their data continue to reap the collective benefits (such as in medicine) of data left in the commons, yet those benefits are threatened and will degenerate as data subjects opt out. Others strike a different warning, arguing that the anonymization of identity leads to crowd behaviour and subjects taking less responsibility for what they say and do and increases the likelihood of their misbehaving.[34]

Both the arguments for and against anonymization as a solution presume that what is at issue is protecting the 'data doubles' of citizen subjects.[35] However, the predominant objects of datafying that are of interest to governments, corporations, or platform designers are discrete digital actions such as searching, messaging, clicking, blogging, purchasing, linking, tweeting, and posting. These data are often not connected to individuals or even populations. That some can be associated with specific subjects who have committed an action is relevant, but it is not a given or necessary logic of the tracking of digital actions.[36] Instead, traces of digital actions are often 'decoupled' from identifiable subjects, which is the working logic of data mining where inferences and predictions are made based on associations between actions across multiple aggregated data sets.[37] Through combining actions such as tweeting, purchasing, and messaging, patterns and associations can be identified, and profiles of particular subject positions (as being made up of sets of digital actions) can be generated. Louise Amoore thus argues, 'The one-to-one match with an identified individual gives way to what Gilles Deleuze calls the "dividual"—a "torn chain of variables" dividing the subject within herself, recombining with the divided elements of others. The signature of the dividual that is sought by the security software does not "belong" to a subject as such—it does not sign off on past events, it signals possibilities.'[38] That is, past associations and patterns between the digital actions of numerous and often anonymous bodies are the basis on which profiles of subjects can be composed and predicted and their digital and other actions acted upon. Consequently, once separated, the anonymized digital traces of multiple citizen subjects can be linked, analysed, and made actionable and have effects on the lives of citizens. Through this action, citizens become subjects not of disciplinary power but a mode of cybernetic or soft control;[39] rather than embodied subjects, modulations, patterns, and associations between multiple digital actions are the sites of often predictive analyses and interventions. These interventions can have real effects on lives and opportunities, from the mundane predictive algorithms of search engines that prefill queries and regulate access to knowledge to the more serious pre-emptive security decisions of border agencies that regulate movement or the decisions of credit and insurance brokers that evaluate the worthiness of applicants.

Datafying is thus performative in two ways. First, within the workings of particular platforms, through feedback loops and recursive iterations, datafying shapes actions and conduct. An algorithm such as 'People You May Know' may prompt connecting with a friend on the Internet, for example.[40] In relation to sorting, the performative force of filters involves directing the knowledge of citizen subjects and closes off and encloses their worlds (filter bubble). Second, as Amoore suggests, with the move from embodied subjects to their multiple digital traces, anonymization cannot adequately address the circulation, aggregation, and various repurposing to which individual digital traces may be put. This leads to a different kind of closure, perhaps the one that Yakowitz warns about, that of citizen subjects making new demands to further close their 'open' digital traces through laws on consent and data rights (an issue we address in chapter 7). But this demand is also fed by another action, that of the commodification of data.

In addition to owning and mediating the platforms that make up the dominant conventions of cyberspace, corporations monetize the data generated by the digital actions of citizen subjects. These digital traces are often referred to as big data and are popularly discussed as a resource, a raw material with qualities to be mined and capitalized, the new oil to be tapped to spur economies. Through a variety of practices of valuation, corporations not only exploit the digital traces of their customers to maximize their operations but also sell those traces to others. For that reason, citizen subjects who use platforms such as Google are sometimes referred to not as its customers but as its product.[41]

Digital traces are widely bought and sold. Twitter Inc., for example, makes only small amounts of its data available through its application programming interfaces (APIs), and access to larger volumes comes at a high cost that only large corporations, governments, or major funded research projects can afford.[42] The valuation of digital traces has also given rise to numerous data brokers, from small-scale resellers and repackagers of tweets to the large-scale operations of Acxiom, which tracks millions of consumers.[43] Acxiom is the second-largest broker of personal data in the world; it joins data from public records such as data on home valuation and vehicle ownership, customer surveys, and 'offline' buying behaviour with data on digital behaviour compiled via cookies and across multiple devices to generate 'master profiles.'[44]

For some critics, value generation is not the only consequence of these actions, which are organized by platform owners; they also 'subsume the potential diversity of social life to narrower commercial interests.'[45] In exchange for the 'free' use of platforms and the values of connecting (via email or social media, for example), subjects submit to forms of online monitoring, advertising, and data monetization.[46] Whether or not subjects accept this exchange, the right to use and sell digital traces is mostly reserved for platform owners, and few terms of service include the rights of subjects to even access their data.[47] Be that as it may, such submission needs to be understood in relation to the callings of openness and its associated digital acts of participating, connecting, and sharing. That is, rather than a simple question of choice or exchange economy, citizen subjects are caught between the demands to participate and connect—and all the reasons and values they attach to this—and the interests, imperatives, and trade-offs configured by platform owners. But it would be wrong to reduce this to merely the interest of platform owners, which are only one element in the make-up of conventions such as browsing. The conventions of social networking inevitably embody the social and cultural norms, rules, and customs of which citizen subjects are a part and take part.[48]

Because of the different ways that data is being generated and the myriad ways that it circulates and gets analysed, the term 'dataveillance' has been coined to distinguish the actions of reusing bits of data generated by and for purposes such as social networking from other specific, targeted surveillance practices. This is the distinction that David Lyon makes when he argues that digital traces are being taken up by various 'big data practices' and are extending and accentuating the character of surveillance. He summarizes this extension as involving the ever-growing reliance on algorithms, software, and automated analytics, such that discretion is being further circumscribed; a focus on the anticipatory and the future such that more emphasis is given to predicting, intervening, and managing consequences rather than understanding causes; and the

more easy and successful adoption and adaption of data to different
fields with little risk.[49]

The actions of datafying, commodifying, and dataveilling also remain
relatively invisible. This includes covert forms of dataveilling such as
spyware that reports digital actions back to an installer. However, even
when consensually installed, users rarely understand how spyware
works and often forget about its presence.[50] Cookies are the most pervasive form. They are bits of data stored on devices and sent to browsers by
websites that are visited or through techniques like 'device fingerprint-
ing', which enables watching subjects who delete or do not store cookies.[51] They are used not only for monitoring digital actions but also for
tracking preferred language, login, and other personal settings such as
search preferences and for targeting advertising and tracking numbers of
visits to sites.[52] Digital traces picked up by cookies have also been repurposed by security agencies, such as the NSA's utilization of Google's
advertising cookies to track targets.[53]

Concerns about online tracking and the use of spyware along with
limited citizen awareness of cookies, how they are used, and options for
managing them have been some of the reasons that many states have
introduced regulations. For citizen subjects in the European Union, the
European Commission E-Privacy directive was enacted in 2009.[54] It requires that consent must be obtained for the use of cookies and similar
technologies, which governments in the EU had to implement by May
2011.[55] Importantly, the rules were designed not to restrict the use of
these actions but to prevent their use without the knowledge and agreement of users. As a consequence, websites now include pop-up windows
that advise visitors through messages such as: 'We use cookies to provide
you with a better service. Carry on browsing if you're happy with this, or
find out how to manage cookies.'[56] These come in various forms, such as
one on the 'allaboutcookies' website, which demands the action of granting permission to the site's use of cookies.

This action is now a regularized part of the conventions of cyberspace,
where consent can be understood as a form of submission. Consent—
while often considered as a right—also places obligations on citizen subjects to decipher the various models of opting in (such as the two referenced above) and to remember their choices. But more significantly, as
we noted in the discussion of datafying, consent does not mean citizen
subjects control their individual digital traces or can ever fully be aware

of what their consent unleashes. Unknown are the dispersed sites where their traces may travel or be aggregated and the purposes for which they may be analysed. The circulation of digital traces is extensive, and rather than regulating, consent involves the regularizing, authorizing, and normalizing of the tracking and circulation of the digital traces of citizen subjects.

NORMALIZING

Acts of normalizing also join the logic of closure by performing actions in relation to the acts of filtering and tracking in a number of ways. We will illustrate this by referring again to some of the points raised above. Consent, for instance, is an action that is part of widespread protocols that call upon citizen subjects to permit other actions such as automatic software updates. In general, normalizing actions produce tractable subjects 'who comply with the requirements of authorization protocols and refrain from behaviours that are unauthorized or simply anomalous.'[57] Cohen argues that these form 'regimes of authorization' that operate on difference and unpredictability with the effect of producing 'more homogeneous, more carefully modulated behavior.'[58] But in order to operate or be effective, they require the repetitive and normalized actions of subjects, such as the granting of consent discussed above.

While it may sound contradictory, even personalization is a normalizing action. The personalized profiles or 'filter bubbles' generated by platforms such as Google and Facebook operate on standardized algorithms; while the predictions about 'who you are and what you'll do and want next' may be unique for different subjects, they are unique only in line with the rules of the algorithm. Just as Twitter trends normalize what constitutes a trend, so, too, does Google normalize 'who you are'. And continuing with the analysis of filtering, this also applies to the rules and protocols that sort and narrow what is known by search engines that act as amplifiers and filters of information.[59]

Normalizing actions can also be taken up in relation to participating, connecting, and sharing discussed in chapter 4. For instance, Campanelli argues that Facebook's 'frictionless sharing' presents sharing as normal and even desirable and that it simply involves using trivial data such as purchases to develop profiles that can then be linked to likely political orientations, genders, or religions.[60] While this is certainly a privacy concern, Campanelli argues that a greater danger is the narrowing of horizons whereby subjects encounter cultural products that reflect only the presumed preferences of their profile as interpreted by marketing interests: 'the more predictable result would be a gradual desertification of the cultural life of individuals no longer able to encounter what is unusual, unexpected, and surprising.'[61] Rather than individualized bubbles, sharing segregates social network users into cultural bubbles of preferences, products, and knowledge.

If we explore another bubble that normalizes, an enclosed 'virtual world' much like that of Second Life, this becomes clearer. It picks up on the discussion of teens in chapter 4 and recalls the imaginary of cyberspace as open and liberating. Buckingham and Rodriguez criticize the educational uses of 'virtual worlds' that ostensibly provide children with a space of freedom that is more open to innovation rather than more controlled 'offline' pedagogical contexts.[62] They also challenge celebratory assertions about the emergence of participatory culture, amateur creativity, user-generated content, and 'prosumption' (the combination of production and consumption). They do so through a case study of Habbo Hotel, an internationally popular 'virtual world' mainly aimed at teenagers where '[u]sers create digital avatars and furnish virtual "rooms" in which they live, and are able to engage in a range of interactions (including chat, competitions and names) with other users.'[63] Rather than a self-regulating community as promoted by the owners, the researchers conclude that the site advances an imaginary of the 'model citizen' built on expectations that subjects internalize rules by engaging in self-surveillance and self-policing, and when these self-regulatory mechanisms fail, subjects are disciplined by moderators (e.g., sanctioned, expelled, or banned).[64] Their argument is that what teens learn are particular economic lessons such as how to be diligent consumers and how to construct their identities through the virtual products that they purchase.

This convention illustrates a number of issues we have raised. First, Habbo Hotel normalizes participating, regulating, moderating, posting, blocking, purchasing, and reporting that make up this and other conventions. So while we might take issue with the conclusions Buckingham and Rodriguez draw, it is the normalizing effects of conventions that we think their study highlights. Second, as the other examples we have cited also illustrate, platforms are but one part of conventions—the rituals, customs, practices, traditions, laws, institutions, technologies, and protocols—that configure cyberspace. That is, notwithstanding what we have stated above in regard to normalization, it is wrong to confine the consequences of platforms to the actions of their designers and technologies; instead, their performative force springs from the actions of citizen subjects. For instance, through the conventions of Habbo Hotel, teens regularly test the boundaries of the rules of being a citizen and are invited to report inappropriate conduct on the part of others and participate in forums where they complain, challenge, and criticize the rules of the convention, including decisions of moderators. That is, they learn that being a citizen involves not simply obedience but also submission to a number of actions (e.g., reporting) in which they participate but which they also attempt to subvert by breaking conventions and resignifying actions.

The performative force of actions also opens the possibilities for subversive and transgressing actions on 'others.' While citizen subjects must be between thirteen and eighteen years of age, in 2012 a news investigation revealed that would-be predators were engaging in routine sexualized or violent online chatting and making sexual approaches to young participants.[65] This exposé lead to new measures being introduced as part of the conventions of Habbo Hotel towards creating a 'protected democracy': 'a regulated environment that protects the free speech, as well as the safety and interests, of the legitimate user community.'[66] After the exposé, Habbo Hotel turned off the chat function for several weeks and called upon its citizen subjects to make submissions during a six-hour period to a forum called 'the great unmute', where they could express the values and benefits of the convention and propose ideas about how safety could be revised. This led to the introduction of a slew of new measures with the understanding that a protected democracy 'can only be realised through a mix of technology, moderation, education and engagement.'[67] Through an assemblage of algorithms, humans, rules, norms, and sanctions, the conventions of Habbo Hotel were changed not just once but through an ongoing process of refinement in relation to the digital actions of citizen subjects.

But more significantly for our argument and to repeat what we have said in chapters 2 and 3, both the logic and embodiment of conventions involve agreement, but performing them also produces disagreement. It is through their repetitive actions that teens in Habbo Hotel come to experiment, push the limits, question rules, and subvert authority, not as claims separate from but very much part of their embodied lives, where bullying, disruption, sexualization, harassment, and hate speech are also part of their experience. Rather than operating through disciplinary power and categories of normality or abnormality or spaces of enclosure such as the school and prison, in Habbo Hotel control is modulated where new actions are constantly being incorporated, an inventive power that is working by inclusion, as Foucault illustrated, and 'whose effect will be greater than the sum of its component parts', as Deleuze argued.[68]

The normalizing actions of Habbo Hotel illustrate what is often overlooked: citizen subjects usually engage with multiple and disconnected conventions composed of similar actions. Habbo Hotel, Google, Facebook, reddit, Twitter, and YouTube are some of the multiple conventions through which subjects inhabit and negotiate relations and knowledge through cyberspace. Those who claim that [Google] is 'altering the very ways we see our world and ourselves' overstate the case and assume it is the only and dominant platform.[69] Citizen subjects navigate cyberspace through many conventions—blogs, Twitter, Facebook, and media and institutional sites they bookmark and connect to. And while each of these conventions embodies similar actions, from reporting functions to consenting to cookies, the kinds of citizen subjects they cultivate are not homogeneous and universal but fragmented, multiple, and agonistic.

Consider election campaigns that involve the mining of data. These do not rely on one source but on the data of multiple platforms to interpret the voting intentions of citizens. Campaigns in the United States, for example, have involved continuous recalibration—a 'permanent beta in politics'—in response to instant online polls, fund-raising drives, comments lists on YouTube video pages, and blog and forum posts.[70] But the terminology of a 'permanent beta in politics' can be taken up in other ways that usefully draw attention to how conventions modulate through the digital actions of citizen subjects. British prime minister Tony Blair's e-petitions initiative, launched in November 2006, saw petitions go exclusively to the prime minister's office. Using open-source code, it was launched by the charity mySociety and remained in a beta version but was suspended by the coalition government with its election in 2010.[71] The suspension was tied to the high volumes of prank petitions and negative publicity that resulted from allowing any petition to be posted and directed to the prime minister's office, which resulted in embarrassing demands and a high number of rejections.[72] The new site is now owned and operated by the United Kingdom government, and petitions can be submitted to only specific ministries and departments of government and must go through a checking and approval process before being posted.[73]

Through the actions of citizen subjects, e-petitions were contested and then recalibrated. Rather than simply participating on a platform, through the actions of citizen subjects, the conventions of e-petitioning were followed but also subverted. Like the 'edit wars' of Wikipedia, conventions are not fixed, and in fact, the digital actions they permit are the very means through which the conventions also are exceeded. As van Dijck has noted in relation to social media, citizen subjects develop forms of protest about user interfaces and negotiate their relations to conventions through appropriation and protest.[74] While there certainly are big differences in the relations of power between citizen subjects and platform owners, actions can and do exceed the affordances of their conventions. It is in relation to the normalizing tendencies of cyberspace—from those that format the actions that make up participating, connecting, and sharing to those of filtering and tracking—that tensions arise and citizen subjects engage in the play of obedience, submission, and subversion.

Coming at this same issue in relation to everyday practices, Cohen argues that more opportunity is needed in cyberspace to counter the 'innate tendency to naturalize' or 'take the current technological landscape as given.'[75] Instead, she calls for mechanisms that preserve 'room for the acts of tactical evasion and situated creativity' that allow citizen subjects to 'tinker, repurpose, and adapt' and push 'against those structures, sometimes conforming to them and sometimes finding ways to work around them.'[76] Citing Jonathan Zittrain, Cohen notes his principle of the 'generativity' of technologies, which refers to the capacity of a technology to allow its users to tinker, revise, and make new things that were never anticipated by their designers.[77]

RUPTURES

Tinkering is what citizen subjects are inevitably and always doing, intentionally or unintentionally, through many of their digital actions.[78] Conventions such as search engines and trends are recursively calibrated in relation to the modulating actions of citizen subjects. Others such as social networking are responsive to the demands and challenges of their members or face mutinies, such as the outcries against Twitter, Facebook, or Habbo Hotel. Citizen subjects have challenged conventions, such as the storm around the introduction of an application called 'Girls Around Me' in 2012 that scraped public Foursquare and Facebook check-ins onto a map displaying people—but in particular, women—in one's vicinity.[79] While technically within privacy laws, the case highlighted how data generated by and publicly available on platforms can be freely accessed by applications and used for other purposes than originally intended. But it was in response to the objections of citizen subjects who called it a 'stalker app' that Foursquare and Facebook closed the app's access to their APIs. Of course, there are many counterexamples, such as tracking and filtering or the workings of regimes of authorization. But there are also those acts of citizen subjects that go beyond tinkering, which, as described by Cohen, is more a form of submission than of subversion. Like our submission to the blocking actions of the British Library, tinkerers inevitably work within the logic and configuration of the conventions of which they are a part.

Yet citizen subjects come into being through the subversion of conventions that call them into obedience or submission in the first place. Through creating openings for thinking, speaking, and acting differently, citizen subjects resignify conventions rather than just tinker with them. As we argued in chapter 3, the force of the performative issues from the rupturing of given conventions. While still calling for their obedience and submission—for inevitably they are always in relation to conventions—at the same time, citizen subjects create possibilities of subversion. Indeed, it is this possibility (and the citizen subjects that have exercised it) that many of the closings we have noted target. In relation to anxieties about 'superusers' and morality plays of the hacker, the pirate, and the terrorist, securitization has been invoked and then extended to other citizen subjects who cannot be trusted as they will resort to illegality when and if given the opportunity.[80] This just highlights another aspect of the play of actions between and among bodies acting through the Internet where closings are intricately tied to callings but also give rise to openings.

NOTES

1. E. Morozov, *To Save Everything, Click Here: The Folly of Technological Solutionism* (PublicAffairs, 2013). Morozov argues that even critics such as Lawrence Lessig accept openness as an inevitable and built-in feature of the Internet (quoting his statement

that 'the network is not going away'). He notes that other champions of openness argue that the disclosure benefits of transparency outweigh the costs.

2. J. E. Cohen, *Configuring the Networked Self: Law, Code, and the Play of Everyday Practice* (Yale University Press, 2012), 1.

3. R. Deibert, "The Geopolitics of Internet Control: Censorship, Sovereignty, and Cyberspace," in *Routledge Handbook of Internet Politics*, ed. Andrew Chadwick and Philip N. Howard (Routledge, 2009), 324.

4. R. Deibert and R. Rohozinski, "Beyond Denial: Introducing Next-Generation Information Access Controls," in *Access Controlled: The Shaping of Power, Rights, and Rule in Cyberspace*, ed. R. Deibert et al. (MIT Press, 2010).

5. Ibid., 21.

6. Ibid., 23. 'In Chinese-style filtering, lists of Internet protocol (IP) addresses, keywords, and/or domains are programmed into routers or software packages that are situated at key Internet choke points, typically at international gateways or among major Internet service providers (ISPs).' Deibert and Rohozinski, "Beyond Denial: Introducing Next-Generation Information Access Controls," 4.

7. Deibert makes this point based on David Lyon's analyses of everyday surveillance. See, for example, D. Lyon, "Everyday Surveillance: Personal Data and Social Classifications," *Information, Communication & Society* 5, 2 (2002).

8. Haggerty and Ericson make this argument in relation to surveillance and what they call a 'surveillant assemblage.' K. D. Haggerty and R. V. Ericson, "The Surveillant Assemblage," *British Journal of Sociology* 51, 4 (2000).

9. Banksy is an internationally recognized British graffiti artist whose works challenge political authority.

10. Webstart Studios, *The Web Blocker*, 2014 [accessed 13 November 2014], www. thewebblocker.com.

11. Cohen, *Configuring the Networked Self*, 188.

12. E. Morozov, "The Rise of Data and the Death of Politics," *Guardian*, 20 July 2014 [accessed 7 August 2014], bit.ly/1rf3LiV.

13. S. Vaidhyanathan, *The Googlization of Everything: (And Why We Should Worry)* (University of California Press, 2011), 2.

14. T. Gillespie, "Can an Algorithm Be Wrong?," *Limn*, 2 (2012).

15. R. König and M. Rasch, eds., *Society of the Query Reader: Reflections on Web Search* (Institute of Network Cultures, 2014), 16. See also M. Fuez et al., "Personal Web Searching in the Age of Semantic Capitalism: Diagnosing the Mechanisms of Personalisation," *First Monday* 16, 2 (2011).

16. E. Pariser, *The Filter Bubble: What the Internet Is Hiding from You* (Viking, 2011), 8.

17. Fuez et al., "Personal Web Searching."

18. Gillespie, "Can an Algorithm Be Wrong?"

19. As Gillespie notes, these are just some of the disclosed criteria provided by Twitter, whose interests would not be served by revealing the workings of the algorithm as this would risk opening up the platform to being 'gamed'. Ibid.

20. A submission's score is the number of upvotes minus the number of downvotes. reddit inc., *Frequently Asked Questions*, 2014 [accessed 13 November 2014], www. reddit.com/wiki/faq.

21. The US Public Access to Court Electronic Records (PACER) platform redacts personal identifiers before a federal court record is made accessible. Administrative Office of the U.S. Courts, *Public Access to Court Electronic Records*, 2014 [accessed 13 November 2014], www.pacer.gov/. To protest PACER's paywall that charges users for

downloading documents that are in the public domain and not covered by copyright, in 2008 Internet hacktivist Aaron Swartz downloaded millions of records during an initial free trial period for libraries. While the FBI investigated his action, no charges were ever filed.

22. Examples of 'Internet trolls' targeting women with threats of violence are plentiful. One instance concerned threats against freelance journalist Caroline Criado-Perez, who successfully campaigned for Jane Austen's picture to be put on a new ten-pounds United Kingdom banknote. She suffered a deluge of threats, which eventually led to the arrest of two men and to Twitter's improving its report function.

23. König and Rasch, *Society of the Query Reader*, 13.

24. In one of the more hyperbolic accounts, personalized filters are described as leading to a kind of 'global lobotomy' instead of a 'worldwide metabrain', which was the promise first held out by the Internet. Additionally, how this shaping relates to 'offline' lives—for a separation is maintained—remains unexamined. Pariser, *The Filter Bubble*.

25. Ibid., 124. On the question of 'citizenship', Pariser reduces this to Facebook reminding people to vote and Google helping citizens find their polling station. Ibid.

26. A. Preston, "The Death of Privacy," *Observer*, 3 August 2014 [accessed 7 August 2014], bit.ly/1pdlWFs.

27. J. van Dijck, *The Culture of Connectivity: A Critical History of Social Media* (Oxford University Press, 2013), 12.

28. For discussions of the social lives of data, see E. Ruppert et al., "Reassembling Social Science Methods: The Challenge of Digital Devices," *Theory, Culture & Society, Special Issue on The Social Life of Methods* 30, 4 (2013); D. Beer and R. Burrows, "Popular Culture, Digital Archives and the New Social Life of Data," *Theory, Culture & Society* 30, 4 (2013).

29. The term 'datafication' has been used by a number of authors, such as Mayer-Schönberger and Cukier, and in the media by Bertolucci. Of course, datafication does not only refer to digital formats; historically and currently, subjects and objects can be rendered into analogue data formats. V. Mayer-Schönberger and K. Cukier, *Big Data: A Revolution That Will Transform How We Live, Work and Think* (John Murray, 2013); J. Bertolucci, "Big Data's New Buzzword: Datafication," *Information Week*, 25 February 2013 [accessed 20 August 2014], ubm.io/XzSrn2.

30. A. Chadwick and P. N. Howard, eds., *Routledge Handbook of Internet Politics* (Routledge, 2009), 6.

31. P. Ohm, "Broken Promises of Privacy: Responding to the Surprising Failure of Anonymization," *UCLA Law Review* 57 (2010): 1701. Cited in J. Yakowitz, "Tragedy of the Data Commons," *bePress*, February 2011 [accessed 11 July 2014], bit.ly/1vvv1ud.

32. Yakowitz, "Tragedy of the Data Commons."

33. For a related argument about the values of open data for research, see D. Watts, "Stop Complaining about the Facebook Study: It's a Golden Age for Research," *Guardian*, 7 July 2014 [accessed 31 July 2014], bit.ly/1nWhefR.

34. D. Rushkoff, *Program or Be Programmed: Ten Commandments for a Digital Age* (OR Books, 2010), 83–84.

35. 'Data doubles' refers to an assembly of data to generate a subject's identification profile. Didier Bigo writes that 'data doubles' arise from 'the knowledge of computer systems, the capacity to create and manage, through statistics, groups of populations—groups that are constituted through algorithms and profiling, connecting otherwise unrelated individuals who happen to have more or less similar "data dou-

bles".' D. Bigo, "The (in)Securitization Practices of the Three Universes of EU Border Control: Military/Navy—Border Guards/Police—Database Analysts," *Security Dialogue* 45, 3 (2014): 217.

36. Ruppert et al., "Reassembling Social Science Methods: The Challenge of Digital Devices." Many digital traces are of the 'internet of things' that can make up networks and display patterns not directly associated with data subjects.

37. In relation to security practices, Louise Amoore argues that this decoupling produces 'data derivatives' and 'fractionated subjects.' L. Amoore, "Security and the Claim to Privacy," *International Political Sociology* 8, 1 (2014).

38. Ibid., 109.

39. T. Terranova, *Network Culture: Politics for the Information Age* (Pluto, 2004), 11.

40. Van Dijck, *Culture of Connectivity*, 157.

41. Vaidhyanathan, *Googlization of Everything*, 3.

42. Tweets are also compiled, organized, and resold by a number of marketing companies such as Retweets.Pro.

43. E. Steel, "Acxiom to Create 'Master Profiles' Tying Offline and Online Data," *Financial Times*, 23 September 2013 [accessed 21 August 2014], on.ft.com/1ljiZ6N. Other examples include Experian's Mosaic program that generates and maps consumer segments based on hundreds of 'online' and 'offline' data sets.

44. Acxiom has records on 'hundreds of millions of Americans, including 1.1 billion browser cookies (small pieces of data sent from a website, used to track the user's activity), 200 million mobile profiles, and an average of 1,500 pieces of data per consumer.' It sells consumer profiles based on this data to its customers, 'who include twelve of the top fifteen credit card issuers, seven of the top ten retail banks, eight of the top ten telecom/media companies, and nine of the top ten property and casualty insurers.' A. E. Marwick, "How Your Data Are Being Deeply Mined," *New York Review of Books*, 9 January 2014 [accessed 21 August 2014], goo.gl/SPfukV.

45. M. Andrejevic, "Social Network Exploitation," in *A Networked Self: Identity, Community and Culture on Social Network Sites*, ed. Z. Papacharissi (Routledge, 2011), 83.

46. Ibid. In exchange for a 'free' Google mail account, Google can track every action and link actions across its various platforms (mail, browser, maps, etc.) as well as target advertising. See also P. Mirowski and D. Plehwe, eds., *The Road from Mont Perlerin: The Making of the Neoliberal Thought Collective* (Harvard University Press, 2009), 224.

47. Van Dijck, *Culture of Connectivity*, 39. In response to concerns about its brokerage activities, Acxiom, in line with relevant data protection laws, introduced options for how personal data is collected and used. Individuals can opt out of cookies and digital advertising (i.e., so that Acxiom no longer can collect or share digital advertising data about them with clients) and can access or correct their personal data or withdraw their consent by contacting Acxiom. Acxiom UK, *UK Privacy Policy*, 2014 [accessed 13 November 2014], bit.ly/1vvy8Cc.

48. As discussed in chapter 4, citizen subjects continue to participate in various conventions even when made aware of surveillant or economic effects; teens, for example, are compelled to maintain their digital connections in order to remain part of their communities. See d. boyd, *It's Complicated: The Social Lives of Networked Teens* (Yale University Press, 2014).

49. D. Lyon, "Surveillance, Snowden, and Big Data: Capacities, Consequences, Critique," *Big Data & Society* 1 (2014).

50. P. N. Howard, "Deep Democracy, Thin Citizenship: The Impact of Digital Media in Political Campaign Strategy," *Annals of the American Academy of Political and Social Science* 597 (2005): 164.

51. Morozov, *To Save Everything*. 'A cookie is a small file, typically of letters and numbers, downloaded on to a device when the user accesses certain websites. Cookies are then sent back to originating website on each subsequent visit. Cookies are useful because they allow a website to recognize a user's device.' UK Information Commissioner's Office, *Guidance on the Rules on Use of Cookies and Similar Technologies*, May 2012 [accessed 22 August 2014], bit.ly/1IcjAfM.

52. Google, Privacy & Terms: "How Google Uses Cookies," 2014 [accessed 13 November 2014], bit.ly/1sHDt73.

53. R. Feloni, "The NSA Is Using Google's Advertising Cookies to Track Its Targets," *Business Insider*, 11 December 2013 [accessed 22 August 2014], read.bi/1s94Zuw. One consequence of cookies is the rise of anti-spyware software.

54. 'The 2003 Regulations implemented a European Directive—2002/58/EC—which is concerned with the protection of privacy in the electronic communications sector. In 2009 this Directive was amended by Directive 2009/136/EC. This included a change to Article 5(3) of the E-Privacy Directive.' UK Information Commissioner's Office, *Guidance on the Rules on Use of Cookies and Similar Technologies*.

55. Ibid.

56. John Lewis, 'What Are Cookies?' [accessed 12 November 2014], bit.ly/1sCIXQe.

57. Cohen, *Configuring the Networked Self*, 207.

58. Ibid., 209.

59. Clay Shirky, referenced in V. Campanelli, "Frictionless Sharing: The Rise of Automatic Criticism," in *Society of the Query Reader: Reflections on Web Search*, ed. René König and Miriam Rasch (Institute of Network Cultures, 2014), 45.

60. Ibid.

61. Ibid.

62. D. Buckingham and C. Rodriguez, "Learning about Power and Citizenship in an Online Virtual World," *Comunicar*, 40 (2013). They make this point based on the review of a number of scholarly articles which argue that 'online' worlds are spaces of freedom for children.

63. Ibid., 51. Sulake, the Finnish owner of Habbo Hotel, reports that as of August 2012, the platform had eleven language versions, customers in more than 150 countries, 273 million registered users, and more than 5 million unique visitors per month. Sulake Corporation, "Habbo Hotel—Where Else?," 2012 [accessed 13 November 2014], www.sulake.com/habbo/.

64. Buckingham and Rodriquez conclude that Habbo Hotel is less open to negotiation than 'offline' contexts such as schools, where the consent of those who would be governed has to be won. Reasons for being banned include transgressing rules concerning disruption, sexually explicit behaviour, personal identifying information, harassment, hate speech, scamming, terms and conditions, and inappropriate name, room, or group. Buckingham and Rodriguez, "Learning about Power and Citizenship in an Online Virtual World." Habbo Hotel grants 'Habbo Citizenship' to subjects who have reached a designated level of achievements and badges based on factors such as amount of time spent in the hotel and earning the right to trade. Sulake Corporation, "Get Your Habbo Citizenship Now!," 2014 [accessed 13 November 2014], bit.ly/1oQcIAN.

65. P. Walker, "Habbo Hotel: NSPCC Urges Government and Technology Industry to Act," *Guardian*, 14 June 2012 [accessed 23 August 2014], bit.ly/1vvk2Rr.

66. Sulake Corporation, "Response to the Great Unmute and a New Era of 'Protected Democracy' for Habbo Hotel," 2012 [accessed 13 November 2014], bit.ly/1vvpIe5.

67. Ibid. New measures included: users to complete a new responsible use test prior to re-entering the site; active and visible staff moderators to be present in a wider range of rooms across the site; user community volunteers to be given the opportunity to qualify as 'Guardians' (a user-populated virtual police force); all users to begin on limited chat and earn their way to filtered chat through responsible interaction; basic level algorithmic chat solution to alert moderators to inappropriate content; and increased prominence of emergency button to encourage active use.

68. M. Foucault, *Security, Territory, Population*, ed. A. Davidson, trans. G. Burchell, Lectures at the Collège de France, 1977–78 (Palgrave Macmillan, 2007), 45; G. Deleuze, "Postscript on Control Societies," in *Negotiations* (Columbia University Press, 1990), 177.

69. Vaidhyanathan, *Googlization of Everything*, 7. Vaidhyanathan's analysis of Google is focused on detailing and interpreting its technocultural structure and corporate ideology and dominance.

70. Chadwick and Howard, *Routledge Handbook of Internet Politics*, 6.

71. Myfanwy, "What We Learned from ePetitions," *mySociety*, 4 August 2011 [accessed 23 August 2014], bit.ly/1tDmq7B.

72. J. Robinson, "E-Petitions Website Shelved," *Guardian*, 22 November 2010 [accessed 23 August 2014], bit.ly/1tDjDLu.

73. HM Government, "E-Petitions—Create and Sign Petitions Online," 2014 [accessed 13 November 2014], epetitions.direct.gov.uk/. The platform also lists 'trending e-petitions'—the most active e-petitions in the past hour.

74. Van Dijck, *Culture of Connectivity*, 160.

75. Cohen, *Configuring the Networked Self*, 197.

76. Ibid.

77. J. Zittrain, *The Future of the Internet and How to Stop It* (Yale University Press, 2008).

78. 'Tinkering' is a term that Annemarie Mol and others deploy to describe a political strategy of intervening in technologies through experimentation and adaptation. A. Mol, I. Moser, and J. Pols (eds.), *Care in Practice: On Tinkering in Clinics, Homes and Farms* (Transcript, 2010).

79. A. C. Madrigal, "Deconstructing the Creepiness of the 'Girls Around Me' App—and What Facebook Could Do about It," *Atlantic*, 2 April 2012 [accessed 23 August 2014], theatln.tc/1oiX9e4.

80. Cohen, *Configuring the Networked Self*, 200.

SIX

Openings

Witnessing, Hacking, Commoning

If making rights claims in or by saying and doing 'I, we, or they have a right to' enacts people as citizen subjects, it also creates openings. For citizen subjects to come into being, certain conventions are invoked, provoked, and ruptured. To recall, these conventions are typically sociotechnical arrangements that embody norms, values, affects, laws, ideologies, and technologies. If rights claims gain ground, become articulable through digital acts, and find addressees, their effects create openings that can be understood as experiments that exceed existing conventions. These openings are not groundless, normless, and lawless experiments, though these properties may sometimes feature in them. Above all, openings are moments and spaces when and where thinking, speaking, and acting differently become possible by resisting and resignifying conventions. Such resignification might feel like freedom for subjects, as if they involve neither obedience nor submission. Yet resignification creates its demands and calls for obedience and submission while at the same time creating possibilities of subversion. Effects depend on how resignification plays out.

We can speak about many openings that the Internet has made possible, but witnessing, hacking, and commoning are perhaps the most important digital acts.[1] Each of these acts has made possible recognizable citizen subjects: citizen journalist, citizen activist, and citizen producer. To be sure, each of these citizen subjects existed before cyberspace. The traditions of community newspapers entirely run by citizen journalists, protests and demonstrations organized by citizen activists, and the cooperative movements of citizen producers are prominent examples. However, each of these has been resignified through cyberspace. The rise and impact of WikiLeaks and whistle-blowing as forms of citizen journalism have dramatically altered the politics of knowledge and the right to know. The emergence of hacker cultures and movements such as Anonymous has dramatically transformed the meaning and function of protest. The emergence of Wikipedia has spectacularly upstaged the subjects and agents of knowledge production and dissemination. We have given only a few examples to illustrate each of these openings, but in this chapter we will discuss various conventions of cyberspace that have made digital acts of witnessing, hacking, and commoning possible. To do so, we are going to work through the theoretical apparatus we have developed to understand the Internet and the space of relations that acting through the Internet has produced—cyberspace. We are going to discuss a class of acts—making rights claims—and demonstrate how in or by saying and doing something through the Internet people have resignified conventions and enacted ways of being citizen subjects. In doing so, we shall also pay close attention to legal, performative, and imaginary forces through which digital acts have become possible. The primary aim of this chapter is to illustrate the usefulness of approaching openings in relation to the conventions they resignify rather than approaching them with already-established categories of thought and practice. As we shall see, approaching myriad actions on the Internet that produce acts of witnessing from the perspective of professional journalism and labelling them as citizen journalism limits our understanding of the new subject positions and ways of being that these actions are opening.

WITNESSING

One of the most oft-cited definitions of citizen journalism states that it is 'the act of a citizen, or group of citizens, playing an active role in the process of collecting, reporting, analyzing and disseminating news and information. The intent of this participation is to provide independent, reliable, accurate, wide-ranging and relevant information that a democracy requires.'[2] This characterization was made relatively early in the development of citizen journalism, when many platforms and digital technologies were in their initial stages of development. Still, in identifying a shift from professionally produced news to hybrid amateur-professional production and even almost entirely amateur production, this moment signalled that the Internet was loosening the grip of professional journalism on the production and dissemination of news and truth telling. Since then, much has been written on whether this is indeed the case or whether professional journalism has now consolidated its grip. But there is no doubt that however it is defined—alternative journalism, citizen's media, citizen journalism, democratic media, and radical media—something new is afoot in journalistic truth telling and knowledge production through cyberspace.[3]

Let us return to the definition of citizen journalism that captured our imagination. There are two aspects of the definition. First, the focus is on acts performed by subjects called citizens. But what is exactly the act? The answer that was originally offered was that of 'participatory journalism'. The idea is that the participation of audiences becomes part of journalism. Those audiences are no longer passive recipients of information and news but actively participate in its production. So the act of participation breaks the established convention of journalism to produce news and 'create' events for an audience that is used to merely receiving it. It is then that those audiences who participate in the production of news become citizens. Many media scholars have questioned for years whether journalism actually worked within such an established convention and whether audiences were as passive as imagined, but the recognition here is that the Internet now makes it possible at least to participate directly in the production of news. Still, what is exactly the act? Is it participation? Can its subjects be called citizens? We think that this is rather a weak characterization of what is arguably a radical shift. This is because participation often calls for, as we discussed earlier, involvement in already-established conventions. From our perspective, participation is a submissive (though not obedient) act in or by which a citizen subject performs a claim. There ought to be something broader than connecting it to journalism alone to characterize acts by which citizens produce knowledge about events. Moreover, the association of the term 'citizen' with this rather submissive participation overlooks the radical potential of the figure of the citizen subject as an agent of submission *and* subversion and thus subject *of* power.

We will shortly return to this, but now let us take a look at the second aspect of the definition. It proposes that the intent of participation is about providing accurate, reliable, independent information for democracy. This is the conventional imaginary of professional journalism—its objectivity. Many media scholars question journalistic objectivity not because they disagree with it but because they do not think professional journalism achieves it. Bolette Blaagaard, for example, argues that the contribution of citizen journalism has been to challenge the ostensible objectivity of professional journalism.[4] She argues that in creating a journalistic objectivity, professional journalism portrayed a knowing subject that is detached, unemotional, neutral, unbiased, and independent. By contrast, citizen journalism's contribution has been to demonstrate that passionate, attached, affective, and biased yet fair reporting can result from journalistic subjectivity.[5] She illustrates this using a famous case of citizen journalism where a bystander citizen recorded with his mobile phone the London police assault on Ian Tomlinson that resulted in his death. Blaagaard argues that this was not accidental journalism, but its intent was to demonstrate the consequences of the police action of kettling.[6] She also illustrates with the website CrisisJam that journalistic subjectivity can call for political solidarity and bring political interests into the public in ways that journalistic objectivity often fails to accomplish.[7] Similarly, Chris Atton notes that citizen journalism has inevitably created multiple versions of events, which highlights how news is socially constructed by selecting, filtering, and presenting.[8] We now recognize the regime of objectivity is only one of the ways in which we know about the world of events. Atton asks, '[O]nce we acknowledge the social construction of news, why should we then reject alternative journalism simply because it is not subject to the same normative and epistemological limits of mainstream journalism?'[9]

So by imposing the conventional idea of professional journalism and characterizing digital journalism as participation, the performative and imaginary forces of a digital act are practically neutralized. How do we then characterize citizen journalism? To answer this is to engage in a social struggle and not merely an intellectual exercise. As Michael Meadows says, 'The shibboleth "citizen journalism" now seems to refer to virtually anyone writing anything that bears some resemblance to "the facts" or "the truth", however they are defined.'[10] Similarly, Linda Steiner and Jessica Roberts say that 'as with public journalism, citizen journalism's philosophy is somewhat unclear; its definition is still emerging.'[11] Yet 'citizen journalism understands people as having political roles, interests and relationships, and as actively interested in sharing news they deem relevant. It understands, or perhaps intuits, that a knee-jerk definition of all forms of journalism as acquiring and distributing information misses the point.'[12] There is a recognition that it is difficult to define citizen journalism without making some investment in one or another aspect of it. Rather than attempting to define it, let us see what the main arguments are for and against 'it' so far and how we can tease out the act that constitutes it.

The literature on citizenship journalism is already vast, but it will be helpful to outline the various actions that have become possible and how they have created conventions that have come to be named citizen journalism. Let us start with some events. Beginning with the Southeast Asia earthquake and tsunami in 2004 and accelerating with major events such as the Iranian uprising in 2009, uprisings in Libya, Tunisia, and Egypt, and the civil war in Syria since 2011, a new kind of reporting has increasingly incorporated images, video footage, and reportage by ordinary or amateur observers or participants in these events. Many have commented on the difference, for example, between the Afghan and Iraq wars earlier in the same decade and these later events. Simultaneously, citizen journalism became prominent in other instances depicting racism, xenophobia, misogyny, homophobia, or police conduct against protesters, demonstrators, and activists around the world.[13] While these were often called 'accidental journalism', citizen journalism also began creating new conventions—made up of actions, norms, values, protocols, and practices—using Internet platforms.[14] Most of these platforms, or at least the ones that have gained prominence, are closed (proprietary) platforms, which means their protocols, algorithms, and procedures are under the control of their owners. As the difference between open and closed platforms or conventions is not straightforward, we will discuss both and indicate their main tendencies.[15]

Among the most famous platforms is the South Korean OhMyNews, which arguably became a social movement and is considered a pioneer.[16] OhMyNews advanced a direct challenge to professional journalism in South Korea by registering thousands of citizen journalists, enabling them to write their own stories, and developing an editorial process by which they were curated and audited. By contrast, what some call 'mobi journalism' in Slovenia accomplished an opposite effect by a major television channel (Kanal A) that uses citizen journalism as a shield to produce a tabloid news programme.[17]

Since then, many platforms have been established that follow similar conventions, such as YouTube, IndyMedia, Digg.com, Global Voices, Newsvine, and Guerrilla News Network (GNN).[18] But there are also interesting differences among these platforms, especially in terms of algorithms and codes that determine 'newsworthy' reporting and footage by ranking, ordering, and grouping. Luke Goode, for example, discusses how different platforms produce different sociotechnical arrangements—rules, norms, procedures, protocols, code, and algorithms—in order to create an effective presentation for their users. These arrangements, or what we call conventions, accomplish not only a sense of fairness but also strong hierarchies through which news is produced.[19] There is no reason to believe that these platforms feature flat hierarchies or smooth spaces of dialogue; rather, they are hierarchical and striated. The issues of status and gatekeeping are as prominent in these platforms as they are elsewhere.[20] Thus, there is also no reason to think that citizen journalism—at least as it is practiced in these platforms—is intrinsically counterhegemonic. Rather, we would investigate the rationalities of these conventions, the way they are taken up by subjects in obedient, submissive, and subversive ways, and the effects they produce. Yet these are difficult investigations not only because these platforms proliferate and change so rapidly but also because the gatekeepers and proprietors of these platforms display varying degrees of transparency and openness about them (as we discussed in chapter 5).

Concern also arises as to whether the openings for citizen journalism are being already incorporated or co-opted by professional journalism. One of the prominent examples of such co-optation is CNN's iReport platform.[21] Launched in 2006, iReport ostensibly provides a platform for amateur journalists and ordinary citizens to engage in news production. But analyses of the platform urge caution about whether and to what extent CNN provides a democratic, unfiltered, and uncensored form of reportage and expression. Faroq Kperogi, for example, argues that CNN deploys a sophisticated journalistic hegemony—much akin to the imaginary of the definition with which we began this discussion on participation and intent—that while legitimizing a conventional imaginary of journalism, it benefits from the unpaid labour of a vast army of people who provide its material.[22] Similarly, by investigating CNN's reporting of the uprising in Iran in 2009, Lindsay Palmer reports that 'CNN simultaneously denigrates and depends on the unpaid labour of its iReporters, especially when covering a political uprising.'[23] Yet she also concludes with a thought that rather forcefully expresses our view of the modern citizen as subject *of* power. She writes, '[M]y case study reveals that citizen coverage of global conflict is a story of both exploitation and subversion, since hegemonic journalistic representations of world events ultimately unfold within the increasingly disruptive informational milieu that is the product of network culture.'[24] From our perspective, this is both the promise and the danger of being subjects *of* power: what separates submission from subversion is a fleeting moment. But by submitting to the authority of platforms such as Digg, GNN, or iReport, citizen subjects also engage in the possibilities of subversion, inventing ways of breaking conventions to which they have submitted but from within the possibilities and affordances of those very conventions.

We can also observe this in several other hybrid forms of journalism. Research on various hybrid forms of journalism in Australia, Germany, the Netherlands, and the United States conclude that 'for all its success, citizen journalism remains dependent to a significant extent on mainstream news organizations, whose output it debates, critiques, recombines, and debunks by harnessing large and distributed communities of users.'[25] Similarly, news organizations are increasingly relying on citizen journalism, and this includes not only national outlets such as BBC's 'Have Your Say' but also local outlets such as Citizens' Eye of Leicester News.[26] Citizens' Eye, an independent citizen journalist platform, is now incorporated into the *Leicester Mercury*, which is a major local newspaper but one facing losses.[27] Nevertheless, rather than assimilating Citizens' Eye, the *Leicester Mercury* finds it more effective to present it as its citizen journalist component.

Although these examples of citizen journalism predominantly focus on platforms that either serve as independent or hybrid journalism, the Internet raises an outstanding issue that Goode calls 'metajournalism'. We have seen some platforms that include algorithms and code that rank, order, and group items submitted as news stories and where the logics of these algorithms inevitably involved striating the cyberspace they have created. The presence and persistence of such algorithms also creates new actions such as tagging or aggregating. These actions involve neither the production nor consumption of news but its dissemination, classification, and curating or, as we have put it, involve acting not only in or by saying things but also in or by doing things. As Goode illustrates when he calls this activity metajournalism, many actions on the Internet involve subjects tagging, aggregating, redirecting, liking, ranking, rating, and reposting news items produced by citizen journalists.[28] These actions by which people submit to conventions are how the subject, the citizen journalist, is enacted. Of note, these actions are not limited to bespoke news platforms but normalized actions of other platforms such as Twitter, Facebook, YouTube, Flickr, and Instagram that may not have had citizen journalism in mind when they were created. Yet people often subvert the original aims of these platforms and use them for other purposes. Again, that such subversion takes place is no guarantee that the platforms are either progressive or counterhegemonic, but it is to mark that citizen metajournalism is perhaps just as significant as citizen journalism. The retelling or resignification of news stories raises the question of whether such subjects who engage in these actions should be called citizen journalists. Or, as Goode writes, it raises the question 'whether we should restrict its definition to practices in which citizens act as content creators, producing original news material.'[29] More importantly, it also exposes an aspect of professional journalism—its supposed objectivity—that has been kept hidden from open view: that professional journalism, too, is an agent of aggregating, filtering, and ranking rather than merely disclosing or revealing events.[30] If that's the case, we question whether there should be a different label for curators and aggregators for two reasons. As we have argued, digital acts involve doing something through various actions not confined to language but including images and sounds as well as the coding, linking, and classifying of content. Second, these actions resignify questions of anonymity, extensity, traceability, and velocity. They enable the dissemination of news with anonymity at almost instantaneous speed through numerous networks, and they leave traces along the way. As we shall now argue, this is indeed a distinctly cyberspace enactment of citizen witnessing.

The question that we posed, though, still persists: What exactly is the act that citizen journalists perform to constitute themselves as digital citizens? What rights claims do citizen journalists perform? This is where we find the literature on citizen journalism too narrowly focused on the journalism aspect rather than the citizen aspect.[31] The impact of citizen journalism on professional journalism's monopoly on telling truths about events and producing and disseminating knowledge is certainly momentous and significant. But when we think about the citizen subject that it gives rise to, matters appear rather differently.

We can approach citizen journalism from our perspective, that is, from the perspective of not the subject but the act itself. Leaving aside the question whether WikiLeaks is an instance of citizen journalism, an early reflection by Julian Assange, a cofounder of WikiLeaks, is appropriate. He writes, '[E]very time we witness an act that we feel to be unjust and do not act we become a party to injustice.'[32] Now, two things are said at once here. There is an act that involves an injustice. There is also an act that involves witnessing it. There are two dimensions here that we can term political and ethical. The political involves the judgement on justice and injustice. The ethical involves the call to act as bearing witness. The ethical dimension becomes even clearer when Assange says, 'Those who are repeatedly passive in the face of injustice soon find their character corroded into servility.'[33] To put it in our words, citizen subjects, precisely because of their capacity to judge, are not merely obedient (or servile) but also subversive. This is because submission to conventions requires using judgement on the terms of submission. Although the citizen subject submits to conventions, because of this capacity, the call of subversion to rupture a convention always retains its force. Assange clearly appeals here to an aspect of journalistic ethics—bearing witness—but he resignifies it politically by identifying it as a call to act. The debate over whether WikiLeaks is a platform for journalism or whistle-blowing overlooks that it primarily enables witnessing—that the world may know (differently). It is often argued that such whistle-blowing exposes classified secrets and endangers the intelligence work of the state. But what whistle-blowing exposes is that there are those who find it intolerable to witness abuses and misuses of authority and not share them. If bankers deceive, soldiers massacre, agencies snoop, and diplomats lie, citizens have the right to know that. Citizens have a right to know what state and corporate authorities are doing in, and often with, their name. WikiLeaks and whistle-blowing in general are essentially claiming this right to know.

We also think that witnessing is the act that calls for both content creation and transmission. It is unnecessary to differentiate citizen journalists and citizen metajournalists as both depend on similar actions, invoke, provoke, and break similar conventions, and enable citizen sub-jects to bear witness. Acts of witnessing are making rights claims in the sense that they enact a right to witness an injustice and share it (so that the world may know) as both a political and an ethical act. Their primary orientation is not towards the ethics of a profession but the right to wit-ness and share acts of injustice. This way, it also invokes a complex as-semblage of legal, performative, and imaginary forces. Making a rights claim to witness a police injustice against a protest may invoke legal citizenship rights, but it may also perform citizenship rights that as yet do not exist (performative) or even call for rights to come (imaginary).

For these reasons, we think Stuart Allan's suggestion to think of citi-zen journalism as 'citizen witnessing' is both powerful and yet inade-quate.[34] Allan describes citizen journalism 'as a type of first-person re-portage in which ordinary individuals temporarily adopt the role of a journalist in order to participate in news making, often spontaneously during a time of crisis, accident, tragedy or disaster.'[35] This is powerful because it recognizes the significance of the act that brings citizen subjects into being as witnessing. It is vitally important to recognize that citizen witnessing responds to a call whose imaginary force, what James Dawes names as 'that the world may know', ought to remain and has been the ethical core of being citizen subjects.[36] This is one of the reasons why singular acts of citizen witnessing enacted through blogs have received as wide attention as collaborative or crowd-sourced platforms. The celebrat-ed Baghdad blogger Salam Pax, who has written his blog on everyday life in the city immediately before and after the American invasion, is an example of this.[37]

Yet Allan's characterization of citizen witnessing has three weak-nesses. First, Allan imagines citizen witnessing as a 'first-person' report-age. We have already argued that making rights claims, as a class of acts that Austin overlooked, in or by saying and doing 'I, we, or they have a right to', enacts people as citizen subjects. Making rights claims does not need to be performed in the first person. Second, Allan neglects citizen metajournalists whose performative force we have already discussed. We consider curation and aggregation as digital actions that enact citizen subjects as witnesses in an especially forceful manner through the Inter-net. Third, it is not clear why citizen witnessing must be restricted to either temporary or crisis moments. In those moments, the meaning and force of citizen witnessing may gain an additional and important strength as the Internet and the space of relations acts have created—cyberspace—has shown. Sasha Costanza-Chock's objection to using citizen journalism because most acts of witnessing involve subjects who are actually noncitizens ought not to deter us from using the term. She warns that 'those tied to the "citizen journalist" label might want to publicly rethink their reasons for conceptually linking the right to speak in new communication spaces to legal membership in the nation-state.'[38] As we affirm in chapter 2, we think that the citizen subject is not the exclusive property of the nation-state. On the contrary, the nation-state may have become a liability for upholding the subject *of* power we have inherited. As Allan writes, many of the issues that citizen journalism raises are 'set against the backdrop of incidents around the globe where the nation-state's ideological appropriation of citizenship—from outright attacks on its legitimacy to the steady erosion of its protections, typically (and ironically) in the name of national security—has made journalism as a struggle over "the right to bear witness".'[39] Citizen witnessing is an ongoing and crucial aspect of democratic citizenship. The Internet, by creating openings for digital citizens, has made citizen witnessing an indispensable part of a political imaginary. This is not without its dangers and perils (co-optation, assimilation, infiltration, taming, blocking, filtering, and so on), but that's what also makes it a site of political struggles.

HACKING

To understand the emergence of citizen subjects acting through the Internet as subjects *of* power requires investigating the conventions that call them forth as digital citizens and the digital acts they perform to say and do things. No doubt, the birth of a subject position called 'hacker' and the digital acts with which it came into being present a challenge. The stories that have been told about hackers make it difficult to resignify this subject *of* power afresh. Since the 1980s, the image of hackers has dominated fictional and semifictional worlds of writing and filmmaking. Our focus here, though, is to get a grip on the openings that 'acts of hacking' have created.

Much has been written about hackers and hacking.[40] Since the 1950s with the emergence of large-scale computers (mainframes), we have seen not only programmers but also those who were intrigued by the possibilities of accessing, controlling, and generally hacking into these computers. But first, with the networking of these large-scale infrastructures and then, second, the progressive miniaturization of them (personal computers, laptops, hand-held, and eventually wearable devices), the challenges and possibilities of programming and hacking software and hardware became exponentially huge. For us, probably the most pertinent distinction is between programmers and hackers. In or by saying something in code performs both illocutionary and perlocutionary acts. The difference between programmers and hackers is, however, the effects of their acts, which have dramatically changed over time. Programmers are those — either employed by software companies or working independently — who make a living by writing code, which includes anything between snippets (short code) and apps. Hackers may also program code in this fashion, but the culture that gives them the name emanates from a distinct set of ethical and aesthetic values that combine to create a different kind of politics than programming does. This difference is hard to express, but it is also the difference that is of interest to us. It is hard to express perhaps because so much has been said and written about hackers — mostly negative. As a consequence, a unified, typically clandestine, selfish, young, male, and outlaw image has become dominant, which more recent studies have shown is grotesquely simplified. We want to argue that hackers are those whose acts break conventions of programming.

Even a pioneering and dominant, if not sympathetic and celebratory, account provides an image of such a unified culture that it has recently been questioned by scholars who have wondered about its popularity. Interestingly, it was in that intriguing year of 1984 (*The Postmodern Condition, Neuromancer, Cyborg Manifesto*) that Steven Levy published his *Hackers: Heroes of the Computer Revolution.*[41] Levy drew a more nuanced and panoramic view of hackers yet still practically reproduced the clandestine image. Critiquing this image, Tim Jordan and Paul Taylor argue that various classes of hackers emerged over time and need to be distinguished.[42] They note that although hackers gradually formed a dissident culture in the 1980s, they were also incorporated into a massive workforce as 'microserfs' programming for global corporations and security states in the emerging software and application industries.[43] By the 1990s, hackers were already functioning in at least four ways: original hackers (dissident and libertarian), microserfs (subservient and submissive), a growing group of open-source software developers (critical and resilient), and politically motivated hacktivists (political and subversive).[44] These two last groups—open-source developers and hacktivists—constitute the most significant groups for understanding the emergence of citizen subjects in cyberspace.

Although many of the examples that have gained notoriety in the media about hackers—attacks, encryption, decryption, and disclosure—are typically clandestine and negative, hacker culture also has shown itself to be passionately committed to the collaborative development and free dissemination of software for many purposes. These are known as free software and open-source software (not to be conflated) and cover considerable ground in providing reusable programming. Often strong values are developed and codified through such development. Gabriella Coleman gives the example of Linux (an operating system), especially a version known as Debian. She says, '[T]hese values are reflected in a pair of charters—the Debian Constitution and the Debian Social Contract—that articulate an organizational vision and formulate a set of promises to the wider free software community.'[45] Coleman argues that by mostly circumventing copyright laws with their commitment to the free circulation of intellectual property, hackers contradict the existing liberal conception of intellectual property as the right to exclude and control. Yet by advancing values of civil liberties and promoting individual autonomy and, above all, a commitment to free speech, hackers are the most ardent promoters of liberal values. Thus, for Coleman, hackers occupy both a central and marginal—we might say a paradoxical—place within the liberal tradition.

We are not convinced that interpreting both the ethics and aesthetics of hacker cultures as advancing liberal values captures their originality. These 'values' are inherited by the figure of the citizen within a much longer historical and wider geographic experience than liberal values extending from universal law to equal opportunity. Coleman says that hackers 'tend to value a set of liberal principles: freedom, privacy, and access.' It is difficult for us to see freedom, privacy, and access as either values or principles, though they express certain values. From our point of view, things such as freedom, privacy, and access are rights, and, like all rights, they are born of social and political struggles, and these struggles both predate and are wider than what liberalism implies. Thus, we wonder whether it is possible to understand hacking cultures in ethical and aesthetic terms without also considering their broader politics. The joy (deep hack mode) that hackers experience in creating a collaborative culture by sharing their skills and talents is wonderful, but understanding the ways in which this joy can be assimilated into obedient, submissive, or subversive ways of being hackers requires a broader perspective.

One aspect of hacker culture that Coleman highlights is the slogan 'code is speech'.[46] Code is indeed the language of the Internet. But is it speech? Following Austin, we argue that through speech acts we do something in or by saying something. Similarly, we would argue that programmers are doing something in or by coding something. Yet, to articulate this more precisely, code is *not* speech: it is a language in or by which speech acts are performed. Just as in human languages, the decisive things here are not only the linguistic conventions that animate speech acts but also the social conventions that they bring about. For Coleman, 'the key point is that the multifaceted pleasures of hacking signal that utility is not the only driving force in hackers' creative acts.' Thus, 'for many free software hackers, the act of writing software and learning from others far exceeds the simple enactment of an engineering ethic, or a technocratic calculus for the sake of becoming a more proficient as well as efficient programmer or system administrator.'[47] That's true, but what differentiates hackers from programmers is that in or by saying something through code, hackers challenge, if not subvert, conventions in which they find themselves. Hackers are those whose acts subvert conventions governing themselves and digital citizens. Coleman recognizes that 'many hackers are citizens of liberal democracies, and have drawn on the types of accessible liberal tropes—notably free speech—as a means to conceptualize their technical practice and secure novel political claims.' But given the extensity of the Internet, while this statement may have been true in the past, it would be hard to substantiate today that hackers are only citizens of liberal democracies, meaning they are legal holders of citizenship status in liberal democratic states. If we think about being citizens not only in legal terms but also in relation to performative and imaginary forces, we cannot agree that hackers are only citizen subjects of liberal democracies. Coleman notes this by emphasizing that there are genres of hacking and that hackers embody enormous political, regional, national, and cultural differences. She notes, for example, that southern European hackers are more overtly political (leftist and anarchist) than their northern counterparts. Similarly, while Chinese hackers are nationalistic, Americans tend to be anti-authoritarian.

Still, we need to recognize that the effects of digital acts performed by hackers, not who they supposedly are, is what distinguishes them from programmers.

What are the effects of digital acts of hacking? What conventions do these acts break? What conventions do these acts resignify? They are as broad as there are types of hackers. Take, for example, the difference between 'white hats' and 'black hats'. This difference pertains to whether acts of hacking use legal or illegal actions. It can also refer to the extent to which its collaborative conventions remain transparent. Those who mainly operate in the information security field are often called 'infosec' hackers. Yet another group called 'antisec' hackers are against just about all security measures on the Internet and aim to dismantle them. Among these groups various actions, such as deliberately releasing security vulnerabilities, are debated passionately. We want to consider these combined and diffuse effects of acts of hacking in terms of actions against closings such as filtering, tracking, and normalizing. These actions that feed the imaginary force of acts of hacking perhaps explain the joy of the deep hack mode that Coleman documents. Yet a generalized conclusion cannot be reached since hackers can create dangerous effects that also participate in closings of the Internet.[48]

These actions are becoming intensified around the question of encryption, which is not simply a technology of being able to keep digital information secret but also one of being able to communicate without incrimination and with privacy, confidentially, and, if one chooses, anonymously. The battle over encryption is the link between hacking and hacktivism. Many readers will be already familiar with BitTorrent, Tor, and cypher (an algorithm for encrypting and decrypting digital data): technologies that enable people on the Internet to perform various actions, from communicating to downloading, privately and anonymously.[49] Although these can be used for actions such as 'illegal' downloading through Pirate Bay, these technologies have also facilitated WikiLeaks and dissident communication throughout the world.[50] Through these technologies, many activists are able to circumvent authorities and their filtering and tracking. When Iran or Turkey blocks communication platforms, for example, hacktivists are able to bypass such blocks through these technologies. These technologies of evasion have profound implications for privacy, anonymity, and access to the Internet. It would not be an exaggeration to say that the main battlefield of cyberspace is these technologies of evasion.[51] A fascinating example of a new convention is DissidentX, which is being developed by the creator of BitTorrent, Bram Cohen, and being watched carefully or anxiously, depending on who is watching.[52] This algorithm offers the ability to conceal a message inside another message. The point of communication is to conceal that there is a communication by including in it various messages that can also be red herrings. Sharing a sound file, for example, can involve sending a message. Apparently inspired by a pioneering algorithm by Julian Assange, the invention of this convention on the Internet can have major consequences.[53] For this reason, perhaps, Julian Assange argues that today's hackers are cypherpunks.[54]

At any rate, this brings us to the second group we mentioned earlier: hacktivists. The term is not an elegant one, and it has had a limited traction, probably for that reason. But it introduces a vital distinction in terms of understanding the effects of what hackers do in or by saying something and thus doing something with code. Jordan and Taylor captured this vital difference by designating hacktivists as rebels with a cause and yet posing this statement with a question mark to indicate that the effects are not straightforward to interpret. For example, they admit that although hacktivism arises from hackers, it is difficult to draw the line between the two: '[B]ecause hacktivism uses computer techniques borrowed from the pre-existing hacker community, it is difficult to identify definitively where hacking ends and hacktivism begins.'[55] They understand hacktivism as 'the emergence of popular political action, of the self-activity of groups of people, in cyberspace. It is a combination of grassroots political protest with computer hacking.'[56] Jordan and Taylor also provide a historical overview of dissent and civil disobedience as repertoires of politics, which we would call 'acts of digital citizens'. They discuss how, for example, electronic civil disobedience by Zapatistas, the Mexican dissident group, changed the terms of policies by engaging incipient Internet technologies in the 1990s to argue that Zapatismo—the convention combined of grassroots and electronic activism—was in many ways the birthplace of hacktivism as a disruptive convention.[57] Many forms of activism that followed in subsequent decades bear the marks of the convention that emerged during the Zapatista uprisings. One of its activists, for example, already suggested in 1998 that the state was intent on capturing the dissemination and exchange of information on the Internet, especially among activists: 'We must begin to invent other methods of Electronic Civil Disobedience. . . . The Zapatista Networks, in the spirit of Chiapas are developing methods of electronic disturbance as sites of invention and political action for peace. At this point in time it is difficult to know how much of a disturbance these acts of electronic civil disobedience specifically make. What we do know is that neoliberal power is extremely concerned by these acts.'[58]

The virtue of hacktivism is that it reminds us that activism on the Internet and the political cyberspace that it creates share a lineage with especially the social struggles against racism, misogyny, inequality, exploitation, xenophobia, homophobia, and other forms of oppression and injustice that defined the twentieth century. If indeed the nineteenth century was defined by the struggles between working classes and privileged classes of the bourgeoisie and aristocracy, a result of which was the expansion of modern citizenship to nonpropertied classes, we have witnessed these struggles of the twentieth century as the expansion of the meaning and function of citizenship rights.[59] If we say that we have inherited the figure of citizen as a subject *of* power, this was possible because of the activism of the working classes and their organizations in the nineteenth century. Similarly, we inherit from the twentieth century civil rights movements, women's movements, queer movements, environmental movements, and social justice movements. Seeing hacktivism connected with these movements and their extension to a new site of politics that hitherto did not exist has the advantage of maintaining a vital and crucial perspective on the effects of the acts of hacking. As Marianne Franklin reminds us with Donna Haraway, being able to differentiate between hacking for and without a cause is as important as ever for enacting political subjectivity.[60] So when we see Russian women taking on an oppressive regime with an act of singing (Pussy Riot) or Turkish women taking on a misogynist political establishment by performing massive Twitter laughter, these acts both resignify conventions and iterate a struggle that is already in our imaginary.

Hackers thus contribute to upholding the subversive image of being digital citizens, but by doing so they also painstakingly make rights claims through cyberspace as a commons. This leads us to the last exploration of acts in this chapter.

COMMONING

We mentioned above free software and open-source software developers and the hacker cultures that they come from. We also mentioned one of the significant accomplishments, Linux, an operating system developed by the contributions of thousands of developers. Another aspect of this development is its distribution, which has challenged the convention of copyright and the development of the idea of digital commons. It is worth briefly reflecting on copyright law as a modern invention to understand how the digital commons creates a direct challenge to copyright's hegemony. Copyright derives its legal force from laws that protect exclusive rights to and control of intellectual property. Even if its origins can be traced to early modern Europe (sixteenth to eighteenth centuries), it is modern in the sense that the formation of intellectual property—that is, the conversion of creative products such as words, data, images, and sound into property for exchange—is a result of the accumulation of capital in modern societies. This is what Lyotard highlighted as the commodification of knowledge in what he then called computerized societies. The conversion of intellectual or, more broadly, cultural capital into economic capital is possible under the protection of copyright laws. This is the force of copyright law. Since it introduces a tension between creativity and calculability, it is doubtful that copyright law either protects or encourages creativity. Instead, creativity is commodified by copyright. The performative force of copyright is that both the creator and consumer must—knowingly and unknowingly—repeat and iterate it. The force of copyright law would be nothing if it were not performed. That is the reason why maintaining its imaginary force requires enormous energy: copyright mobilizes massive efforts to maintain its legal, performative, and imaginary force. If creativity were not commodified, copyright would not exist. Commodification transforms the use value of things into exchange value for being sold and bought.

For many scholars, this snippet on copyright will be too simple.[61] They will argue that originally copyright laws did indeed favour creators and that it was for their protection. That intellectual property actually predates modern societies and that it is only very recently—perhaps with the rise of the digital economy—that copyright laws became (marginally) counterproductive and restrictive. All is well taken. After all, copyright law and intellectual property laws are among the most debated contemporary issues. Yet the digital commons—the rise of an international movement to create, contribute, share, and distribute digital objects—is a more fundamental challenge than a reaction to the more recent restrictions of copyright law. The challenge is against the relentless drive to convert knowledge into capital over the past two centuries.[62]

The Internet, however, disrupted more than the convention of copyright. As we discussed, acting through the Internet has raised political questions about anonymity, extensity, traceability, and velocity. The production and dissemination of digital words, data, images, and sound intensified these questions. Arguably, one action more than any other indicates how the legal, performative, and imaginary force of copyright has been severely disrupted: it is 'copying'. The digital has made copying an obsolete act. Instead, the digital always involves replication, remixing, mashing, and recombining of the original. That's why Walter Benjamin's celebrated reflections on art in the age of mechanical reproduction became a source of inspiration in the age of digital replication.[63] As Lawrence Lessig puts it starkly, '[E]very act on the Internet is a copy. Every act in a digital network produces a copy.'[64] This results in the creation of something called digital commons: a commons produced by the participation of creators and commoners.[65] The very principle that creates digital commons also creates tendencies against commodification: its very production entails creators contributing resources without the direct monetization of their contributions and commoners enjoying the benefits of these resources. Thus, digital commons constitutes a major challenge to the commodification of creative or immaterial labour, and this is why the battle over intellectual property law has become decisive.[66]

The alternative and challenging conventions against copyright law are many. Perhaps the two best known are copyleft, which concerns open-source software, and creative commons, which concerns broader creative production in digital commons. There is also a more recent convention, which is a digital or crypto-currency, especially Bitcoin. We briefly discuss all three conventions because they resignify conventions by which software, creativity, and money are respectively valued.

To start with, copyleft is significant since it arises from a particular political struggle around software production and dissemination on the Internet. In the 1980s, copyright laws quite dramatically changed in the United States and Europe. The gist of these changes was that intellectual property became much more exclusive and controlled with the extension of rights to their creators. From an original fourteen-year protection of intellectual property rights throughout the 1980s and 1990s, American law increased to fifty and then fifty plus seventy years, which in effect made it impossible for intellectual rights to pass into the public domain. At the same time, an increased concentration in media ownership meant that a huge proportion of intellectual production remained in the hands of a few conglomerates.[67] While much of the focus on the digital commons has focused on it as the cause of intellectual copyright problems, arguably it is the other way around: digital commons arose as a challenge to this concentration and usurpation of creative production. How rapidly this concentration happened over three decades and how the digital commons emerged as a challenge to this oligopolistic system is a significant aspect of understanding acts of commoning.

The first such act was performed by the invention of copyleft. It was 'a brilliant notion given that the accepted convention at the time was proprietary software code, and in most instances, licenses placed strict limitations on software users as to where the software could be installed.'[68] Instead, copyleft granted liberties to remix, reuse, and repurpose software but mandated that such liberties continue to be inherited by future versions of the software.[69] The inventor of the idea, software programmer Richard Stallman, argued that 'copyleft is a general method for making a program free software and requiring all modified and extended versions of the program to be free software as well.'[70] For Stallman, 'the simplest way to make a program free is to put it in the public domain, uncopyrighted. This allows people to share the program and their improvements, if they are so minded.' But the problem with this approach was that 'it also allows uncooperative people to convert the program into proprietary software. They can make changes, many or few, and distribute the result as a proprietary product. People who receive the program in that modified form do not have the freedom that the original author gave them; the middleman has stripped it away.'[71] So the problem that copyleft solved was how to provide free software but maintain its freedom. The idea of copyleft became the foundation of a general public licence known as GPL and spurred global free software and open-source software movements.[72] As Stallman puts it, the GPL's aim was 'to give all users the freedom to redistribute and change GPL software. If middlemen could strip off the freedom, we might have many users, but those users would not have freedom.' For Stallman, the core idea was that 'anyone who redistributes the software, with or without changes, must pass along the freedom to further copy and change it. Copyleft guarantees that every user has freedom.'[73] This licence was mobilized by hackers who eventually became the creators of successful operating systems such as Linux, especially the Debian version, which we mentioned earlier, and web server software such as Apache. It is not an exaggeration to say that the Internet, and especially the infrastructure of digital commons, is mostly run by open-source software such as WordPress, Wikimedia, Joomla, and Drupal, which are the results of the contributions of many programmers. Open-source software repositories such as GitLab, Savannah, Ourproject.org, and SourceForge, to give just a few examples, are a testimony to the resilience of the digital commons. It is no wonder, then, that it would be the subject of intense political economy analyses of its gift economy and also its ethics and aesthetics.[74]

The copyleft convention was taken in another direction by the founding of Creative Commons. Arguing that the debate (or battle) over copyright in the 1990s was being increasingly polarized into 'all rights reserved' versus 'no rights reserved' extremes, Lessig and his colleagues founded the Creative Commons convention in 2002 to enable digital creators to maintain certain rights for their intellectual labour while providing its dissemination and circulation.[75] While it has its critics (who argue that it reproduces the flaws of copyright laws), Creative Commons is an ingenious convention that ruptures (resignifies radically) a copyright convention and provides various actions by which a creator is able to specify rights that she wants to retain by visiting its site, making her choices, creating code and embedding it in her code, and thereby setting the terms of the distribution and circulation of her digital labour—and thus enacting herself as both a creator and commoner of the digital commons. Of course, being founded in the United States, Creative Commons was limited by being a representative and expression of an American approach to digital creativity. But it soon spread to other countries through the iCommons moniker and now constitutes an international movement for creative freedom.[76]

Another fascinating convention was invented in the digital commons in 2009. In that year, a person with the pseudonym Satoshi Nakamoto announced a new convention by which person-to-person payments could now eliminate the third party, such as a bank, from a transaction. Nakamoto called this convention Bitcoin. Although immediately defined as a 'digital currency', Bitcoin is different. Nakamoto also posted the details of this convention in a brilliant eight-page document.[77] Nakamoto defined his proposal as 'a system for electronic transactions without relying on trust.'[78] What Nakamoto meant is the absence of a third party. Clearly, for any digital transaction to be possible between two parties there has to be a third party which both parties trust and which underwrites the transaction. This usually means a financial institution. For Nakamoto, what was needed was 'a purely peer-to-peer version of electronic cash [that] would allow online payments to be sent directly from one party to another without going through a financial institution.'[79] How Nakamoto achieves this is beyond our comprehension, but the effects of this convention are radical. If there were a way to bypass existing financial institutions and achieve person-to-person payments, it would be a more radical invention than the invention of money. Bitcoin not only resignifies anonymity, extensity, traceability, and velocity of a digital act but also ruptures the existing monopoly over transactions held by financial institutions. The interesting aspect of the system is that it requires keeping all transactions on a public ledger since this is the only way to maintain proof of its work. Yet although all transactions are public, the parties in these transactions remain anonymous, represented only by public encryption keys.

The potential of this resignification of a convention can be found in the example of the WikiLeaks release of Iraq war documents in 2010, which lead to international financial institutions freezing its accounts and all donations to it.[80] This action was later interpreted as an instance of how international financial institutions can collude with national authorities to charge someone or something as guilty before/until proven innocent. Through a convention such as Bitcoin, not only WikiLeaks but other bodies can bypass such collusion. There is, of course, concern that not only legal but also illegal transactions of payments will happen through Bitcoin. As some scholars say, '[I]n the world of Bitcoin, there are goldbugs, hippies, anarchists, cyberpunks, cryptographers, payment systems experts, currency activists, commodity traders, and the curious.'[81] There is also concern about misuses of the system that will seek to defraud it. But its 'practical materialism', or what Nakamoto calls its 'unstructured simplicity', depends on more honest nodes in the system than dishonest ones.[82] We don't understand how this is achieved technically, but theoretically it is not an unreasonable assumption. But the real interest in this convention, whether it is Bitcoin or any other digital currency, is what, once again, it demonstrates: that in the digital commons there is an inexhaustible ingenuity, and people are willing to contribute to its expansion and maintenance as a public domain. To do so, they are resignifying conventions using open-source software, and with these conventions they are inviting others to transform cyberspace for digital citizens committed to the digital commons.

CLAIMS

Witnessing, hacking, and commoning are three digital acts that have become possible over the past few years and have created openings for being digital citizens in or by making rights claims. The resignification of existing or the introduction of new conventions made these acts possible: Bitcoin, copyleft, Creative Commons, Digg, GitHub, GNN, GNU, WikiLeaks, and many others. No doubt some of these conventions will be replaced or displaced by others. Some will become defunct. Some will perhaps persist as a testament to the digital commons. There will certainly be new conventions. What endures is the performative force that has gone into making these openings possible. If we understand cyberspace as a space of relations between and among bodies acting through the Internet, witnessing, hacking, and commoning resignify or invent conventions and make possible the emergence of new ways of being citizen subjects in cyberspace.

As we discussed earlier, just as many efforts are being expended on closings as these openings, cajoling and coercing them in various submissive ways and generally blocking possibilities. The digital commons is certainly a new frontier for struggles over commodification.[83] The main challenges to these creative forces emanate from state-security apparatuses and commercial-legal apparatuses. We have covered some of these closings, but here we want to restate the importance of open versus closed conventions of the Internet. Much has been said about Facebook, Flickr, Google, Tumblr, Twitter, and YouTube and their activities for tracking the conduct of people for advertising revenues and collecting big data. Let us emphasize that among one of the most important reasons that both state and corporate apparatuses are able to do this is because these are designed as proprietary and closed conventions. Unlike open conventions such as WordPress or Wikimedia, these conventions require submitting to end-user licences and user contracts that not only severely restrict actions but also appropriate their results as data. There is a massive difference between the digital commons created by open-source code and its increasing zoning, appropriation, sequestration, and enclosure through closed conventions.

We now conclude this book with a chapter focusing on making digital rights claims to draw out both our theoretical and empirical interventions. Let us remember that cyberspace is a fragile if not a precarious space. This makes its protection as an open-source digital commons a political question—a question that those who are making digital rights claims are enacting with increasing effectiveness but also with urgency.

NOTES

1. For accounts of the openings that the Internet has made possible, see E. G. Coleman, *Coding Freedom: The Ethics and Aesthetics of Hacking* (Princeton University Press, 2013); T. Jordan, *Cyberpower: The Culture and Politics of Cyberspace and the Internet* (Routledge, 1999).

2. S. Bowman and C. Willis, *We Media: How Audiences Are Shaping the Future of News and Information*, ed. J. D. Lasica (Media Center at the American Press Institute, 2003), 9. Scholars who take this as their starting point include M. G. Antony and R. J. Thomas, "'This Is Citizen Journalism at Its Finest': YouTube and the Public Sphere in the Oscar Grant Shooting Incident," *New Media & Society* 12, 8 (2010), 1284; and F. A. Kperogi, "Cooperation with the Corporation? CNN and the Hegemonic Cooptation of Citizen Journalism through iReport.Com," *New Media & Society* 13, 2 (2011): 317.

3. C. Atton, "Alternative and Citizen Journalism," in *The Handbook of Journalism Studies*, ed. K. Wahl-Jorgensen and T. Hanitzsch (Routledge, 2009), 265.

4. B. B. Blaagaard, "Situated, Embodied and Political Expressions of Citizen Journalism," *Journalism Studies* 14, 2 (2013).

5. Ibid., 194.

6. Ibid., 194–95.

7. Ibid., 196.

8. Atton, "Alternative and Citizen Journalism," 272.

9. Ibid.

10. M. Meadows, "Putting the Citizen Back into Journalism," *Journalism* 14, 1 (2013): 48.

11. L. Steiner and J. Roberts, "Philosophical Linkages between Public Journalism and Citizen Journalism," in *Media Perspectives for the 21st Century*, ed. S. Papathanassopoulos (Routledge, 2011), 192.

12. Ibid.

13. S. Costanza-Chock, "The Immigrant Rights Movement on the Net: Between 'Web 2.0' and *Comunicación* Popular," *American Quarterly* 60, 3 (2008); G. Mythen, "Reframing Risk? Citizen Journalism and the Transformation of News," *Journal of Risk Research* 13, 1 (2010); Antony and Thomas, "'This Is Citizen Journalism at Its Finest'";

L. Canter, "The Source, the Resource and the Collaborator: The Role of Citizen Journalism in Local UK Newspapers," *Journalism* 14, 8 (2013).

14. T. Gillespie, "The Politics of 'Platforms'," *New Media & Society* 12, 3 (2010).

15. We recognize that the distinction we are making here is not watertight. With open access and source content management platforms such as Joomla, Drupal, and WordPress, it is also possible to create proprietary and closed platforms. Nevertheless, the difference is significant between a blogger on a proprietary platform such as Twitter and an independent blogger who uses WordPress.

16. T. Kern and S. Nam, "The Making of a Social Movement: Citizen Journalism in South Korea," *Current Sociology* 57, 5 (2009).

17. M. P. Kovačič and K. Erjavec, "Mobi Journalism in Slovenia: Is This Really Citizen Journalism?," *Journalism Studies* 9, 6 (2008): 875.

18. M. Deuze et al., "Preparing for an Age of Participatory News," *Journalism Practice* 1, 3 (2007).

19. L. Goode, "Social News, Citizen Journalism and Democracy," *New Media & Society* 11, 8 (2009).

20. Ibid., 1302.

21. Kperogi, "Cooperation with the Corporation?"

22. Ibid., 321.

23. L. Palmer, "'iReporting' an Uprising: CNN and Citizen Journalism in Network Culture," *Television & New Media* 14, 5 (2013): 367.

24. Ibid., 370.

25. Deuze et al., "Preparing for an Age of Participatory News," 335.

26. Canter, "The Source, the Resource and the Collaborator," 1097–98; M. Gillespie, "BBC Arabic, Social Media and Citizen Production: An Experiment in Digital Democracy before the Arab Spring," *Theory, Culture & Society* 30, 4 (2013).

27. Canter, "The Source, the Resource and the Collaborator," 1093.

28. Goode, "Social News, Citizen Journalism and Democracy," 1291.

29. Ibid., 1290.

30. Ibid., 1291.

31. This is perhaps expected since media and journalism scholars write almost all the literature and seem to use the term 'citizen' as nothing more than a metaphor indicating either 'amateur' or ordinary. Their gaze is really focused on the threat that 'citizen' journalism poses to professional journalism as a genre of news production conducted by non-expert, non-elite, non-gatekeeper subjects. So the term seems to cover these aspects of citizen journalism rather than citizens making rights claims. Exceptions are those who, partially for this reason, reject the term altogether. We will discuss these exceptions later.

32. J. Assange, "Conspiracy as Governance," Archive.org, 3 December 2006 [accessed 7 August 2014], goo.gl/4l8lA.

33. Ibid.

34. S. Allan, *Citizen Witnessing: Revisioning Journalism in Times of Crisis* (Polity Press, 2013).

35. Ibid., 9.

36. J. Dawes, *That the World May Know: Bearing Witness to Atrocity* (Harvard University Press, 2007). We question, however, why such a strong call to bear witness should be restricted to witnessing only atrocities. Such bearing witness is often what calls people to question authority and the terms under which they have submitted to con-

ventions. Many aspects of whistle-blowing are also related to this call 'that the world may know'. It is ultimately the basic ethical aspect of being citizen subjects.

37. Goode, "Social News, Citizen Journalism and Democracy," 1290; Mythen, "Reframing Risk? Citizen Journalism and the Transformation of News," 50.

38. Costanza-Chock, "The Immigrant Rights Movement on the Net," 863.

39. Allan, *Citizen Witnessing*, 206.

40. The original and classic account still remains: S. Levy, *Hackers*, 25th anniversary ed. (O'Reilly, 2010). More recent accounts are Coleman, *Coding Freedom*; G. Coleman, "The Hacker Conference: A Ritual Condensation and Celebration of a Lifeworld," *Anthropological Quarterly* 83, 1 (2010), and R. Deibert, *Black Code: Inside the Battle for Cyberspace* (McClelland & Stewart, 2013).

41. Levy, *Hackers*.

42. T. Jordan and P. A. Taylor, *Hacktivism and Cyberwars: Rebels with a Cause?* (Routledge, 2004).

43. Ibid., 6–12.

44. Ibid., 13.

45. Coleman, *Coding Freedom*, chapter 4.

46. Ibid., chapter 5.

47. Ibid., introduction.

48. The documentary *We Are Legion: The Story of the Hacktivists* reminds us of two significant points. First, the transformation of a group of people called Anonymous from a group whose members were most interested in pranks and hacks to an international political movement supporting a wide range of political protests such as WikiLeaks, Arab revolutions, and Occupy movement was neither inevitable nor an accidental transformation. It indicates, among other things, that for the emergence of a social group with an identifiable political purposiveness, a whole lot of skills had to be developed and sharpened. If the conditions of possibility of Anonymous lay in the development of skills in 4chan and 4chan/b/, its members becoming political was certainly related to the censorship and surveillance to which they became subject. Then the emergence of accidental adversaries such as Scientology and Garry may well have accelerated such processes of becoming political. The upshot is that however objectionable or nihilist its early development may have been, its culture of dissension and irreverence are what made its subsequent politicization possible. Second, the moment when Anonymous made a call to protest against Scientology on the streets where Scientology centres are located and the large number of people responding to this call is the moment that demonstrates how cyberspace is a space of relations between and among bodies acting through the Internet. B. Knappenberger, *We Are Legion: The Story of the Hacktivists*, USA (2012), documentary, 93 min.

49. A good overview of these technologies is S. Davidoff and J. Ham, *Network Forensics: Tracking Hackers through Cyberspace* (Prentice Hall, 2012). Although it bills itself as a guide to tracking hackers, it is really an overview since those who want to track hackers will have begun their training elsewhere than in this book.

50. S. Devilette, ed., *Handbook for Bloggers and Cyber-Dissidents* (Reporters without Borders, 2005).

51. Deibert, *Black Code*.

52. A. Greenberg, "BitTorrent Creator's New Software DissidentX Hides Secrets in Plain Sight," *Forbes*, 15 January 2014 [accessed 26 July 2014], onforb.es/1gMc0wh. DissidentX is available at GitHub, github.com/bramcohen/DissidentX.

53. Ibid.

54. J. Assange et al., *Cypherpunks: Freedom and the Future of the Internet* (OR Books, 2012). See a much earlier manifesto: E. Hughes, *The Cypherpunk's Manifesto*, Activism.net, 9 March 1993 [accessed 10 July 2014], bit.ly/1psQizP.

55. Jordan and Taylor, *Hactivism*, 2.

56. Ibid., 1.

57. Ibid., 164.

58. R. Dominguez, "Digital Zapatismo," *Electronic Civil Disobedience*, 1998 [accessed 14 August 2014], bit.ly/1kE1UUk. Also quoted in Jordan and Taylor, *Hactivism*, 166.

59. A. McNevin, *Contesting Citizenship: Irregular Migrants and New Frontiers of the Political*; Rygiel, *Globalizing Citizenship* (Columbia University Press, 2011); A. Shachar, *The Birthright Lottery: Citizenship and Global Inequality* (Harvard University Press, 2009); J. Stevens, *States without Nations: Citizenship for Mortals* (Columbia University Press, 2009); B. S. Turner, "Citizenship Studies: A General Theory," *Citizenship Studies* 1, 1 (1997); B. S. Turner, "Outline of a Theory of Citizenship," *Sociology* 24 (1990).

60. M. I. Franklin, *Digital Dilemmas: Power, Resistance, and the Internet* (Oxford University Press, 2013), 202; D. J. Haraway, *Simians, Cyborgs and Women: The Reinvention of Nature* (Free Association, 1991).

61. See B. Atkinson and B. Fitzgerald, *A Short History of Copyright* (Springer, 2014); R. Deazley, *Rethinking Copyright: History, Theory, Language* (Edward Elgar, 2006).

62. We are able to make this claim thanks to the great contribution made by Lessig. Yet, at the same time, Lessig remarkably remains within contemporary intellectual property debates without seeing the broader (and more radical) challenge that the digital commons poses to the very idea of creativity. L. Lessig, *The Future of Ideas: The Fate of the Commons in a Connected World* (Random House, 2001); L. Lessig, *Free Culture: How Big Media Uses Technology and the Law to Lock Down Culture and Control Creativity* (Penguin, 2004).

63. W. Benjamin, "The Work of Art in the Age of Mechanical Reproduction," in *Illuminations*, ed. H. Arendt (Pimlico, 1999). The genius of this 1936 article by Walter Benjamin was to have observed the radical change mechanical reproduction brought to the dissemination of art. But for Benjamin, the radicality was not about dissemination; it was about the very nature of art.

64. L. Lessig, "The Creative Commons," *Montana Law Review* 65 (2004): 6.

65. A. Wittel, "Counter-Commodification: The Economy of Contribution in the Digital Commons," *Culture and Organization* 19, 4 (2013): 320.

66. The battle over intellectual property law is obviously beyond the scope of our argument, but we shall return to it in the last chapter to discuss making digital rights claims.

67. M. Garcelon, "An Information Commons? Creative Commons and Public Access to Cultural Creations," *New Media & Society* 11, 8 (2009): 1308.

68. C. M. Schweik and R. C. English, *Internet Success: A Study of Open-Source Software Commons* (MIT Press, 2012), 5.

69. Garcelon, "An Information Commons," 1314.

70. R. M. Stallman, *Free Software, Free Society: Selected Essays*, ed. J. Gay (GNU Press, 2002), 91.

71. Ibid.

72. General public licence (GPL) is also known as GNU or GNU/GPL licence. GNU is a computer operating system like Unix, but it is not Unix, hence the recursive acronym.

73. Stallman, *Free Software, Free Society: Selected Essays*, 91.

74. Fuchs provides an especially insightful account by discussing not only classic political economy but also gift economy. C. Fuchs, *Digital Labour and Karl Marx* (Routledge, 2014). Coleman has provided an insightful account of the aesthetic and ethics of the digital commons. Coleman, *Coding Freedom*.

75. Lessig, "The Creative Commons"; M. Kim, "The Creative Commons and Copyright Protection in the Digital Era: Uses of Creative Commons Licenses," *Journal of Computer-Mediated Communication* 13, 1 (2007).

76. Garcelon, "An Information Commons," 1317.

77. S. Nakamoto, "Bitcoin: A Peer-to-Peer Electronic Cash System," Bitcoin.org, 2009 [accessed 18 August 2014], bitcoin.org/bitcoin.pdf. Nakamoto's identity has been the subject of international speculation. The fact that its creator is anonymous makes it more interesting for retelling this story as the invention of a convention.

78. Ibid., 8.

79. Ibid., 1.

80. B. Maurer et al., "'When Perhaps the Real Problem Is Money Itself!': The Practical Materiality of Bitcoin," *Social Semiotics* 23, 2 (2013): 266.

81. Ibid., 262.

82. Ibid. The term 'practical materialism' to describe the workings of Bitcoin is from Maurer et al.

83. Wittel, "Counter-Commodification: The Economy of Contribution in the Digital Commons," 329.

SEVEN
Making Digital Rights Claims

Three rights—expression, access, and privacy—have emerged as the most often debated digital rights. To these, openness and innovation have recently been added. All together, these five rights have come to constitute digital rights in cyberspace.[1] Yet cyberspace is undoubtedly a complex space, which we defined as a space of relations between and among bodies acting through the Internet. It is even more complex for understanding the birth of the citizen subject in or by making digital rights claims. By focusing on digital acts that constitute cyberspace, we have reoriented the theorizing of cyberspace and its politics towards digital acts and making rights claims. Not surprisingly, then, much of our attention has been on exploring digital acts in relation to the constitutive forces that we designated as legal, performative, and imaginary. We have given an account of how callings summon subjects to act through the Internet, how these callings create openings *and* closings that configure cyberspace, and how these dynamics create citizen subjects in or by their making of rights claims. Although expressed as separate, these rights are undoubtedly related. The right to equal access to the Internet, for example, may appear a more fundamental right than freedom of speech since without access there can be no speech. But since cyberspace is a space of relations between and among bodies acting through the Internet, access can take different forms. Although the right to access the Internet evokes the image of a smooth cyberspace of flat hierarchies where everyone can enjoy that access without fetters, it turns out to be more complicated than that. The term 'equal access' stands as both a normative claim and want.

We have argued that such a smooth cyberspace probably never existed except in its imaginary force; rather, cyberspace has always been striated since it is neither separate nor an independent space from the power and knowledge relations that constitute it.

We could, of course, continue here and discuss these five digital rights and the tensions that arise from their advocacy.[2] We could, for example, discuss the tensions that arise between the right to own and use the big data generated in or by saying and doing things through the Internet and the right to create knowledge that contributes to a cyberspace commons. We could discuss the tensions that arise between claims such as the right to be forgotten versus calls for a collective memory and archive.[3] These tensions are undoubtedly intense and the object of debates (and political struggles) over the conventions and governance of the Internet. They are debates that are already well under way. But we now want to return to the question we alluded to in chapter 3: Who is the subject of these digital rights? Since we are interested in the processes through which these rights are enacted rather than their substance, our question of 'who' concerns that of political subjectivity through the Internet.[4] As we have expressed it in various ways, 'who' does not correspond to an already formed political subject but a figure: How is a political subject being constituted as a claimant of digital rights? We have illustrated throughout this book that digital acts traverse multiple national borders and legal orders. Yet making rights claims that traverse borders is often addressed through sovereign regional or national legal orders and their particular understanding of rights.

So the question of 'who' the subject is of digital rights is both an analytical but also an urgent political question that requires addressing. If we use 'citizen' as the subject of these rights, clearly it does not capture how both the enactment of the political subject and of cyberspace cut across national borders and legal orders. Today, the citizen functions as a member of a nation-state, and there are no corresponding rights and obligations beyond the nation-state that can govern subjects whose acts traverse international spaces. Yet if we use the 'human' to denote the subject of these rights, clearly this is a subject as yet without digital rights. To clarify this problem, we first turn to the 'digital rights movement'. If indeed it is possible to identify a social movement around digital rights, we want to see how the movement envisages and negotiates between the figure of the citizen and the human. We then turn to Jacques Rancière's thoughts concerning 'who is the subject of rights' and Jacques Derrida's thoughts on the performativity of declarations, bills, charters, and manifestos to think about digital rights. What we gather from Rancière and Derrida is the importance of refusing to make a choice between the citizen and the human as the subject of digital rights. Instead, we anticipate a new figure of a citizen yet to come as the subject of digital rights.

WHO IS THE SUBJECT OF DIGITAL RIGHTS?

What was described at the end of the twentieth century as 'electronic civil disobedience' was transformed into a veritable 'digital rights movement' in the first decade of the twenty-first century. Appealing to the concept of 'civil disobedience' has been a common trope since the beginnings of Internet activism. The Critical Art Ensemble (CAE), a collective of political art performers, produced arguably one of the most prescient statements about 'electronic civil disobedience'.[5] Their view on electronic civil disobedience was predicated on the decentralization of power in contemporary societies and the ineffectiveness of traditional civil disobedience.[6] For the collective, it was no longer effective to focus on streets and squares as the sites of civil disobedience since power was dispersed elsewhere through information networks. If there is to be disruption of this dispersed power of information networks, acts of disobedience, too, must be dispersed and seek power disruption in these networks. The dispersal of power was such that 'if mechanisms of control are challenged in one spatial location, they simply move to another location. As a result, CD [civil disobedience] groups are prevented from establishing a theater of operations by which they can actually disrupt a given institution.'[7] For the collective, 'nothing of value to the power elite can be found on the streets, nor does this class need control of the streets to efficiently run and maintain state institutions.'[8] The collective understood cyberspace as a separate and independent space from physical space and argued that the 'degree of access to the information located in cyberspace suggests how institutions are configured in real space.'[9] For this reason, 'blocking information access is the best means to disrupt any institution, whether it is military, corporate, or governmental. When such action is successfully carried out, all segments of the institution are damaged.'[10] Having settled the issue of how power was exercised in contemporary societies (dispersed, informational, and cybernetic), the pressing issue then was who was the subject of 'electronic civil disobedience': Who could be capable of disrupting this dispersed power? For CAE, the emerging culture of hackers was at once a promise and a problem for political activism. The promise was that hackers understood better than anybody else how and where power was dispersed. The problem was that most, if not all, of these hackers were American teenagers who 'work out of their parents' homes and college dormitories to breach corporate and governmental security systems. Their intentions are vague. Some seem to know that their actions are political in nature.'[11] It was concluded that 'the problem of letting children act as the avant-garde of activism is that they have not yet developed a critical sensibility that would guide them beyond their first political encounter. Ironically enough, they do have the intelligence to realize where political action must begin if it is to be effective — a realization that seems to have eluded leftist sophisticates.'[12]

Two decades later, CAE's view on 'electronic civil disobedience' seems both prescient and naïve.[13] It seems prescient in face of the emergence and transformation of hacktivist groups such as Anonymous, Demand Progress, and WikiLeaks, which have developed new political subjectivities. Also, it can hardly be said that such hacking remains the domain of 'teenagers', let alone American teenagers.[14] CAE's idea that a technocratic avant-garde may emerge as a political subject has also been borne out in some ways. Their idea of small cells of subjects of politics can also be said to anticipate the emergence of hacktivist groups,[15] composed of 'activist, theorist, artist, hacker, and even a lawyer . . . knowledge and practice should mix'. Yet it seems naïve at the same time for its rigid turn away from streets and squares as sites of dissent. Time and again, contemporary events have shown us the importance of streets and squares for enacting dissent, and even simply mentioning Tahrir Square, Taksim Square, Maidan Square, Occupy Wall Street, or Puerta del Sol immediately emphasizes this point without belabouring it. Moreover, as we have argued throughout this book, to imagine cyberspace as separate and independent from an ostensible physical space is both empirically questionable and theoretically indefensible. Nevertheless, the Critical Art Ensemble also ushered in a different way of conceiving performing politics and must be seen as a precursor to the subsequent development of digital political activists as subjects of a new politics of dissent.[16]

Today, using the term 'digital rights movement' to replace 'electronic civil disobedience' can be misleading. It may imply that all of the struggles of cyberspace concern copyright and downloading. Although the digital rights movement includes these struggles, today it is broadly conceived to include the rights to produce, disseminate, and share digital information.[17] If there is indeed a digital rights movement, it is itself dispersed, decentralized, and heterogeneous, involving many groups, tactics, visions, and demands. Although its activists are increasingly coalescing around specific claims, including privacy, anonymity, sharing, and access by engaging people through instituting and enacting changes, it also spawns contradictory imaginary and performative forces. We want to read the emergence and transformations of the digital rights movement from the perspective of digital acts as one of the necessary elements for making digital rights claims. Whether these acts cumulatively constitute a digital rights movement comparable to other social movements will concern scholars in the foreseeable future, and we cannot address that question here. Instead, we want to gather from disparate and dispersed digital acts the recognition of a dimly emerging figure as the subject of digital rights. It is the emergence of this specific political subjectivity around digital rights and the claims through which it has emerged—and the openings and closings it has instigated—that forms the central question of this book. Understood as both an individual and collective political subjectivity, it has been enacted over the past two decades. But as we have already intimated, to address this enactment is not as straightforward as it may seem. For that reason, we will step back to briefly consider the political subjects who have brought themselves into being with both performative and imaginary force.

Julian Assange, who began his active life as a hacker, became a conduit to some of the most significant revelations of state secrets in history through a platform called WikiLeaks. He is languishing in the Ecuadorian embassy in London.[18] Aaron Swartz began his active life as a hacker and transformed himself into a digital rights activist through various involvements and organizations and released a trove of academic articles into the public domain. In the face of an unrelenting force of the law, he ended his own life.[19] Edward Snowden, a security operative working for the FBI, released classified information about how state agencies are involved in massive surveillance and are spying on their own and other countries' citizens with impunity at a scale hitherto unknown. He is now a fugitive in Russia with an uncertain future.[20] Laura Poitras now lives in Berlin as a digital exile for making a film about Edward Snowden.[21]

Chelsea Manning is serving a jail sentence for leaking military secrets, revealing the impunity with which the wars in Iraq and Afghanistan have been conducted. Peter Sunde, who co-founded Pirate Bay for free culture, co-invented a digital payment system (Flattr), and created an end-to-end encrypted messaging system (Hemlis), served several months of a prison sentence for being a conduit in downloading copyrighted material.[22] Ilham Tohti, a former economics professor at Minzu University of China in Beijing, began a website in 2006, which was closed in 2008 by the Chinese government; he was sentenced to life imprisonment for inciting youth online with the aim of making domestic issues international.[23] We can add to this list of names those figures who continue to have force, such as Richard Stallman, who founded the free software movement; Jimmy Wales, who not only founded WikiPedia as a free encyclopaedia but has waged a resilient battle to keep it that way by organizing hundreds of thousands of contributors; Jacob Appelbaum, who continues to campaign for anonymous browsing for privacy and security with the Tor Project; and Phil Zimmerman, who made possible end-to-end encryption in email by fighting off the FBI's best efforts to stop his inventiveness.[24] That almost all these individuals are men says much about how the heroic figure of digital rights claims is gendered. But this list is a fraction of the countless and diverse Internet activists who through sheer inventiveness, creativity, and autonomy make digital rights claims in or by saying and doing something through the Internet. It is tempting to interpret them as the members of an emerging avant-garde technocracy. It is also tempting to interpret them as hacktivists. But when we interpret their digital acts through the Internet, they embody all the characteristics of citizen subjects: they enact citizenship as subjects of power with responsibility in ways that are instantly recognizable and yet cannot be bounded by their identity as military or security personnel. If the performative force of their code is louder than their words, the imaginary force of their words is not so weak, either.

These observations practically apply to all political subjects that the digital rights movement has spawned. Anonymous, a collective group that began its existence as hackers intent on pranks, quite rapidly transformed into a hacktivist group with political subjectivity.[25] Remarkably, the public image of hackers has an inverse relationship to their acts. When hackers were more intent on 'we do because we can' politics, their public image was mysterious, revered, and appreciated. Yet once hackers turned into hacktivists with political subjectivity, their public image suffered, and it became tainted with criminality. There is a lesson to be learned about how new political subjects encounter criminalization when both the performative and imaginary force of their acts come up against the force of law. Yet it is not only Anonymous or Lulzsec, its breakaway version, that the digital rights movement has produced as its collective subjects. The number of non-governmental and activist organizations dedicated to various digital rights, from anonymity to privacy and access, is staggering. They range from advocacy and lobbying organizations such as the Electronic Frontier Foundation and the Open Rights Group to activist groups such as Riseup.net and the Tactical Technology Collective. The large number of digital rights organizations—large and small—is probably already beyond the climax of ecological rights or animal rights movements and is as of yet to be collectively researched and interpreted.

Taken together, these individual and collective bodies begin to give a glimpse of the incipient political subject of digital rights. Can we say something general about the political subjects that spawn making digital rights claims? Our question here deliberately echoes a question Jacques Rancière asks about the rights of humans.[26] His critique of the difference between the rights of humans and the rights of citizens in French (and by extension in American and British) declarations of rights in the seventeenth and eighteenth centuries resonates with our concern here. Rancière's take on the figure of the citizen as we have inherited it echoes with ours, but we read Rancière through performativity. Rancière's take is that what makes the subjects of politics cannot be described independently of how those subjects perform themselves as subjects of politics, and politics itself should be defined through that performance. Rancière does not use our language of the legality, performativity, and imaginary aspects of political subjectivity, but the spirit, if not the letter, is similar.

Rancière proposes to resolve the so-called paradox of the subject of rights introduced by Hannah Arendt.[27] Rancière argues that Arendt is perplexed about human rights precisely because she understands them only in legal and not performative terms. The assumption that there can be no human rights without citizenship rights is a trap that neglects how rights can be brought into being performatively.[28] Arendt, Rancière says, assumes that 'either [human rights are] the rights of those who have no rights or the rights of those who [already] have rights [who are citizens].[29] Instead, Rancière proposes that 'the rights of [hu]man[s] are the rights of those who have not the rights that they have and have the rights that they have not.'[30] The proposition has two parts. The first is those rights that are enacted by subjects who are not included in what counts as subjects of these rights. The second concerns those rights enacted by subjects who are counted in what counts but who do not have the rights that they are supposed to have. In our words, we would describe the first as the imaginary force of rights and the second as the performative force of rights. First, when subjects are acting as political subjects, it is not even imagined or imaginable—given how a society is instituted—that they have a right to do so. Second, only when subjects perform themselves as political subjects do their acts become political. Politics, then, is about bringing both imaginary and performative forces into being. In our words, when citizen subjects claim 'I, we, or they have a right to', they are claiming both rights they don't have and rights that they have. Rancière explains this with women's rights. First, women demonstrate that they are denied the rights that they have by making reference to the declaration of rights. This is to say, if indeed rights are universal (as affirmed by declarations), then women (should) have a right to count themselves in those rights. Second, women can also enact rights that are already in the declaration naming them. So Rancière says that '[women] could act as subjects of the rights of [hu]man[s] in the precise sense that . . . they acted as subjects that did not have the rights that they had and had the rights that they had not.'[31] Rancière calls bringing these two aspects of rights together as dissensus. It is dissensus rather than consensus because politics is always a contestation over *who* is counted and *what* counts. For Rancière, a political subject involves the *capacity* for staging such scenes of dissensus. Thus, 'political subjects are not definite collectivities. They are surplus names, names that set out a question or a dispute about who is included in their count.'[32]

Conceiving the enactment of rights as dissensus is more powerful than understanding dissent as civil disobedience. For all its illustrative history, civil disobedience still evokes a reactionary politics, whereas dissensus is creative and affirmative. Although significant as a specific act, civil disobedience is rather too narrow to understand political acts in general. Staging dissensus brings into play the imaginary, performative, and legality of rights all at once and constitutes subjects as citizen subjects of power. Julian Assange, Edward Snowden, Anonymous, Aaron Swartz, and Open Rights are not *only* definite individuals or collectives of civil disobedience but stand for a political subjectivity enacting rights as the staging of dissensus. This is what we gather from their acts. When they enact rights that they do not have and the rights that they should have, they bring into being political subjects who cannot be known in advance. Their acts are contestations over *who* is counted as political and *what* counts as politics. To put it slightly differently, the performative and imaginary force of rights lies in the double movement between their inscription and enactment. For Rancière, 'these rights are theirs when they can do something with them to construct a dissensus against the denial of rights they suffer.'[33] And, perhaps more importantly, 'there are always people among them who do it.'[34] That there will always be an Aaron Swartz or a Julian Assange should not undervalue the courage summoned by Aaron Swartz or Julian Assange in staging the scenes of dissensus that they have enacted. Without the courage of their bodies, neither the force of their imaginary or performativity alone could stage dissensus against the force of law.

It is clear that the proliferation of making digital rights claims through the Internet has produced a multitude of acts in or by saying and doing something. We don't mean that these acts are intentional claims, but the acts themselves produce effects of making rights claims. So what brings these citizen subjects into being are the digital acts that they enact as dissensus. A parallel development to the emergence of these citizen subjects has been the proliferation of declarations, manifestos, bills, and charters that make specific claims to cyberspace. The aim of these declarations, bills, charters, and manifestos has been to constitute various 'universal' subjects of rights in or by saying something, and we next discuss a select few to interpret the subject of digital rights incipient in them.

BILLS, CHARTERS, DECLARATIONS, AND MANIFESTOS

We have witnessed numerous bills of rights, charters of demands, declarations of principles, and manifestos as callings on the Internet that it is about time we ask what they repeat, cite, iterate, and eventually resignify. It is really important to consider them as speech acts and ask what claims they bring into being in or by making declarations about rights. It is easy to dismiss these declarations that the Internet has occasioned, but they also beg examination. Some dismiss them for their ostensible ineffectiveness, but this is understood in terms of constative rather than performative effects. The question we'd rather ask is what, if any, imaginary and performative if not legal force do they have? We have earlier discussed John Parry Barlow's 'the declaration of independence of cyberspace'. Although it is perhaps the best-known declaration, it is astounding how many more declarations have been proclaimed. It is worth recalling that for Barlow, cyberspace was 'a world that is both everywhere and nowhere, but it is not where bodies live'; this may not have had much legal or even performative force, but it certainly had an imaginary force.[35] This declaration has been followed by numerous other declarations and various bills of rights that, taken together, provide a glimpse into how making digital rights claims has evolved over the past twenty years. Yet we have been unable to find a repository or catalogue of such bills, charters, declarations, and manifestos. The most prominent have been declarations on cyberspace, various hacker manifestos, numerous bills of rights, charters of rights, and supplements to the existing conventions of human rights.[36] Now, we don't want to imply that we will treat them as a homogenous group. On the contrary, each of these declarations belongs to particular speech situations: after all, a United Nations resolution is radically different from a hacker manifesto. However, the relation of ethics to politics in summoning a political subject—though it has not been expressed this way—has been an important element across all of these declarations. So we are going to mention a few almost arbitrarily, and then we will begin to differentiate them. With Derrida, we will then see how we can interpret their imaginary and performative force in summoning a political subject as yet without a name.

It is really difficult to know where to start, but Richard Stallman's manifesto for free software proved resilient in its imaginary force. What he considers as a 'golden rule' requires, in his words, 'that if I like a program I must share it with other people who like it.'[37] For Stallman, 'software sellers want to divide the users and conquer them, making each user agree not to share with others.' By contrast, Stallman 'refuse[s] to break solidarity with other users in this way. [He] cannot in good conscience sign a nondisclosure agreement or a software licence agreement.[38] That Stallman acts with conscience and declares solidarity with users is the imaginary force of this declaration and has retained its resilience remarkably well over the past twenty years.[39] One feels this force when Laura Poitras credits various free and open-source software for making possible her film on Edward Snowden, *Citizenfour*.[40]

One also feels this force in Edward Snowden's open letter to explain his act when he emphatically states that 'citizenship carries with it a duty to first police one's own government before seeking to correct others.'[41] Obviously, he is not speaking here as an American citizen as such. Yet the source of authority for enacting this citizen subject is ambiguous. When Snowden continues to declare that 'I understand that I will be made to suffer for my actions, and that the return of this information to the public marks my end. I will be satisfied if the federation of secret law, unequal pardon, and irresistible executive powers that rule the world that I love are revealed for even an instant.'[42] This is, then, roughly the ethical stance of that ambiguous citizen subject who speaks. Similarly, when Aaron Swartz states in his Guerrilla Open Access Manifesto that 'there is no justice in following unjust laws', one feels that he is moved by this imaginary force. For Swartz, 'all of this action [of sharing] goes on in the dark, hidden underground. It's called stealing or piracy, as if sharing a wealth of knowledge were the moral equivalent of plundering a ship and murdering its crew. . . . There is no justice in following unjust laws. It's time to come into the light and, in the grand tradition of civil disobedience, declare our opposition to this private theft of public culture.'[43] The United States legal authorities apparently used this manifesto to lay charges against him.[44]

It is noteworthy that these declarations have similar imaginary but very different performative force from those of collective declarations. A recent and powerful Declaration of Internet Freedom states, 'We stand for a free and open Internet.'[45] Its signatories include Aaron Swartz, Ai Weiwei, Amnesty International, Digital Sisters, Electronic Frontier Foundation, John Perry Barlow, openDemocracy, Tim Berners-Lee, and hundreds more signers. It declares five principles as digital rights: '**Expression**: Don't censor the Internet. **Access**: Promote universal access to fast and affordable networks. **Openness**: Keep the Internet an open network where everyone is free to connect, communicate, write, read, watch, speak, listen, learn, create and innovate. **Innovation**: Protect the freedom to innovate and create without permission. Don't block new technologies and don't punish innovators for their users' actions. **Privacy**: Protect privacy and defend everyone's ability to control how their data and devices are used.'[46] The declaration rejects singularizing itself and recognizes that it is a reiteration in the sense that '[w]e are not the first nor will we be the last to attempt to articulate basic principles to guide Internet policy and promote the rights of Internet users around the world. This Declaration of Internet Freedom is part of that ongoing global conversation, and we recognize and rely on these previous efforts.'[47] This sensibility is also a key to understanding how these declarations are cumulatively bringing a political subject, as yet unnamed, into being.

Does involving more than five hundred of the world's leading authors in signing an open letter that requests the passing of a bill of digital rights for the Internet have any performative force?[48] To whom is it addressed when the letter declares that 'WE DEMAND THE RIGHT for all people to determine, as democratic citizens, to what extent their personal data may be legally collected, stored and processed, and by whom; to obtain information on where their data is stored and how it is being used; to obtain the deletion of their data if it has been illegally collected and stored'?[49] When it calls on states and corporations to respect these rights and on the United Nations to acknowledge the importance of protecting these civil rights through an International Bill of Digital Rights, who is the democratic citizen it is summoning?

As we mentioned, these individual and collective declarations—of which we could give many more examples—are often dismissed for their lack of legal, if not performative, force. We believe that their imaginary force should not be so easy to dismiss. They not only create a cumulative force but also disseminate this force into other practices and acts. A case in point is the growing political struggle over governing the Internet pursued through international law and institutions. Often named as 'governing the Internet,' scholars have focused on sovereignty games, including those among states staking their claims to the Internet, the actions of international bodies, and negotiations over various protocols.[50] It is well worth considering the international digital rights regime that has been emerging, especially over the past decade and especially centred on the World Summit on the Information Society (WSIS) and the Internet Governance Forum (IGF), both organized by the United Nations.[51]

The United Nations World Summit on the Information Society (WSIS), held in December 2003 in Geneva, is widely recognized as a 'constitution for cyberspace.'[52] The importance of WSIS is that it draws its imaginary force from the Universal Declaration of Human Rights (1948) and institutes parallels between those rights and digital rights.[53] The organization of the summit and the declaration of its principles were the results of years of work. Its sixty-seven principles have more clauses than many constitutions include. It is an ambitious document, and its first principle affirms that

> We, the representatives of the peoples of the world, assembled in Geneva from 10–12 December 2003 for the first phase of the World Summit on the Information Society, declare our common desire and commitment to build a people-centred, inclusive and development-oriented Information Society, where everyone can create, access, utilize and share information and knowledge, enabling individuals, communities and peoples to achieve their full potential in promoting their sustainable development and improving their quality of life, premised on the purposes and principles of the Charter of the United Nations and respecting fully and upholding the Universal Declaration of Human Rights.

The most important principles that evince digital rights involved five rights: connectivity, access, capacity, security, governance, equity, and diversity.[54] The document does not specify digital rights as such, but importantly it recognizes that what was then called 'the information society' constitutes an international resource and that this calls for international responsibility. In subsequent initiatives and declarations, these five rights have become building blocks of claiming digital rights.

Although the WSIS declaration in 2003 in Geneva was a pivotal moment, the struggles leading up to and at the 2005 assembly in Tunis were transformative moments in the emergence of a new political subject of digital rights. As Marianne Franklin has documented, in Tunis WSIS began involving a much broader spectrum of civil society organizations where local activists presented alternative programs and dissenting declarations to those from the official proceedings.[55] This broader involvement was then reflected in the make-up of the Internet Governance Forum, which followed the 2005 Tunis meeting. The WSIS meetings in 2003 and 2005 as well as the constitution and meetings of the IGF, which followed, can be said to have eventually spurred the Charter of Human Rights and Principles for the Internet.[56] The charter builds on the WSIS Declaration of Principles of Geneva and the Tunis Agenda for the Information Society, which both articulated emerging digital rights. Like the WSIS declaration, the charter draws parallels with fundamental human rights that are enshrined in the Universal Declaration of Human Rights (UDHR).

The charter includes nineteen rights and one set of duties, which are important to outline.[57] The charter rights include right to access to the Internet (choice, inclusion, neutrality, equality); right to nondiscrimination in Internet access, use, and governance; right to liberty and security on the Internet (protection); right to development through the Internet (sustainability and development); freedom of expression and information on the Internet (freedom to protest, right to information, freedom from censorship, freedom from hate speech); freedom of religion and belief on the Internet; freedom of online assembly and association; right to privacy on the Internet (anonymity, freedom from surveillance, freedom from defamation); right to digital data protection (protection of personal data, use of personal data, obligations of data collectors); right to education on and about the Internet; right to culture and access to knowledge on the Internet; rights of children and the Internet; rights of people with disabilities and the Internet; right to work and the Internet; right to online participation in public affairs; rights to consumer protection on the Internet; right to health and social services on the Internet; right to legal remedy and fair trial for actions involving the Internet; and right to appropriate social and international order for the Internet (governance, multilingualism, pluralism). The duties and responsibilities include respect for the rights of others and the responsibilities of power holders.

The charter is clearly an ambitious and comprehensive claim to digital rights. It has the advantage of gathering together the experience of the past twenty years concerning not only the usage of the Internet but also how states and corporations have staked their claims to cyberspace. Much can be discussed about each of the claims to digital rights and the subjects that these claims call upon. The charter addresses itself to states and individuals as it argues that 'human rights govern the relationship between the State and the individual, so human rights obligations bind states.'[58] It claims that since the charter is based on human rights, its provisions would be binding on states. It recognizes that the charter does not and cannot address violations of rights claimed in the charter, but it cites the UN 'Protect, Respect and Remedy' framework as a mechanism to address those violations. We will shortly discuss the legal, performative, and imaginary force of the charter, but first, let us consider the following two charter initiatives.

The first is a joint academic initiative to develop a bill of rights for the Internet in 2007 advanced by Italian and Brazilian scholars.[59] This Internet Bill of Rights argued that it was not to be conceived as a transposition of the traditional logic of international conventions to the Internet. Instead, it argued, a bill of rights for the Internet must conceive of genuinely digital rights that are not covered by traditional conventions.[60] Recognizing that such a bill will not have the force of law, it argued that the Internet constitutes a world without borders and will require a new cultural model of making digital rights claims from the bottom up. Although this initiative was not developed further, an American scholar and blogger proposed a bill of rights for cyberspace based on this model, which is the second charter initiative.[61] Combining principles and rights, Jeff Jarvis proposed that any bill of rights should include, 'We have the right to connect. We have the right to speak. We have the right to speak in our languages. We have the right to assemble. We have the right to act. We have the right to control our data. We have the right to our own identity. What is public is a public good. The Internet shall be built and operated openly.'[62]

It is worth mentioning the Deauville Declaration proclaimed at the G8 meeting in Paris in 2011. Although criticized by civil society groups for not explicitly adopting a human rights perspective, the declaration nevertheless presents access to the Internet as a fundamental aspect of its commitment to freedom and democracy. The German minister of foreign affairs, in addressing freedoms in cyberspace, proposed that access to the Internet should be now considered a human right.[63]

Against the background of these developments—albeit related to them and perhaps spurred by them—the United Nations Human Rights Council has been gradually assuming an active (though limited) role in establishing digital rights as human rights. In 2009, the special rapporteur issued an important report raising concerns about privacy on the Internet and concluded that 'the Article 17 of the International Covenant on Civil and Political Rights is flexible enough to enable necessary, legitimate and proportionate restrictions to the right to privacy.'[64] In 2010, the Human Rights Council followed this up by documenting 'good practices' in protecting privacy.[65] In 2011, the UN report of the special rapporteur on the promotion and protection of the right to freedom of opinion and expression followed WSIS.[66] This report goes beyond privacy and argues for 'the right of all individuals to seek, receive, and impart information and ideas of all kinds through the Internet.'[67] The report emphasizes the unique and transformative nature of the Internet to enable individuals to exercise not only their rights to freedom of opinion and expression but also a range of other human rights. It reports on the applicability of international human rights norms and standards on the rights to freedom of opinion and expression on the Internet as a communication medium and sets out the exceptional circumstances under which the dissemination of certain types of information may be restricted. It highlights two aspects of access to the Internet: access to content and access to connectivity. It then reports how states are increasingly censoring information online through arbitrary blocking or filtering of content, criminalization of legitimate expression, imposition of intermediary liability, and disconnecting users from Internet access, including the basis of intellectual property rights law, cyberattacks, and inadequate protection of the right to privacy and data protection. This report was debated at the seventeenth session of the United Nations Human Rights Council in June 2011. On 5 July 2012, the UN Human Rights Council also adopted a resolution on the promotion, protection, and enjoyment of human rights on the Internet, affirming that human rights apply to both online and offline activities.[68] This unanimously adopted resolution to protect the free speech of individuals on the Internet is the first such UN resolution of its kind.[69] The Human Rights Council continued to be active and issued two further reports in 2013 and 2014 that lead to other resolutions in 2014. The first report investigated the impact of the surveillance of communications on the exercise of the human rights to privacy and to freedom of opinion and expression.[70] It identified an urgent need to revise national laws regulating surveillance practices in line with human rights standards. The second report practically enjoined Edward Snowden's revelations and investigated the impact of mass surveillance.[71] This came during the same year when the UN Human Rights Council adopted a resolution on 'the right to privacy in the digital age.'[72]

As these bills, charters, declarations, and manifestos gather momentum, the OpenNet Initiative (ONI), a joint project to monitor and report on Internet filtering and surveillance practices by nations that we discussed in chapter 5, has demonstrated that cyberspace is being increasingly closed. By deploying sophisticated filtering and blocking technologies, many states are both conducting surveillance of their citizens and determining their citizens' access to the Internet.[73] The sovereignty games of states are constantly reterritorializing cyberspace along state territories.[74] Some may see the openings and closings of the Internet as related developments, a sign of social and political struggles over its control. Others may dismiss these bills, charters, declarations, and manifestos for their lack of legal or even performative force. They may argue that regardless of such declarations, or even perhaps in the face of them, states and corporations continue to colonize cyberspace and play sovereignty games. They may argue that it is no longer just states such as China, which pioneered filtering and blocking (euphemistically called the Great Firewall), but also a huge range, including the United Kingdom, United States, and European states that are engaged in this battle for control. Moreover, this is not a struggle between states and their citizens but a struggle involving the collusion and complicity of especially American corporations in various roles as service providers or consultants for filtering, blocking, and censoring.[75]

These criticisms have considerable merits. It is true that any human digital rights-based declarations would suffer from the same criticisms as other human rights declarations, such as their lack of enforceability (perlocutionary force) and effectiveness (illocutionary force) to influence states. Moreover, human rights also suffer from a performative contradiction in that they end up reinforcing the very system of states that they seek to protect people from while often leaving corporations largely outside their purview.

We, of course, agree with these concerns. But our primary concern is a different one. The figure of the citizen, which is a fundamental figure for conceiving politics and rights in cyberspace, is practically absent from the digital rights discourse. The key question, 'Who is the subject of digital rights?' goes amiss. We have mentioned earlier that the bills, conventions, charters, and declarations claiming rights—with all the symbolic dates associated with them of 1689, 1776, 1789, 1835, 1945—are largely about enacting repeatedly the legality, performativity, and imaginary of rights as a contested field of social and political struggles whose both cause and effect are the figure of the citizen. Yet, ironically, this figure disappears from the charters claiming digital rights and instead is replaced by the human rights of 'individuals'. We think that this is radically reducing the imaginary force of these declarations to affirm and assert the figure of the citizen as both the subject and agent of these rights, not merely as a subject of nationality (nation-state), or a subject of humanity (human rights), or a bearer (or holder) of rights but as a historical subject that we inherit and who has a right to claim rights.[76]

Some may object to this by saying that 'we' inherit this as European or Euro-American subjects and that its universalism should be called into question. We have quoted in chapter 2 Mark Poster saying, 'Western concepts and political principles such as the rights of [hu]man[s] and the citizen, however progressive a role they played in history, may not provide an adequate basis of critique in our current, increasingly global condition.'[77] By advancing the figure of the citizen that we have inherited, aren't we risking using 'Western' concepts? This is, of course, a legitimate objection and requires a response. When we use 'we' as the subject who is inheriting the figure of the citizen subject, we have in mind a broader conception than a European or Euro-American conception. Although we give seemingly European and American events—1689, 1776, 1789, 1835, 1945—for its formation, it depends on how we understand those events that makes them belong to European or world histories. Clearly, it is beyond the task of this book to address that issue. Our argument here is that bills, charters, declarations, and manifestos ought to not only enact universal principles but also require regional enactments. There must be a reflexive sensitivity about differentiated experiences, and it should guide our understanding of digital citizens. One of the weaknesses, then, of the contemporary digital rights discourse is precisely in not articulating the subject of these rights as a citizen—albeit a different, if not alternative, one than that which we are accustomed to as a member of the nation-state. Where, or perhaps more importantly, how do we look for the figure of a citizen subject of cyberspace?

We are concerned that the divide between the enactment and inscription of digital rights remains dangerously open. Those whose attempt to inscribe rights in law work with the assumption that their enactment will follow their inscription. Those whose acts enact digital rights work with the conviction that their inscription will follow their enactment. With Rancière, we can say that their inscription is a prelude to their enactment while their enactment inspires their inscription. Those who are making digital rights claims *in* saying something (inscription) are on a separate but necessarily related path from those who are making digital rights claims *by* saying something (enactment). Let us consider more closely making rights claims in saying something and by saying something.

For this, Jacques Derrida's remarkably short piece on the Declaration of Independence is again very close to the spirit, if not the letter, of our interpretation.[78] It was Derrida who thought that such declarations as speech acts could be considered in their performative force for the effects that they create.[79] He thought that a declaration such as the Declaration of Independence cannot be read as a constative speech act describing the state of affairs of which it speaks but a performative act, which 'performs, it accomplishes, it does what it says it does; that at least would be its intentional structure.'[80] The question that concerns Derrida is 'Who is the actual signer of such acts?'[81] If indeed a declaration constitutes a claim 'I, we, they have a right to', by what right do these signatories constitute themselves as political subjects becomes the question. When a declaration such as this is claimed, one cannot know whether its performative force is able to produce the effect that it promises, that of instituting a political subject of rights. Even if it is done in the name of the people, a declaration has no way of guaranteeing that in fact its people exist or will exist as a fact. Rather, and this is Derrida's intervention, the act brings the people, its political subject, into being through the act. The people a declaration names do not exist. Derrida writes, '[People] do *not* exist as an entity, it does *not* exist, *before* this declaration, not as such. If it gives birth to itself, as free and independent subject, as possible signer, this can hold only in the act of the signature. The signature invents the signer.'[82] That the signature invents the signer can be easily misinterpreted to mean that before the signature, the signer does not exist; but for Derrida it means that 'there was no signer, by right, before the text of the Declaration which itself remains the producer and guarantor of its own signature.'[83] On the contrary, the signature gives itself a name, a name by which a people, a political subject, is named. The force of a declaration, its performative 'force makes right, founds right or the law, gives right, brings the law to the light of day, gives both birth and day to the law.'[84] By bringing into play a chain of events, delegation, representation, naming, signature, and citations, a declaration enacts a signature that restores, by right, to political subjects their subjectivity.

Derrida's take on declarations as performative acts teaches us two important lessons about the proliferation of declarations, bills, charters, and manifestos on the Internet and its subjects. First, it is undecidable whether an act is indeed capable of producing a subject that it names. For that reason, without guarantees, it must be done regardless of its actual effects, for the effects of citation and iteration are as much about bringing the political subject thus named into being as about making an attempt to remind ourselves that 'I, we, they have a right to' must be performed.

Second, without naming the political subject, without citing and iterating yet again that 'I, we, they have a right to', its eventual effect will not be accomplished, that is, bringing the force of law into being. With Rancière we can say that staging this dissensus brings together the two necessary aspects of a declaration as a performative act that bridges the gap between inscription and enactment. So although we said that bills, charters, declarations, and manifestos enact an imaginary force by which political subjects are named and claims made, we must now admit that indeed without the imaginary force of these bills, charters, declarations, and manifestos, there can be no performative or legal effects that bring its political subjects into being.

Our argument is that bills, charters, declarations, and manifestos would have stronger imaginary force if they also derived their performative force from everyday acts through the Internet: how people uptake positions as citizens of cyberspace, how they respond to callings to participate in cyberspace, how they create openings for constituting themselves differently, how they struggle for and against closings, and how they make digital rights claims in or by performing digital acts.[85] They would also have more performative if not legal force if they arose from not only a universal commitment but also regional commitments to understanding how the figure of the citizen is being articulated differently in cyberspace and how this figure is essential for bringing the force of law into being. The most significant space for thinking about the politics of the Internet and the political subject it has given rise to—the digital citizen— is the space between the inscription of rights and their enactment. Those who imagine the inscription of digital rights—privacy, access, protection—often assume that the fact of this inscription is also their guarantee. This may not be stated explicitly, but the discourse on inscribing digital rights as human rights in international human rights law often assumes that the force of such laws will guarantee that individuals, states, corporations, and other bodies will perform them. This assumption fails to recognize that how people experience being digital citizens and how they perform rights by bringing them into being through enacting themselves are the grounds on which rights will be guaranteed. How people experience performing rights is the key to understanding how they inhabit that space of rights and develop a political subjectivity necessary to making rights claims 'I, we, they have a right to'. Without such understanding and without developing concepts and methods appropriate to such an understanding, most efforts to inscribe rights, we are afraid, would remain inadequate, for these would be rights without political subjects. Conversely, the same can be said for those who assume that the enactment of rights, of imaginatively and performatively bringing rights into being, would guarantee their inscription. Without understanding the legality of claims and their scope or substance, such enactments would remain inadequate, too. Without the force of law, this would amount to subjects without political rights. It is that space between inscription and enactment that provides clues to understanding how digital citizens are emerging as political subjects of our era and those whose politics side with either inscription or enactment are somewhat missing the significance of that relation.

THE FIGURE OF A CITIZEN AS YET TO COME

There is then no reason to separate political subjects who make digital rights claims in or by acting through the Internet from those who make digital rights claims in and what they say through bills, charters, declarations, and manifestos. These are two moments of dissensus, and without each other, neither would be possible or practicable. As we have illustrated, if no people were acting by witnessing, hacking, and commoning, it would be well nigh impossible to articulate by what performative force they are making claims to 'I, we, they, have a right to'. Conversely, without declarations, bills, charters, and manifestos, it would be impossible to call upon the multitude of people to act in certain ways, give meaning and imaginary force to their actions, and enable the articulation of the figure of citizen as a subject of politics.

What is the force of law that guarantees, then, the imaginary and performative force of digital acts of making rights claims? There is also no reason to assume that the subject of rights is a citizen as we know it—a member of a nation-state. As Franklin says, '[S]tate actors such as the United States, China, United Kingdom, South Korea, or India, for instance, have markedly different ideas about who should control the Internet, however defined, and on whose terms web-based goods and services are to be made available to their citizens.'[86] Moreover, as Deibert has shown, states and corporations on grounds of security and profits are not exactly impeccable guarantors of rights.[87] Yet we would err to assume that the subject of digital rights is *only* a subject of nationality or human rights. What the emerging citizen subjects are bringing into being by enacting their rights through traversing state and national boundaries is precisely a figure of a citizen yet to come. We cannot decide in advance what figure of citizen they are bringing into being when the political subjects of cyberspace enact 'I, we, they have a right to' claims. To think that digital rights in cyberspace can be guaranteed and secured by inscription in charters, declarations, and manifestos of rights is to neglect that the daily enactment of rights is a necessary but not sufficient guarantee. Conversely, to think that the daily enactment of rights in cyberspace is the guarantee of freedom is to neglect that without inscription, enactment would not have its performative force. Being digital citizens requires staging scenes of dissensus by acting as subjects that do not have the rights that they do and have the rights that they should. The most effective guarantee of rights is both their inscription (citation, repetition, and iteration in declarations) and enactment (resignification through acts).

What the figure of the citizen—as we inherited and as yet to come—accomplishes is the bridging of these two forms of politics that has emerged in the enactment of cyberspace: those who enact themselves as political subjects and make digital rights claims in or by saying and doing something through the Internet (enactment) and those who make digital rights claims in or by what they say in bills, charters, declarations, and manifestos (inscription). Having distinguished themselves from hackers, hacktivists—those whose acts disrupt corporate, governmental, and military organizations—acting through the Internet continue to imagine themselves as enacting freedom, privacy, and anonymity. Similarly, having distinguished themselves from libertarians, advocates of human rights for the Internet imagine themselves to be entrenching rights for already-existing subjects. But rarely does the question appear: Where does the right to freedom come from? Where does the freedom to say 'I, we, they have a right to' come from? Can we found a politics on our supposed impulse for freedom by forgetting that this freedom has a history—or, better, multiple histories? Making rights claims in or by saying and doing 'I, we, they have a right to' is not founded in isolation or as if it sprang from nowhere: citizen subjects are often ordinary rather than heroic subjects who have struggled to articulate, claim, and make these rights through multiple and overlapping legal orders. The disappearance or absence of the figure of a citizen that we have inherited and who can make claims to 'I, we, they have a right to' is not simply a politics of tradition: it is also a politics of a citizen to come.

NOTES

1. Free Press, "Declaration of Internet Freedom," *Free Press Action Fund*, 2012 [accessed 24 September 2014], bit.ly/1u3msI7. We discuss various declarations below.

2. A veritable literature on jurisdictions of digital rights is now available. See H. Postigo, *The Digital Rights Movement: The Role of Technology in Subverting Digital Copyright* (MIT Press, 2012); R. F. Jørgensen, *Framing the Net: The Internet and Human Rights* (Edward Elgar, 2013); M. Godwin, *Cyber Rights: Defending Free Speech in the Digital Age*, 2nd ed. (MIT Press, 2003); M. Klang and A. Murray, eds., *Human Rights in the Digital Age* (GlassHouse, 2005); G. Ziccardi, *Resistance, Liberation Technology and Human Rights in the Digital Age* (Springer, 2013); B. D. Herman, *The Fight over Digital Rights: The Politics of Copyright and Technology* (Cambridge University Press, 2013).

3. R. K. Walker, "The Right to Be Forgotten," *Hastings Law Journal* 64, 1 (2012); A. Manteleyo, "The EU Proposal for a General Data Protection Regulation and the Roots of the 'Right to Be Forgotten'," *Computer Law & Security Review* 29, 3 (2013).

4. On the substance and scope of specific digital rights, see S. Trepte and L. Reinecke, eds., *Privacy Online* (Springer, 2011); D. C. Nunziato, *Virtual Freedom: Net Neutrality and Free Speech in the Internet Age* (Stanford University Press, 2009); W. van de Donk et al., eds., *Cyberprotest: New Media, Citizens and Social Movements* (Routledge, 2004); Walker, "The Right to Be Forgotten"; K. A. Belton, "From Cyberspace to Offline Communities: Indigenous Peoples and Global Connectivity," *Alternatives* 35, 3 (2010); E. Wilkinson, "'Extreme Pornography' and the Contested Spaces of Virtual Citizenship," *Social & Cultural Geography* 12, 5 (2011); V. Eubanks, *Digital Dead End: Fighting for Social Justice in the Information Age* (MIT Press, 2011).

5. N. Triscott, "Performative Science in an Age of Specialization: The Case of Critical Art Ensemble," in *Interfaces of Performance*, ed. M. Chatzichristodoulou et al. (Ashgate, 2009); T. Jordan and P. A. Taylor, *Hactivism and Cyberwars: Rebels with a Cause?* (Routledge, 2004), 69, 139; M. Wark, *A Hacker Manifesto* (Harvard University Press, 2004), 182.

6. Critical Art Ensemble, "Electronic Civil Disobedience," *Autonomedia*, 1996 [accessed 15 September 2014], bit.ly/ZgpMo2.

7. Ibid., 9.

8. Ibid., 11.

9. Ibid., 13.

10. Ibid.

11. Ibid., 15.

12. Ibid.

13. J. Hawkins, "When Taste Politics Meets Terror: The Critical Art Ensemble on Trial," in *Critical Digital Studies: A Reader*, ed. A. Kroker and M. Kroker (University of Toronto Press, 2013).

14. We earlier discussed briefly the transformation from hackers to hacktivists and the emergence of new political sensibilities, but it is appropriate here again to highlight Wark, *A Hacker Manifesto*; E. G. Coleman, *Coding Freedom: The Ethics and Aesthetics*

of Hacking (Princeton University Press, 2013); T. Terranova, *Network Culture: Politics for the Information Age* (Pluto, 2004); Jordan and Taylor, *Hactivism and Cyberwars*.

15. Critical Art Ensemble, "Electronic Civil Disobedience."

16. This may well be the reason that the FBI became interested in the group and monitored its activities, eventually arresting and charging one of its members in relation to an apparently separate event, though the coincidence was called into question. See Triscott, "Performative Science."

17. As Hector Postigo argues effectively, a 'digital rights movement' has not yet congealed in political discourse as a recognizable movement compared with, say, ecological rights or animal rights, which were once as fuzzy and unrecognized as digital rights today. As Postigo says, '[W]hat began in the United States as a debate over the acceptable limits of copyright in the digital age has morphed into a global debate about the acceptable limits of law in safeguarding cultural products for large corporations. Debates about net neutrality, copyright, digital rights management, and participatory audience practices are in essence debates about cultural ownership.' Postigo, *Digital Rights Movement*, 7.

18. A. Greenberg, *This Machine Kills Secrets: How Wikileakers, Cypherpunks and Hacktivists Aim to Free the World's Information* (Virgin, 2012).

19. C. Madar, "The Death of Aaron Swartz," *Nation* 296, 6 (2013).

20. G. Greenwald, *No Place to Hide: Edward Snowden, the NSA and the Surveillance State* (Penguin, 2014).

21. C. Cadwalladr, "Berlin's Digital Exiles: Where Tech Activists Go to Escape the NSA," *Guardian*, 10 November 2014 [accessed 10 November 2014], bit.ly/1zGc3Wv.

22. Ernesto, "Pirate Bay Founder Peter Sunde Released from Prison," TorrentFreak, 10 November 2014 [accessed 10 November 2014], bit.ly/1zGc4tM.

23. J. Kaiman, "Peaceful Advocate for Muslim Uighurs in China Sentenced to Life in Prison," *Guardian*, 23 September 2014 [accessed 23 September 2014], gu.com/p/4xnp4.

24. C. M. Kelty, *Two Bits: The Cultural Significance of Free Software* (Duke University Press, 2008); Godwin, *Cyber Rights*; Ziccardi, *Resistance, Liberation Technology*; K. Schmeh, *Cryptography and Public Key Infrastructure on the Internet* (Wiley, 2003).

25. G. Coleman, "Our Weirdness Is Free: The Logic of Anonymous—Online Army, Agents of Chaos, and Seeker of Justice," Triple Canopy, 2012 [accessed 13 September 2014], bit.ly/ZgpvkQ.

26. J. Rancière, "Who Is the Subject of the Rights of Man?," *South Atlantic Quarterly* 103, 2/3 (2004).

27. H. Arendt, *The Origins of Totalitarianism*, 2nd ed. (Harcourt, 1973), 290–302.

28. Bauman et al. argue that 'the 1950s approach to international human rights law was to claim that the instruments do no more than set out principles, they are not "real" law in any significant way and are certainly not available for people to rely upon. This political position has been undermined by the development of very precise international obligations, the establishment of Treaty Bodies with jurisdiction to receive and adjudicate on complaints by individuals regarding alleged breaches of their international human rights and the embrace of international human rights law by national courts.' Z. Bauman et al., "After Snowden: Rethinking the Impact of Surveillance," *International Political Sociology* 8, 2 (2014): 132.

29. Rancière, "Who Is the Subject of the Rights of Man?," 302.

30. Ibid.

31. Ibid., 304.

32. Ibid., 303.

33. Ibid., 305–6.

34. Ibid., 306.

35. J. P. Barlow, "A Declaration of the Independence of Cyberspace," Electronic Frontier Foundation [accessed 11 July 2014], bit.ly/1r41WqG.

36. M. I. Franklin, *Digital Dilemmas: Power, Resistance, and the Internet* (Oxford University Press, 2013). Franklin provides an ethnographic account of the coming into being of the Internet Rights and Principles Coalition and its charter.

37. R. M. Stallman, *Free Software, Free Society: Selected Essays*, ed. Joshua Gay (GNU Press, 2002), 34.

38. Ibid.

39. S. Williams, *Free as in Freedom: Richard Stallman's Crusade for Free Software* (O'Reilly, 2002); Kelty, *Two Bits*.

40. L. Poitras, *Citizenfour* (USA, 24 October 2014), documentary. At the end of her film, she credits specifically PGP, Tor, GNU, and other free software for enabling her privacy and anonymity.

41. Quoted in Greenwald, *No Place to Hide*.

42. Quoted in ibid.

43. A. Swartz, "Guerilla Open Access Manifesto," *Internet Archive*, July 2008 [accessed 23 September 2014], bit.ly/1uWgLvU.

44. D. Kravets, "Feds Used Aaron Swartz's Political Manifesto against Him," *Wired*, 22 February 2013 [accessed 23 September 2014], wrd.cm/1qqXgFk.

45. Free Press, "Declaration of Internet Freedom."

46. Ibid.

47. Ibid.

48. M. Taylor and N. Hopkins, "World's Leading Authors: State Surveillance of Personal Data Is Theft," *Guardian*, 10 December 2013 [accessed 24 September 2014], bit.ly/ZdcV5Q.

49. Writers against Mass Surveillance, "A Stand for Democracy in the Digital Age," Change.org, 2013 [accessed 24 September 2014], chn.ge/1r9rxyN.

50. L. DeNardis, "Hidden Levers of Internet Control," *Information, Communication & Society* 15 (2012): 720–21. Laura DeNardis calls this a hidden struggle over the infrastructure of the Internet. L. DeNardis, *Protocol Politics: The Globalization of Internet Governance* (MIT Press, 2009); L. DeNardis, *The Global War for Internet Governance* (Yale University Press, 2014).

51. Franklin, *Digital Dilemmas*, 103.

52. Ziccardi, *Resistance, Liberation Technology*, 134.

53. World Summit on the Information Society, *Declaration of Principles*, UN-ITU, 12 December 2003 [accessed 29 July 2014], bit.ly/1pA4Iy2.

54. Franklin, *Digital Dilemmas*, 165.

55. Ibid., 227.

56. Internet Rights & Principles Coalition (IRPC), *The Charter of Human Rights and Principles for the Internet* (United Nations Internet Governance Forum [IGF], 2014) [accessed 29 July 2014], bit.ly/ZgqdyC.

57. Ibid., 13–26.

58. Ibid., 2.

59. Ziccardi, *Resistance, Liberation Technology*, 152–54.; S. Rodotà, "Una Carta Dei Diritti Del Web," *Repubblica.it*, 27 November 2007 [accessed 29 July 2014], bit.ly/1xvNYwk.

60. Quoted in Ziccardi, *Resistance, Liberation Technology*, 153.

61. J. Jarvis, "A Bill of Rights in Cyberspace," @BuzzMachine, 27 March 2010 [accessed 29 July 2014], bzzm.ch/I92sZv; J. Jarvis, "Google Is Defending Citizens of the Net," *Guardian*, 29 March 2010 [accessed 29 July 2014], goo.gl/imgj2F.

62. Jarvis, "A Bill of Rights in Cyberspace."

63. Jørgensen, *Framing the Net*.

64. United Nations, *Report of the Special Rapporteur on the Promotion and Protection of Human Rights and Fundamental Freedoms While Countering Terrorism* (United Nations General Assembly, Human Rights Council A/HRC/13/37, 2009).

65. United Nations, *Report of the Special Rapporteur on the Promotion and Protection of Human Rights and Fundamental Freedoms While Countering Terrorism* (United Nations General Assembly, Human Rights Council A/HRC/14/46, 2010).

66. United Nations, *Report of the Special Rapporteur on the Promotion and Protection of the Right to Freedom of Opinion and Expression* (United Nations General Assembly, Human Rights Council A/HRC/17/27, 2011).

67. Ibid., 1–2.

68. United Nations, *The Promotion, Protection and Enjoyment of Human Rights on the Internet* (United Nations General Assembly, Human Rights Council A/HRC/20/L.13, 2012).

69. W. Zeldin, "First Resolution on Internet Free Speech," *Global Legal Monitor*, Law Library of Congress, 12 July 2012 [accessed 2 November 2014], 1.usa.gov/1zYMmlf.

70. United Nations, *Report of the Special Rapporteur on the Promotion and Protection of the Right to Freedom of Opinion and Expression* (United Nations General Assembly, Human Rights Council A/HRC/23/40, 2013).

71. United Nations, *Report of the Special Rapporteur on the Promotion and Protection of Human Rights and Fundamental Freedoms While Countering Terrorism* (United Nations General Assembly, A/69/397, 2014).

72. United Nations, *Resolution Adopted by the General Assembly on 18 December 2013: The Right to Privacy in the Digital Age* (United Nations General Assembly, Human Rights Council A/RES/68/167, 2014).

73. R. Deibert et al., eds., *Access Denied: The Practice and Policy of Global Internet Filtering* (MIT Press, 2008); R. Deibert et al., eds., *Access Controlled: The Shaping of Power, Rights, and Rule in Cyberspace* (MIT Press, 2010).

74. Bauman et al. argue that states such as Brazil and Germany, in the name of protecting the rights of their citizens, are effectively participating in what the authors call the 'thickening of their digital borders.' Bauman et al., "After Snowden," 130.

75. Ronald Deibert has made this point in *Black Code: Inside the Battle for Cyberspace* (McClelland & Stewart, 2013), 28. He argues that 'new companies have sprouted up to serve the growing pressure to "secure" cyberspace, a growth industry now worth tens of billions of dollars annually. Countries that censor the Internet have usually relied on products and services developed by Western manufacturers: Websense in Tunisia, Fortinet in Burma, SmartFilter in Saudi Arabia, Tunisia, Oman, and the United Arab Emirates.'

76. A. Kesby, *The Right to Have Rights: Citizenship, Humanity, and International Law* (Oxford University Press, 2012).

77. M. Poster, "Digital Networks and Citizenship," *Proceedings of Modern Language Association of America (PMLA)* 117, 1 (2002): 99.

78. J. Derrida, "Declarations of Independence," *New Political Science* (1986). See also J. Deville, "Sovereignty without Sovereignty: Derrida's Declarations of Indepen-

dence," *Law and Critique* 19, 2 (2008). Deville argues, however, that this short piece by Derrida should be read in the context of his other writing on legality and performativity, such as J. Derrida, "Force of Law: The 'Mystical Foundation of Authority'," in *Acts of Religion* (Routledge, 2002); J. Derrida, "Before the Law," in *Acts of Literature* (Routledge, 1992).

79. Derrida, "Declarations of Independence," 7.

80. Ibid., 8.

81. Ibid.

82. Ibid., 10.

83. Ibid.

84. Ibid., 10–11.

85. As Franklin argues, visionary declarations, case law, technical standards, and international treaties, while having best intentions, are typically removed from how 'ordinary people use the internet in their everyday life.' Franklin, *Digital Dilemmas*, 140.

86. Ibid., 142.

87. Deibert, *Black Code*; Deibert, "The Geopolitics of Internet Control." Also see Ziccardi, *Resistance, Liberation Technology*; Jørgensen, *Framing the Net*; Eubanks, *Digital Dead End.*

Bibliography

We have included shortened URLs in most cases since full versions become unwieldy. Also, with modern search engines, URLs have become much less significant to locate an online source, which can now be searched and found with the information we have provided even if a URL changes.

PRIMARY AND ONLINE REFERENCES

23andMe. *Find out What Your DNA Says about You and Your Family*. 23andMe, 2014 [accessed 13 November 2014]. www.23andme.com.

Acxiom UK. *UK Privacy Policy*. Acxiom UK, 2014 [accessed 13 November 2014]. bit.ly/1vvy8Cc.

Administrative Office of the U.S. Courts. *Public Access to Court Electronic Records*. PACER, 2014 [accessed 13 November 2014]www.pacer.gov/.

Alberge, Dalya. "Stephen Fry Backs Charter to Switch Mobiles Off before the Curtain Goes Up." *Guardian*, 2 August 2014 [accessed 5 August 2014]. bit.ly/1vm4KOp.

Assange, Julian. "Conspiracy as Governance." Archive.org, 3 December 2006 [accessed 7 August 2014]. goo.gl/4l8lA.

Barlow, John Perry. "A Declaration of the Independence of Cyberspace." Electronic Frontier Foundation, 8 February 1996 [accessed 11 July 2014]. bit.ly/1r41WqG.

Bertolucci, Jeff. "Big Data's New Buzzword: Datafication." *Information Week*, 25 February 2013 [accessed 20 August 2014]. ubm.io/XzSrn2.

Bicknell, David. "Labour Digital Policy Review Examines Continuous Innovation." *Kable*, 15 April 2014 [accessed 30 July 2014]. bit.ly/1kmmKaU.

Blakemore, Eve. "Microsoft Launches Digital Citizenship Resources." Microsoft, 8 September 2011 [accessed 26 September 2014]. wp.me/p4YHEz-lx.

Bowcott, Owen. "Bullied Man Uses Video from Sunglasses to Mount Private Court Case." *Guardian*, 7 October 2014 [accessed 12 October 2014]. bit.ly/ZVoTBF.

Bury, Liz. "Amazon Model Favours Yakkers and Braggers, Says Jonathan Franzen." *Guardian*, 13 September 2013 [accessed 1 August 2014]. bit.ly/1nSpL2x.

———. "Jonathan Franzen Falls Foul of Twitterati after Scorning Social Media." *Guardian*, 3 October 2013 [accessed 1 August 2014]. bit.ly/1nSrnsY.

Cadwalladr, Carole. "Berlin's Digital Exiles: Where Tech Activists Go to Escape the NSA." *Guardian*, 10 November 2014 [accessed 10 November 2014]. bit.ly/1zGc3Wv.

Coleman, Gabriella. "Our Weirdness Is Free: The Logic of Anonymous—Online Army, Agents of Chaos, and Seeker of Justice." Triple Canopy, 2012 [accessed 13 September 2014]. bit.ly/ZgpvkQ.

Critical Art Ensemble. "Electronic Civil Disobedience." Autonomedia, 1996 [accessed 15 September 2014]. bit.ly/ZgpMo2.

Department of Business Innovation & Skills. "Providing Better Information and Protection for Consumers." gov.uk, 2014 [accessed 13 November 2014]. bit.ly/1trM6qB.

Digital Citizens Alliance. "Become a Digital Citizen: Get Involved in Making the Internet Safe." Digital Citizens Alliance, 2014 [accessed 26 September 2014]. bit.ly/1utQ7vz.

Dominguez, Ricardo. "Digital Zapatismo." Electronic Civil Disobedience, 1998 [accessed 14 August 2014]. bit.ly/1kE1UUk.

Dudman, Jane. "Francis Maude: Data Is 'the New Raw Material of the 21st Century'." *Guardian Professional*, 2012 [accessed 31 Oct 2014]. bit.ly/1yLMtfG.

Ernesto. "Pirate Bay Founder Peter Sunde Released from Prison." TorrentFreak, 10 November 2014 [accessed 10 November 2014]. bit.ly/1zGc4tM.

Feloni, Richard. "The NSA Is Using Google's Advertising Cookies to Track Its Targets." *Business Insider*, 11 December 2013 [accessed 22 August 2014]. read.bi/1s94Zuw.

Free Press. "Declaration of Internet Freedom." Free Press Action Fund, 2012 [accessed 24 September 2014]. bit.ly/1u3msI7.

Gibson, William. "Google's Earth." *New York Times*, 31 August 2010 [accessed 9 August 2014]. nyti.ms/1vm4CP7.

Google, Privacy & Terms. "How Google Uses Cookies." Google, 2014 [accessed 13 November 2014]. bit.ly/1sHDt73.

Greenberg, Andy. "BitTorrent Creator's New Software DissidentX Hides Secrets in Plain Sight." *Forbes*, 15 January 2014 [accessed 26 July 2014]. onforb.es/1gMc0wh.

Harding, Luke. *The Snowden Files: The Inside Story of the World's Most Wanted Man* (Vintage, 2014).

Harris, John. "The Year of the Networked Revolution." *Guardian*, 13 December 2011 [accessed 18 July 2014]. bit.ly/1p2lRTC.

Hern, Alex. "Sir Tim Berners-Lee Speaks out on Data Ownership." *Guardian*, 8 October, 2014 [accessed 8 October 2014]. bit.ly/1t2DEPR.

HM Government. "E-Petitions—Create and Sign Petitions Online." HM Government, 2014 [accessed 13 November 2014]. epetitions.direct.gov.uk/.

HM Government. "Identity Assurance: Delivering Trusted Transactions." HM Government, 14 May 2012 [accessed 26 December 2014]. bit.ly/1kmlrc2.

Hughes, Eric. *The Cypherpunk's Manifesto*. Activism.net, 9 March 1993 [accessed 10 July 2014]. bit.ly/1psQizP.

Internet Rights & Principles Coalition (IRPC). *The Charter of Human Rights and Principles for the Internet* (United Nations Internet Governance Forum, [IGF] 2014) [accessed 29 July 2014]. bit.ly/ZgqdyC.

Jarvis, Jeff. "A Bill of Rights in Cyberspace." @BuzzMachine, 27 March 2010 [accessed 29 July 2014]. bzzm.ch/I92sZv.

———. "Google Is Defending Citizens of the Net." *Guardian*, 29 March 2010 [accessed 29 July 2014]. goo.gl/imgj2F.

John Lewis PLC. 'What Are Cookies?' John Lewis [accessed 12 November 2014]. bit.ly/1sCIXQe.

Jurgenson, Nathan. "The IRL Fetish." *New Inquiry*, 28 June 2012 [accessed 8 August 2014]. bit.ly/N57s34.

Kaiman, Jonathan. "Peaceful Advocate for Muslim Uighurs in China Sentenced to Life in Prison." *Guardian*, 23 September 2014 [accessed 23 September 2014]. gu.com/p/4xnp4.

Kiss, Jemima. "Online Privacy: How Secure Are You?" *Guardian*, 2 December 2013 [accessed 30 July 2014]. bit.ly/1kmo11X.

Knappenberger, Brian. *We Are Legion: The Story of the Hacktivists*. USA (2012). Documentary, 93 mins.

Kravets, David. "Feds Used Aaron Swartz's Political Manifesto against Him." *Wired*, 22 February 2013 [accessed 23 September 2014]. wrd.cm/1qqXgFk.

Logicalis. *Realtime Generation: Rise of the Digital First Era*. Logicalis, 2013 [accessed 12 October 2014]. bit.ly/1qL2ToH.

Madrigal, Alexis C. "Deconstructing the Creepiness of the 'Girls Around Me' App— and What Facebook Could Do about It." *Atlantic*, 2 April 2012 [accessed 23 August 2014]. theatln.tc/1oiX9e4.

Mance, Henry. "Consumers More Wary of Sharing Data, Finds Poll." *Financial Times*, 1 December 2013 [accessed 15 July 2014]. on.ft.com/1oWDB2K.

Marwick, Alice E. "How Your Data Are Being Deeply Mined." *New York Review of Books*, 9 January 2014 [accessed 21 August 2014]. goo.gl/SPfukV.

Mayo, Ed, and Tom Steinberg. "The Power of Information: An Independent Review." Office of Public Sector Information, June 2007 [accessed 12 October 2014]. bit.ly/ZVoZct.

Meeks, Elijah. "Digital Literacy and Digital Citizenship." Stanford University, Digital Humanities Specialist, 2013 [accessed 13 November 2014]. stanford.io/1rRME7a.

Milner, Helen. "The Preventative Care Revolution Depends on Closing the Digital Divide." *Guardian Professional*, 1 November 2013 [accessed 17 July 2014]. bit.ly/1wzXWfx.

Morozov, Evgeny. "The Rise of Data and the Death of Politics." *Guardian*, 20 July 2014 [accessed 7 August 2014]. bit.ly/1rf3LiV.

Myfanwy. "What We Learned from ePetitions." mySociety, 4 August 2011 [accessed 23 August 2014]. bit.ly/1tDmq7B.

mySociety. "We Make Websites and Tools That Empower Citizens." mySociety, 2014 [accessed 13 November 2014]. mysociety.org.

Nakamoto, Satoshi. "Bitcoin: A Peer-to-Peer Electronic Cash System." Bitcoin.org, 2009 [accessed 18 August 2014]. bitcoin.org/bitcoin.pdf.

Neale, Mark. *William Gibson: No Maps for These Territories*. Canada (2000). Documentary, 89 mins.

Onwurah, Chi. "Labour's Digital Review: The Emerging Themes." *Kable*, 30 June 2014 [accessed 17 July 2014]. bit.ly/1tUVWlX.

PatientsLikeMe. *Live Better, Together!* PatientsLikeMe, 2014 [accessed 13 November 2014]. www.patientslikeme.com.

Poitras, Laura. *Citizenfour*. USA (2014). Documentary, 114 min.

Preston, Alex. "The Death of Privacy." *Observer*, 3 August 2014 [accessed 7 August 2014]. bit.ly/1pdlWFs.

PricewaterhouseCoopers. "The Five Behaviors That Accelerate Value from Digital Investments: 6th Annual Digital IQ Survey." PwC, March 2014 [accessed 4 August 2014]. pwc.to/119uVyX.

reddit inc. *Frequently Asked Questions*. reddit, 2014 [accessed 13 November 2014]. www.reddit.com/wiki/faq.

Ribble, Mike. *Digital Citizenship: Using Technology Appropriately.* 2014 [accessed 13 November 2014]. digitalcitizenship.net.

Robinson, James. "E-Petitions Website Shelved." *Guardian,* 22 November 2010 [accessed 23 August 2014]. bit.ly/1tDjDLu.

Rodotà, Stefano. "Una Carta Dei Diritti Del Web." Repubblica.it, 27 November 2007 [accessed 29 July 2014]. bit.ly/1xvNYwk.

San Antonio Independent School District. *Creating Responsible Digital Citizens.* SAISD, 2014 [accessed 13 November 2014]. bit.ly/1k6SzUO.

Schneier, Bruce. "NSA Surveillance: A Guide to Staying Secure." *Guardian,* 6 September 2013 [accessed 30 July 2014]. bit.ly/1qKAZZY.

Shubber, Kadhim. "29 Ways to Take Control of Your Social Media." *Guardian,* 2014 [accessed 31 July 2014]. bit.ly/1s5Z0sq.

Steel, Emily. "Acxiom to Create 'Master Profiles' Tying Offline and Online Data." *Financial Times,* 23 September 2013 [accessed 21 August 2014]. on.ft.com/1ljiz6N.

Stewart, Graeme. "The Data Security Threat Is Holding Back Digital Progress in the NHS." *Guardian,* 19 June 2014 [accessed 30 July 2014]. bit.ly/1qL0V7F.

Sulake Corporation. "Get Your Habbo Citizenship Now!" Habbo.com Customer Support, 2014 [accessed 13 November 2014]. bit.ly/1oQcIAN.

————. "Habbo Hotel—Where Else?" Sulake, 2012 [accessed 13 November 2014]. www.sulake.com/habbo/.

————. "Response to the Great Unmute and a New Era of 'Protected Democracy' for Habbo Hotel." Behind the Pixels (blog), 2012 [accessed 13 November 2014]. bit.ly/1vvpIe5.

Swartz, Aaron. "Guerilla Open Access Manifesto." Internet Archive. July 2008 [accessed 23 September 2014]. bit.ly/1uWgLvU.

Taylor, Matthew, and Nick Hopkins. "World's Leading Authors: State Surveillance of Personal Data Is Theft." *Guardian,* 10 December 2013 [accessed 24 September 2014]. bit.ly/ZdcV5Q.

UK Cabinet Office. "Government Digital Inclusion Strategy." Government Digital Service, 2014. bit.ly/1tUZ2GE.

UK Information Commissioner's Office. *Guidance on the Rules on Use of Cookies and Similar Technologies.* Information Commissioner's Office, May 2012 [accessed 22 August 2014]. bit.ly/1IcjAfM.

United Nations. *The Promotion, Protection and Enjoyment of Human Rights on the Internet* (United Nations General Assembly, Human Rights Council A/HRC/20/L.13, 2012). undocs.org/A/HRC/20/L.13.

————. *Report of the Special Rapporteur on the Promotion and Protection of Human Rights and Fundamental Freedoms While Countering Terrorism* (United Nations General Assembly A/69/397, 2014). undocs.org/A/69/397.

————. *Report of the Special Rapporteur on the Promotion and Protection of Human Rights and Fundamental Freedoms While Countering Terrorism* (United Nations General Assembly: Human Rights Council A/HRC/14/46, 2010). undocs.org/A/HRC/14/46.

————. *Report of the Special Rapporteur on the Promotion and Protection of Human Rights and Fundamental Freedoms While Countering Terrorism* (United Nations General Assembly, Human Rights Council A/HRC/13/37, 2009). undocs.org/A/HRC/13/37.

————. *Report of the Special Rapporteur on the Promotion and Protection of the Right to Freedom of Opinion and Expression* (United Nations General Assembly, Human Rights Council A/HRC/23/40, 2013). undocs.org/A/HRC/23/40.

———. *Report of the Special Rapporteur on the Promotion and Protection of the Right to Freedom of Opinion and Expression* (United Nations General Assembly, Human Rights Council A/HRC/17/27, 2011). undocs.org/A/HRC/17/27.

———. *Resolution Adopted by the General Assembly on 18 December 2013: The Right to Privacy in the Digital Age* (United Nations General Assembly, Human Rights Council A/RES/68/167, 2014). undocs.org/A/RES/68/167.

Venkataramanan, Madhumita. "The Data Industry Is Selling Your Life." *Wired*, November 2014, 98–105.

Walker, Peter. "Habbo Hotel: NSPCC Urges Government and Technology Industry to Act." *Guardian*, 14 June 2012 [accessed 23 August 2014]. bit.ly/1vvk2Rr.

Watts, Duncan. "Stop Complaining about the Facebook Study: It's a Golden Age for Research." *Guardian*, 7 July 2014 [accessed 31 July 2014]. bit.ly/1nWhefR.

Webstart Studios. *The Web Blocker*. 2014 [accessed 13 November 2014]. www.thewebblocker.com.

World Summit on the Information Society. *Declaration of Principles*. UN-ITU, 12 December 2003 [accessed 29 July 2014]. bit.ly/1pA4Iy2.

Writers against Mass Surveillance. "A Stand for Democracy in the Digital Age." Change.org, 2013 [accessed 24 September 2014]. chn.ge/1r9rxyN.

Yakowitz, Jane. "Tragedy of the Data Commons." *bePress*, February 2011 [accessed 11 July 2014]. bit.ly/1vvv1ud.

Zeldin, Wendy. "First Resolution on Internet Free Speech." *Global Legal Monitor*, Law Library of Congress, 12 July 2012 [accessed 2 November 2014]. 1.usa.gov/1zYMmlf.

REFERENCES

Allan, Stuart. *Citizen Witnessing: Revisioning Journalism in Times of Crisis* (Polity Press, 2013).

Allen, John. "Three Spaces of Power: Territory, Networks, Plus a Topological Twist in the Tale of Domination and Authority." *Journal of Power* 2 (2009): 197–212.

Amoore, Louise. "Security and the Claim to Privacy." *International Political Sociology* 8, 1 (2014): 108–12.

Andrejevic, Mark. "Social Network Exploitation." In *A Networked Self: Identity, Community and Culture on Social Network Sites*, ed. Zizi Papacharissi, 82–101 (Routledge, 2011).

Antony, May Grace, and Ryan J. Thomas. "'This Is Citizen Journalism at Its Finest': YouTube and the Public Sphere in the Oscar Grant Shooting Incident." *New Media & Society* 12, 8 (2010): 1280–96.

Archibugi, Daniele. *The Global Commonwealth of Citizens: Toward Cosmopolitan Democracy* (Princeton University Press, 2008).

Arendt, Hannah. *The Origins of Totalitarianism*. 2nd ed. (Harcourt, 1973).

Assange, Julian, Jacob Appelbaum, Andy Müller-Maguhn, and Jérémie Zimmermann. *Cypherpunks: Freedom and the Future of the Internet* (OR Books, 2012).

Atkinson, Benedict, and Brian Fitzgerald. *A Short History of Copyright* (Springer, 2014).

Atton, Chris. "Alternative and Citizen Journalism." In *The Handbook of Journalism Studies*, ed. Karin Wahl-Jorgensen and Thomas Hanitzsch, 265–78 (Routledge, 2009).

Austin, J. L. *How to Do Things with Words* (Oxford University Press, 1962).

Balibar, Etienne. "Citizen Subject." In *Who Comes after the Subject?*, ed. Eduardo Cadava, Peter Connor, and Jean-Luc Nancy, 33–57 (Routledge, 1991).

Bartlett, Jamie. *The Dark Net: Inside the Digital Underworld* (Heinemann, 2014).

Bauman, Z., D. Bigo, P. Esteves, E. Guild, V. Jabri, D. Lyon, and R. B. J. Walker. "After Snowden: Rethinking the Impact of Surveillance." *International Political Sociology* 8, 2 (2014): 121–44.

Beer, David, and Roger Burrows. "Popular Culture, Digital Archives and the New Social Life of Data." *Theory, Culture & Society* 30, 4 (2013): 47–71.

Bell, Vikki. *Culture and Performance: The Challenge of Ethics, Politics, and Feminist Theory* (Berg, 2007).

Belton, K. A. "From Cyberspace to Offline Communities: Indigenous Peoples and Global Connectivity." *Alternatives* 35, 3 (2010): 193–215.

Benjamin, Walter. "The Work of Art in the Age of Mechanical Reproduction," in *Illuminations*, ed. Hannah Arendt (Pimlico, 1999), 211–44.

Bigo, Didier. "The (in)Securitization Practices of the Three Universes of EU Border Control: Military/Navy—Border Guards/Police—Database Analysts." *Security Dialogue* 45, 3 (2014): 209–25.

———. "Security, Surveillance and Democracy." In *Routledge Handbook of Surveillance Studies*, ed. Kirstie Ball, Kevin D. Haggerty, and David Lyon, 277–84 (Routledge, 2012).

———. "The Transnational Field of Computerised Exchange of Information in Police Matters and Its European Guilds." In *Transnational Power Elites: The Social and Global Structuration of the EU*, ed. Niilo Kauppi and Mikael Rask Madsen, 155–82 (Routledge, 2013).

Blaagaard, Bolette B. "Situated, Embodied and Political Expressions of Citizen Journalism." *Journalism Studies* 14, 2 (2013): 187–200.

Bourdieu, Pierre. *Distinction: A Social Critique of the Judgement of Taste* (Harvard University Press, 1987).

———. *Language and Symbolic Power* (Harvard University Press, 1993).

Bowman, Shayne, and Chris Willis. *We Media: How Audiences Are Shaping the Future of News and Information*, ed. J. D. Lasica (Media Center at the American Press Institute, 2003).

boyd, danah. *It's Complicated: The Social Lives of Networked Teens* (Yale University Press, 2014).

Braidotti, Rosi. *Nomadic Subjects: Embodiment and Sexual Difference in Contemporary Feminist Theory*. 2nd ed. (Columbia University Press, 2011).

Braudel, Fernand. *On History*, trans. Sarah Matthews (University of Chicago Press, 1980).

Buckingham, D., and C. Rodriguez. "Learning about Power and Citizenship in an Online Virtual World." *Comunicar*, 40 (2013): 49–57.

Bulmer, Martin, and Anthony M. Rees, eds. *Citizenship Today: The Contemporary Relevance of T. H. Marshall* (UCL Press, 1996).

Butler, Judith. *Subjects of Desire: Hegelian Reflections in Twentieth-Century France* (Columbia University Press, 1999).

———. *Bodies That Matter: On the Discursive Limits of "Sex"* (Routledge, 1993).

———. *Excitable Speech: A Politics of the Performative* (Routledge, 1997).

———. *Gender Trouble: Feminism and the Subversion of Identity* (Routledge, 1990).

———. *Undoing Gender* (Routledge, 2004).

Campanelli, Vito. "Frictionless Sharing: The Rise of Automatic Criticism." In *Society of the Query Reader: Reflections on Web Search*, ed. René König and Miriam Rasch (Institute of Network Cultures, 2014): 41–48.

Canter, Lily. "The Source, the Resource and the Collaborator: The Role of Citizen Journalism in Local UK Newspapers." *Journalism* 14, 8 (2013): 1091–1109.

Castoriadis, Cornelius. *The Imaginary Institution of Society*, trans. Kathleen Blamey (Polity, 1987).

———. *World in Fragments: Writings on Politics, Society, Psychoanalysis and the Imagination*, ed. D. A. Curtis (Stanford University Press, 1997).

Cavell, Stanley. *Must We Mean What We Say? A Book of Essays*. 2nd ed. (Cambridge University Press, 2002).

———. *Philosophical Passages: Wittgenstein, Emerson, Austin, Derrida* (Blackwell, 1995).

———. *A Pitch of Philosophy: Autobiographical Exercises* (Harvard University Press, 1994).

Chadwick, Andrew, and Philip N. Howard, eds. *Routledge Handbook of Internet Politics* (Routledge, 2009).

Clarke, John, Kathleen M. Coll, Evelina Dagnino, and Catherine Neveu. *Disputing Citizenship* (Policy Press, 2014).

Cohen, Julie E. *Configuring the Networked Self: Law, Code, and the Play of Everyday Practice* (Yale University Press, 2012).

———. "Cyberspace as/and Space." *Columbia Law Review* 107, 1 (2007): 210–56.

Coleman, E. Gabriella. *Coding Freedom: The Ethics and Aesthetics of Hacking* (Princeton University Press, 2013).

———. "The Hacker Conference: A Ritual Condensation and Celebration of a Lifeworld." *Anthropological Quarterly* 83, 1 (2010): 47–72.

Coleman, Stephen. "The Lonely Citizen: Indirect Representation in an Age of Networks." *Political Communication* 22, 2 (2005): 197–214.

Coleman, Stephen, and Jay G. Blumler. *The Internet and Democratic Citizenship: Theory, Practice and Policy* (Cambridge University Press, 2009).

Collinge, Chris. "The *Différance* between Society and Space: Nested Scales and the Returns of Spatial Fetishism." *Environment and Planning D: Society and Space* 23 (2005): 189–206.

———. "Flat Ontology and the Deconstruction of Scale: A Response to Marston, Jones and Woodward." *Transactions of the Institute of British Geographers* 31 (2006): 244–51.

Costanza-Chock, Sasha. "The Immigrant Rights Movement on the Net: Between 'Web 2.0' and *Comunicación* Popular." *American Quarterly* 60, 3 (2008): 851–64.

Couldry, Nick, Hilde Stephansen, Aristea Fotopoulou, Richard MacDonald, Wilma Clark, and Luke Dickens. "Digital Citizenship? Narrative Exchange and the Changing Terms of Civic Culture." *Citizenship Studies* 18, 6–7 (2014): 615–29.

Curran, James, Natalie Fenton, and Des Freedman, eds. *Misunderstanding the Internet* (Routledge, 2012).

Davidoff, Sherri, and Jonathan Ham. *Network Forensics: Tracking Hackers through Cyberspace* (Prentice Hall, 2012).

Dawes, James. *That the World May Know: Bearing Witness to Atrocity* (Harvard University Press, 2007).

Deazley, Ronan. *Rethinking Copyright: History, Theory, Language* (Edward Elgar, 2006).

Deibert, Ronald. *Black Code: Inside the Battle for Cyberspace* (McClelland & Stewart, 2013).

———. "The Geopolitics of Internet Control: Censorship, Sovereignty, and Cyberspace." In *Routledge Handbook of Internet Politics*, ed. Andrew Chadwick and Philip N. Howard, 323–36 (Routledge, 2009).

Deibert, Ronald, John Palfrey, Rafal Rohozinski, and Jonathan Zittrain, eds. *Access Controlled: The Shaping of Power, Rights, and Rule in Cyberspace* (MIT Press, 2010).
———. *Access Denied: The Practice and Policy of Global Internet Filtering* (MIT Press, 2008).
Deibert, Ronald, and Rafal Rohozinski. "Beyond Denial: Introducing Next-Generation Information Access Controls." In *Access Controlled: The Shaping of Power, Rights, and Rule in Cyberspace*, ed. Ronald Deibert, John Palfrey, Rafal Rohozinski, and Jonathan Zittrain, 3–13 (MIT Press, 2010).
Deleuze, Gilles. "Control and Becoming." In *Negotiations*, 169–76 (Columbia University Press, 1990).
———. *Difference and Repetition* (Columbia University Press, 1995).
———. *Foucault* (University of Minnesota Press, 1986).
———. *The Logic of Sense* (Columbia University Press, 1993).
———. "Postscript on Control Societies." In *Negotiations*, 177–82 (Columbia University Press, 1990).
Deleuze, Gilles, and Félix Guattari. *A Thousand Plateaus* (University of Minnesota Press, 1980).
DeNardis, Laura. *The Global War for Internet Governance* (Yale University Press, 2014).
———. "Hidden Levers of Internet Control." *Information, Communication & Society* 15 (2012): 720–38.
———. *Protocol Politics: The Globalization of Internet Governance* (MIT Press, 2009).
Derrida, Jacques. "Before the Law." In *Acts of Literature*, 181–220 (Routledge, 1992).
———. "Declarations of Independence." *New Political Science* (1986): 7–15.
———. "Force of Law: The 'Mystical Foundation of Authority'." In *Acts of Religion*, 1:230–58, 2:259–98 (Routledge, 2002).
———. *Limited Inc.* Trans. G. Graff (Northwestern University Press, 1988).
———. *Without Alibi.* Ed. Peggy Kamuf (Stanford University Press, 2002).
Deuze, Mark, Axel Bruns, and Christoph Neuberger. "Preparing for an Age of Participatory News." *Journalism Practice* 1, 3 (2007): 322–38.
Devilette, Sylvie, ed. *Handbook for Bloggers and Cyber-Dissidents* (Reporters without Borders, 2005).
Deville, Jacques. "Sovereignty without Sovereignty: Derrida's Declarations of Independence." *Law and Critique* 19, 2 (2008): 87–114.
Dodge, M., and R. Kitchin. *Mapping Cyberspace* (Routledge, 2001).
Dutton, William H. "Internet Studies: The Foundations of a Transformative Field." In *The Oxford Handbook of Internet Studies*, ed. William H. Dutton, 1–23 (Oxford University Press, 2013).
Dutton, William H., and Elizabeth Dubois, eds. *Politics and the Internet.* 4 vols. (Routledge, 2014).
Erel, Umut. *Migrant Women Transforming Citizenship* (Ashgate, 2009).
Ess, Charles, and Mia Consalvo. "Introduction: What Is 'Internet Studies'?" In *The Handbook of Internet Studies*, ed. Mia Consalvo and Charles Ess, 1–8 (Wiley-Blackwell, 2013).
Eubanks, Virginia. *Digital Dead End: Fighting for Social Justice in the Information Age* (MIT Press, 2011).
Felman, Shoshana. *The Scandal of the Speaking Body: Don Juan with J. L. Austin, or Seduction in Two Languages* (Stanford University Press, 2003).

Ford, Richard. "Against Cyberspace." In *The Place of Law*, ed. Austin Sarat, Lawrence Douglas, and Martha Merrill Umphrey, 147–80 (University of Michigan Press, 2003).

Foucault, Michel. *Power/Knowledge*. Ed. C. Gordon (Harvester Wheatsheaf, 1980).

———. *Discipline and Punish: The Birth of the Prison* (Vintage, 1979).

———. *Ethics: Subjectivity and Truth*. Ed. P. Rabinow. Vol. 3, *Essential Works of Foucault, 1954–1984* (New Press, 1997).

———. *Security, Territory, Population*. Ed. Arnold Davidson. Trans. Graham Burchell. Lectures at the Collège de France, 1977–78 (Palgrave Macmillan, 2007).

Franklin, Marianne I. *Digital Dilemmas: Power, Resistance, and the Internet* (Oxford University Press, 2013).

Freedman, Des. "Web 2.0 and the Death of the Blockbuster Economy." In *Misunderstanding the Internet*, ed. James Curran, Natalie Fenton, and Des Freedman, 69–94 (Routledge, 2012).

Fuchs, Christian. *Digital Labour and Karl Marx* (Routledge, 2014).

———. *Internet and Society: Social Theory in the Information Age* (Routledge, 2008).

———. *Social Media: A Critical Introduction* (Sage, 2014).

Fuez, Martin, Matthew Fuller, and Felix Stalder. "Personal Web Searching in the Age of Semantic Capitalism: Diagnosing the Mechanisms of Personalisation." *First Monday* 16, 2 (2011).

Fuller, Matthew, and Andrew Goffey. *Evil Media* (MIT Press, 2012).

Galloway, Alexander R. *Protocol: How Control Exists after Decentralization* (MIT Press, 2006).

Garcelon, M. "An Information Commons? Creative Commons and Public Access to Cultural Creations." *New Media & Society* 11, 8 (2009): 1307–26.

Gerbaudo, Paolo. *Tweets and the Streets: Social Media and Contemporary Activism* (Pluto, 2012).

Gillespie, M. "BBC Arabic, Social Media and Citizen Production: An Experiment in Digital Democracy before the Arab Spring." *Theory, Culture & Society* 30, 4 (2013): 92–130.

Gillespie, Tarleton. "The Politics of 'Platforms'." *New Media & Society* 12, 3 (2010): 347–64.

———. "Can an Algorithm Be Wrong?" *Limn*, 2 (2012).

Godwin, Mike. *Cyber Rights: Defending Free Speech in the Digital Age*. 2nd ed. (MIT Press, 2003).

Goode, Luke. "Social News, Citizen Journalism and Democracy." *New Media & Society* 11, 8 (2009): 1287–1305.

Greenberg, Andy. *This Machine Kills Secrets: How Wikileakers, Cypherpunks and Hacktivists Aim to Free the World's Information* (Virgin, 2012).

Greenwald, Glenn. *No Place to Hide: Edward Snowden, the NSA and the Surveillance State* (Penguin, 2014).

Haggerty, Kevin D., and Richard V. Ericson. "The Surveillant Assemblage." *British Journal of Sociology* 51, 4 (2000): 605–22.

Halford, S., and M Savage. "Reconceptualizing Digital Social Inequality." *Information, Communication and Society* 13, 7 (2010): 937–55.

Haraway, Donna Jeanne. *Simians, Cyborgs and Women: The Reinvention of Nature* (Free Association, 1991).

Hawkins, Joan. "When Taste Politics Meets Terror: The Critical Art Ensemble on Trial." In *Critical Digital Studies: A Reader*, ed. Arthur Kroker and Marilouise Kroker, 447–64 (University of Toronto Press, 2013).

Hayles, N. Katherine. "The Materiality of Informatics." *Configurations* 1, 1 (1993): 147–70.

———. *My Mother Was a Computer: Digital Subjects and Literary Texts* (University of Chicago Press, 2005).

Helbig, N., J. R. Gil-Garcia, and E. Ferro. "Understanding the Complexity of Electronic Government: Implications from the Digital Divide Literature." *Government Information Quarterly* 26, 1 (2009): 89–97.

Herman, Bill D. *The Fight over Digital Rights: The Politics of Copyright and Technology* (Cambridge University Press, 2013).

Herrera, L. "Youth and Citizenship in the Digital Age: A View from Egypt." *Harvard Educational Review* 82, 3 (2012): 333–52.

Hill, Kevin A., and John E. Hughes. *Cyberpolitics: Citizen Activism in the Age of the Internet* (Rowman & Littlefield, 1998).

Howard, Philip N. "Deep Democracy, Thin Citizenship: The Impact of Digital Media in Political Campaign Strategy." *Annals of the American Academy of Political and Social Science* 597 (2005): 153–70.

———. *New Media Campaigns and the Managed Citizen* (Cambridge University Press, 2006).

Huysmans, J. "What's in an Act? On Security Speech Acts and Little Security Nothings." *Security Dialogue* 42, 4–5 (2011): 371–83.

Isin, Engin F., and Peter Nyers, eds. *The Routledge Handbook of Global Citizenship Studies* (Routledge, 2014).

James, Jeffrey. "The Digital Divide across All Citizens of the World: A New Concept." *Social Indicators Research* 89, 2 (2008): 275–82.

Jordan, Tim. *Cyberpower: The Culture and Politics of Cyberspace and the Internet* (Routledge, 1999).

Jordan, Tim, and Paul A. Taylor. *Hacktivism and Cyberwars: Rebels with a Cause?* (Routledge, 2004).

Jørgensen, Rikke Frank. *Framing the Net: The Internet and Human Rights* (Edward Elgar, 2013).

Katz, Jon. "The Digital Citizen." *Wired* 5, 12, December 1997, 68–82.

Kelty, Christopher M. *Two Bits: The Cultural Significance of Free Software* (Duke University Press, 2008).

Kern, Thomas, and Sang-hui Nam. "The Making of a Social Movement: Citizen Journalism in South Korea." *Current Sociology* 57, 5 (2009): 637–60.

Kesby, Alison. *The Right to Have Rights: Citizenship, Humanity, and International Law* (Oxford University Press, 2012).

Kim, M. "The Creative Commons and Copyright Protection in the Digital Era: Uses of Creative Commons Licenses." *Journal of Computer-Mediated Communication* 13, 1 (2007): 187–209.

Kim, Y. M. "The Shifting Sands of Citizenship: Toward a Model of the Citizenry in Life Politics." *Annals of the American Academy of Political and Social Science* 644 (2012): 147–58.

Klang, Mathias, and Andrew Murray, eds. *Human Rights in the Digital Age* (GlassHouse, 2005).

Knorr Cetina, Karin, and Urs Bruegger. "Traders' Engagement with Markets: A Post-social Relationship." *Theory, Culture & Society* 19, 5/6 (2002): 161–85.

König, René, and Miriam Rasch, eds. *Society of the Query Reader: Reflections on Web Search* (Institute of Network Cultures, 2014).

Kovačič, Melita Poler, and Karmen Erjavec. "Mobi Journalism in Slovenia: Is This Really Citizen Journalism?" *Journalism Studies* 9, 6 (2008): 874–90.

Kperogi, Farooq A. "Cooperation with the Corporation? CNN and the Hegemonic Cooptation of Citizen Journalism through iReport.Com." *New Media & Society* 13, 2 (2011): 314–29.

Kroker, Arthur, and Marilouise Kroker. *Critical Digital Studies: A Reader*. 2nd ed. (University of Toronto Press, 2013).

Latour, Bruno. "The Berlin Key or How to Do Words with Things." In *Matter, Materiality and Modern Culture*, ed. Paul Graves-Brown, 10–21 (Routledge, 2000).

———. *Reassembling the Social: An Introduction to Actor-Network-Theory* (Oxford University Press, 2005).

———. *An Ethnography of the Conseil d'Etat* (Polity, 2010).

Latta, Alex. "Environmental Citizenship." *Alternatives Journal* 33, 1 (2007): 18–19.

Law, John. *After Method: Mess in Social Science Research* (Routledge, 2004).

Lefebvre, Henri. *The Production of Space* (Wiley-Blackwell, 1991).

Lessig, Lawrence. *Code: Version 2.0* (Basic, 2006).

———. "The Creative Commons." *Montana Law Review* 65 (2004): 1–13.

———. *Free Culture: How Big Media Uses Technology and the Law to Lock Down Culture and Control Creativity* (Penguin, 2004).

———. *The Future of Ideas: The Fate of the Commons in a Connected World* (Random House, 2001).

———. "The Zones of Cyberspace." *Stanford Law Review* 48, 5 (1996): 1403–11.

Levy, Steven. *Hackers*, 25th anniversary ed. (O'Reilly, 2010).

Lin, W. Y., P. H. Cheong, Y. C. Kim, and J. Y. Jung. "Becoming Citizens: Youths' Civic Uses of New Media in Five Digital Cities in East Asia." *Journal of Adolescent Research* 25, 6 (2010): 839–57.

Lovink, Geert. *Networks without a Cause: A Critique of Social Media* (Polity, 2012).

Luke, Timothy W. "Digital Citizenship." In *Emerging Digital Spaces in Contemporary Society: Properties of Technology*, ed. Phillip Kalantzis-Cope and Karim Gherab Martín, 83–96 (Palgrave Macmillan, 2011).

Lyon, David. "Everyday Surveillance: Personal Data and Social Classifications." *Information, Communication & Society* 5, 2 (2002): 242–57.

———. "Surveillance, Snowden, and Big Data: Capacities, Consequences, Critique." *Big Data & Society* 1 (2014): 1–13.

Lyotard, Jean-François. *The Postmodern Condition: A Report on Knowledge* (University of Minnesota Press, 1984).

Mackenzie, Adrian. *Wirelessness: Radical Empiricism in Network Cultures* (MIT Press, 2010).

Mackenzie, A., and T. Vurdubakis. "Codes and Codings in Crisis Signification, Performativity and Excess." *Theory, Culture & Society* 28, 6 (2011): 3–23.

Mackenzie, Adrian, and Theo Vurdubakis. "The Performativity of Code: Software and Cultures of Circulation." *Theory, Culture & Society* 22, 1 (2005): 71–92.

Madar, C. "The Death of Aaron Swartz." *Nation* 296, 6 (2013): 4–6.

Mahnke, Martina, and Emma Uprichard. "Algorithming the Algorithm." In *Society of the Query Reader: Reflections on Web Search*, ed. René König and Miriam Rasch, 257–70 (Institute of Network Cultures, 2014).

Manteleyo, A. "The EU Proposal for a General Data Protection Regulation and the Roots of the 'Right to Be Forgotten'." *Computer Law & Security Review* 29, 3 (2013): 229–35.

Maratea, R. J. *The Politics of the Internet: Political Claims-Making in Cyberspace and Its Effect on Modern Political Activism* (Lexington, 2014).

Marshall, T. H. *Citizenship and Social Class* (1949). Ed. T. B. Bottomore (Pluto Press, 1992).

Massey, Doreen B. *For Space* (Sage, 2005).

Maurer, B., T. C. Nelms, and L. Swartz. "'When Perhaps the Real Problem Is Money Itself!': The Practical Materiality of Bitcoin." *Social Semiotics* 23, 2 (2013): 261–77.

Mayer-Schönberger, Viktor, and Kenneth Cukier. *Big Data: A Revolution That Will Transform How We Live, Work and Think* (John Murray, 2013).

McNevin, Anne. *Contesting Citizenship: Irregular Migrants and New Frontiers of the Political* (Columbia University Press, 2011).

Meadows, Michael. "Putting the Citizen Back into Journalism." *Journalism* 14, 1 (2013): 43–60.

Miller, Daniel. *Tales from Facebook* (Polity, 2011).

Miller, Toby. *Cultural Citizenship: Cosmopolitanism, Consumerism, and Television in a Neoliberal Age* (Temple University Press, 2007).

Miller, William J. "Digital Citizen." In *Encyclopedia of Social Media and Politics*, ed. Kerric Harvey, 388–90 (Sage, 2014).

Mirowski, Philip, and Dieter Plehwe, eds. *The Road from Mont Perlerin: The Making of the Neoliberal Thought Collective* (Harvard University Press, 2009).

Mitchell, William J. *Me++: The Cyborg Self and the Networked City* (MIT Press, 2003).

Mol, Annemarie, Ingunn Moser, and Jeanette Pols, eds. *Care in Practice: On Tinkering in Clinics, Homes and Farms* (Transcript, 2010).

Morozov, Evgeny. *The Net Delusion: How Not to Liberate the World* (PublicAffairs, 2011).

———. *To Save Everything, Click Here: The Folly of Technological Solutionism* (PublicAffairs, 2013).

Mossberger, Karen, Caroline. J. Tolbert, and A. Hamilton. "Measuring Digital Citizenship: Mobile Access and Broadband." *International Journal of Communication* 6 (2012): 2492–2528.

Mossberger, Karen, Caroline J. Tolbert, and Ramona S. McNeal. *Digital Citizenship: The Internet, Society, and Participation* (MIT Press, 2008).

Mythen, Gabe. "Reframing Risk? Citizen Journalism and the Transformation of News." *Journal of Risk Research* 13, 1 (2010): 45–58.

Negroponte, Nicholas. *Being Digital* (Hodder and Stoughton, 1995).

Ní Mhurchú, Aoileann. *Ambiguous Citizenship in an Age of Global Migration* (Edinburgh University Press, 2014).

Nietzsche, Friedrich. *On the Genealogy of Morality*. Ed. K. Ansell-Pearson. Trans. C. Diethe (Cambridge University Press, 1994).

Nunes, Mark. "Virtual Topographies: Smooth and Striated Cyberspace." In *Cyberspace Textuality: Computer Technology and Literary Theory*, ed. Marie-Laure Ryan, 61–77 (Indiana University Press, 1999).

Nunziato, Dawn C. *Virtual Freedom: Net Neutrality and Free Speech in the Internet Age* (Stanford University Press, 2009).

Nyers, Peter. "Abject Cosmopolitanism: The Politics of Protection in the Anti-deportation Movement." *Third World Quarterly* 24 (2003): 1069–93.
———. "The Accidental Citizen: Acts of Sovereignty and (Un)Making Citizenship." *Economy and Society* 35 (2006): 22–41.
Ohm, Paul. "Broken Promises of Privacy: Responding to the Surprising Failure of Anonymization." *UCLA Law Review* 57 (2010): 1701.
Olsson, Tobias. "'The Architecture of Participation': For Citizens or Consumers?" In *Critique, Social Media and the Information Society,* ed. Christian Fuchs and Marisol Sandoval (Routledge, 2014).
Palmer, Lindsay. "'iReporting' an Uprising: CNN and Citizen Journalism in Network Culture." *Television & New Media* 14, 5 (2013): 367–85.
Papacharissi, Zizi, ed. *A Networked Self: Identity, Community and Culture on Social Network Sites* (Routledge, 2011).
Pariser, Eli. *The Filter Bubble: What the Internet Is Hiding from You* (Viking, 2011).
Phelan, Shane. *Sexual Strangers: Gays, Lesbians, and Dilemmas of Citizenship* (Temple University Press, 2001).
Poster, Mark. "Cyberdemocracy: Internet and the Public Sphere." In *Politics and the Internet,* ed. William H. Dutton and Elizabeth Dubois, 1:199–214.
———. "Digital Networks and Citizenship." *Proceedings of Modern Language Association of America (PMLA)* 117, 1 (2002): 98–103.
Postigo, Hector. *The Digital Rights Movement: The Role of Technology in Subverting Digital Copyright* (MIT Press, 2012).
Rancière, Jacques. "The Thinking of Dissensus: Politics and Aesthetics." In *Reading Rancière,* ed. Paul Bowman and Richard Stamp, 1–17 (Continuum, 2011).
———. "Who Is the Subject of the Rights of Man?" *South Atlantic Quarterly* 103, 2/3 (2004): 297–310.
Relph, E. C. *Place and Placelessness* (Pion, 1976).
Ritzer, George, and Nathan Jurgenson. "Production, Consumption, Prosumption: The Nature of Capitalism in the Age of the Digital 'Prosumer'." *Journal of Consumer Culture* 10, 1 (2010): 13–36.
Rodgers, Jayne. *Spatializing International Politics: Analysing Activism on the Internet* (Routledge, 2003).
Rogers, Richard. *The End of the Virtual: Digital Methods* (Amsterdam University Press, 2009).
Rossiter, Ned. *Organized Networks: Media Theory, Creative Labour, New Institutions* (Institute of Network Cultures, 2006).
Ruppert, Evelyn. "Doing the Transparent State: Open Government Data as Performance Indicators." In *A World of Indicators: The Making of Governmental Knowledge through Quantification,* ed. Richard Rottenburg, Sally E. Merry, Sung-Joon Park, and Johanna Mugler (Cambridge University Press, 2015).
Ruppert, Evelyn, John Law, and Mike Savage. "Reassembling Social Science Methods: The Challenge of Digital Devices." *Theory, Culture & Society, Special Issue on the Social Life of Methods* 30, 4 (2013): 22–46.
Ruppert, Evelyn, and Mike Savage. "Transactional Politics." *Sociological Review* 59, s2 (2012): 73–92.
Rushkoff, Douglas. *Program or Be Programmed: Ten Commandments for a Digital Age* (OR Books, 2010).
Rygiel, Kim. *Globalizing Citizenship* (UBC Press, 2010).

Santora, J. C. "Crossing the Digital Divide: Do All Global Citizens Have Their Pass-ports?" *Academy of Management Perspectives* 20, 4 (2006): 118–19.

Schattle, Hans. *The Practices of Global Citizenship* (Rowman & Littlefield, 2007).

Schlozman, Kay Lehman, Sidney Verba, and Henry E. Brady. "Weapon of the Strong? Participatory Inequality and the Internet." *Perspectives on Politics* 8, 2 (2010): 487–509.

Schlozman, Kay Lehman, Sidney Verba, and Henry E. Brady. "Who Speaks? Citizen Political Voice on the Internet Commons." *Daedalus* 140, 4 (2011): 121–39.

Schmeh, Klaus. *Cryptography and Public Key Infrastructure on the Internet* (Wiley, 2003).

Schweik, Charles M., and Robert C. English. *Internet Success: A Study of Open-Source Software Commons* (MIT Press, 2012).

Shachar, A. *The Birthright Lottery: Citizenship and Global Inequality* (Harvard University Press, 2009).

Shklovski, Irina, Scott D. Mainwaring, Halla Hrund Skúladóttir, and Höskuldur Borg-thorsson. "Leakiness and Creepiness in App Space: Perceptions of Privacy and Mobile App Use." In *ACM Conference on Human Factors in Computing Systems (CHI) 2014* (Toronto: ACM CHI, 2014).

Soja, Edward W. *Thirdspace* (Blackwell, 1996).

Squire, Vicki. *The Exclusionary Politics of Asylum* (Palgrave Macmillan, 2009).

Stallman, Richard M. *Free Software, Free Society: Selected Essays*, ed. Joshua Gay (GNU Press, 2002).

Steiner, Linda, and Jessica Roberts. "Philosophical Linkages between Public Journal-ism and Citizen Journalism." In *Media Perspectives for the 21st Century*, ed. Stylianos Papathanassopoulos, 191–211 (Routledge, 2011).

Stevens, Jacqueline. *States without Nations: Citizenship for Mortals* (Columbia University Press, 2009).

Tartoussieh, K. "Virtual Citizenship: Islam, Culture, and Politics in the Digital Age." *International Journal of Cultural Policy* 17, 2 (2011): 198–208.

Terranova, Tiziana. *Network Culture: Politics for the Information Age* (Pluto, 2004).

Trepte, Sabine, and Leonard Reinecke, eds. *Privacy Online* (Springer, 2011).

Triscott, N. "Performative Science in an Age of Specialization: The Case of Critical Art Ensemble." In *Interfaces of Performance*, ed. M. Chatzichristodoulou, J. Jefferies, and R. Zerihan, 151–66 (Ashgate, 2009).

Tuan, Yi-Fu. *Space and Place: The Perspective of Experience*. 2nd ed. (University of Minne-sota Press, 2001).

Turkle, Sherry. *Alone Together: Why We Expect More from Technology and Less from Each Other* (Basic, 2011).

———. *Life on the Screen: Identity in the Age of the Internet* (Simon & Schuster, 1995).

Turner, Bryan S. *Citizenship and Capitalism: The Debate over Reformism* (Unwin, 1986).

———. "Citizenship Studies: A General Theory." *Citizenship Studies* 1, 1 (1997): 5–18.

———. "Outline of a Theory of Citizenship." *Sociology* 24 (1990): 189–217.

Vaidhyanathan, Siva. *The Googlization of Everything: (And Why We Should Worry)* (Uni-versity of California Press, 2011).

van de Donk, Wim, Brian D. Loader, Paul G. Nixon, and Dieter Rucht, eds. *Cyberprot-est: New Media, Citizens and Social Movements* (Routledge, 2004).

Van der Heijden, Hein-Anton, ed. *Handbook of Political Citizenship and Social Movements* (Edward Elgar, 2014).

Van Dijck, José. *The Culture of Connectivity: A Critical History of Social Media* (Oxford University Press, 2013).

Walker, R. K. "The Right to Be Forgotten." *Hastings Law Journal* 64, 1 (2012): 257–86.

Wark, McKenzie. *A Hacker Manifesto* (Harvard University Press, 2004).

Watts, Duncan. *Six Degrees: The Science of a Connected Age* (Norton 2003).

White, S. *The Ethos of a Late-Modern Citizen* (Harvard University Press, 2009).

Wiener, Norbert. *Cybernetics: Or, Control and Communication in the Animal and the Machine* (Wiley, 1948).

Wiener, Norbert. *The Human Use of Human Beings: Cybernetics and Society*. 2nd ed. (Sphere, 1968).

Wilkinson, Eleanor. "'Extreme Pornography' and the Contested Spaces of Virtual Citizenship." *Social & Cultural Geography* 12, 5 (2011): 493–508.

Williams, Sam. *Free as in Freedom: Richard Stallman's Crusade for Free Software* (O'Reilly, 2002).

Wittel, Andreas. "Counter-Commodification: The Economy of Contribution in the Digital Commons." *Culture and Organization* 19, 4 (2013): 314–31.

Wittgenstein, Ludwig. *Philosophical Investigations*. Ed. P. M. S. Hacker and Joachim Schulte. Trans. G. E. M. Anscombe. 4th ed. (Blackwell, 1998).

———. *Philosophical Investigations*. Trans. G. E. M. Anscombe. 2nd ed. (Basil Blackwell, 1958).

Yang, G. *The Power of the Internet in China: Citizen Activism Online* (Columbia University Press, 2009).

Ziccardi, Giovanni. *Resistance, Liberation Technology and Human Rights in the Digital Age* (Springer, 2013).

Ziewitz, Malte. "Evaluation as Governance: The Practical Politics of Reviewing, Rating and Ranking on the Web." (PhD dissertation, Oxford University, 2012).

Zittrain, Jonathan. *The Future of the Internet and How to Stop It* (Yale University Press, 2008).

Zivi, Karen. *Making Rights Claims: A Practice of Democratic Citizenship* (Oxford University Press, 2012).

Žižek, Slavoj. *The Ticklish Subject: The Absent Centre of Political Ontology* (Verso, 2000).

Index